Thunderation!/Alle Wetter!

Thunderation!
Folk Play with Song and Dance

Alle Wetter!
Volksstück mit Gesang und Tanz

Erich Mühsam

A Dual-Language Edition

Translated, Edited, and with an Introduction
by David A. Shepherd

Lewisburg
Bucknell University Press
London: Associated University Presses

Associated University Presses
440 Forsgate Drive
Cranbury, NJ 08512

Associated University Presses
16 Barter Street
London SC1A 2AH, England

Associated University Presses
P.O. Box 338, Port Credit
Mississauga, Ontario
Canada L5G 4L8

The paper used in this publication meets the requirements of the American National Standard for Permanence of Paper for Printed Library Materials Z39.48-1984.

Library of Congress Cataloging-in-Publication Data

Mühsam, Erich, 1878-1934.
  [Alle Wetter. English & German]
  Thunderation! : folk play with song and dance = Alle Wetter! : Volksstück mit Gesang und Tanz / Erich Mühsam ; translated, edited, and with an introduction by David A. Shepherd.--Dual-language ed.
      p. cm.
  Includes bibliographical references.
  ISBN 0-8387-5416-3 (alk. paper)
    I. Title: Alle Wetter. II. Shepherd, David A., 1953- III. Title.

PT2625.U25 A7413 2001
832'.912--dc21   00-048645

PRINTED IN THE UNITED STATES OF AMERICA

To the memory of
Hans-Joachim Schulz

Contents

Acknowledgments

This edition of *Thunderation/Alle Wetter* would not have been possible without the support and assistance of several people. Above all, I would like to express my thanks to my brother, Howard Shepherd, who located the "lost" microfilm copy of the typescript of *Alle Wetter* in the Library of Congress. Howard's detective work gave me access to the only known authentic copy of this play in North America. I would also like to thank Sabine Kruse and the *Erich-Mühsam-Gesellschaft* of Lübeck, Germany, for generously granting permission to publish this edition. Thanks are due as well to Volker Kahl, director of the archives of the *Deutsche Akademie der Künste* in Berlin, and the *Akademie* as an institution, for their grant of permission to publish. My friend and colleague Thomas Mast helped me decipher more than a few rather exotic German colloquialisms, and I am grateful for his help. Finally, thanks to my wife Barbara Shepherd and my parents Banks and Eulene Shepherd for reading the text and commenting on the fluency of the translation.

Introduction

David A. Shepherd

Erich Mühsam's name is generally known to those who have a fairly thorough knowledge of the German Weimar Republic (1918–33); but if asked to cite more than a couple of his notable achievements, most students of that era would be hard-pressed to do so. Mühsam (1878–1934) is likely to be remembered as one of the leading figures of the leftist revolution in Munich after the First World War, which led to a short-lived soviet republic in Bavaria. Among anarchists and those familiar with the history of political anarchism, he might be known as an early organizer of the *Lumpenproletariat*, the subproletariat, in Munich before the war, or as the publisher of two anarchist periodicals, *Kain. Zeitschrift für Menschlichkeit* (Cain. Journal for Humanity) and *Fanal* (Torch). Aficionados of German cabaret lyric after the turn of the twentieth century might have heard of or read his poem "Der Revoluzzer" (The Revolutionary, 1905), a jaunty, somewhat sardonic satire of "weekend revolutionaries" who were members of the Social Democratic Party. Students of the Third Reich might know him as one of the earliest victims of National Socialist cruelty that was murdered in a concentration camp in July 1934, because he was both an outspoken anarchist and a Jew.

Beyond these few highlights, however, the details of Mühsam's work and life are relatively unknown. This obscurity is remarkable because Mühsam was not only present in, but in fact a central figure of, some of Germany's most significant literary and social-protest movements of the first third of the twentieth century. Mühsam was a consistent and noisy critic of complacent middle-class society: from his early development as a writer in Berlin's bohemian writers' community; to the cabaret scene of Munich; through the First World War, the revolutions of 1918–19, and the Weimar Republic; to the rise of the Nazis. His critical attack was not, however, merely a facile finger-pointing at the rich; it was also an active

11

engagement for the poor, the disenfranchised, the marginalized. Nor did he withhold criticism of the established workers' parties, which he frequently took to task for placing internal party politics and dogma above the concerns of actual workers. For his activism, Mühsam paid a high price. He was never financially comfortable. He was imprisoned several times for lengthy periods. His pure anarchist ideology and critical stance shut him out of the most prominent revolutionary parties (the Communists and the Independent Social Democrats), except for a very brief membership in the Communist Party in 1919. Ultimately his social and political convictions cost him his life at the hands of the Nazis. But none of these difficulties, up to his execution, could silence him. Whether in polemical essays published in his own journals and elsewhere, in both serious and whimsical lyric, or in dramas, Mühsam was a consistent and idealistic voice for justice, freedom, and social equality. *Alle Wetter*, Mühsam's last play, is in many important respects the clearest synthesis of his humor, his boldness, and his pure ideology.

The Career of a Revolutionary

Erich Mühsam was born on 6 April 1878 in Berlin, the son of a middle-class Jewish pharmacist. When Erich was less than a year old, the family moved to Lübeck, where Erich grew up. (Lübeck was also the hometown of Heinrich and Thomas Mann, who lived there as children at the same time as Mühsam.) When he was a seventeen-year-old student in the Katharineum-Gymnasium in Lübeck, Mühsam was kicked out of school for "socialist intrigues" (*sozialistische Umtriebe*). This subversive activity consisted of publishing a satirical portrait of his school's principal in the local Social Democratic newspaper. Thus, he already had a history as a "subversive" writer when he went to Berlin in 1900 to be a pharmacist's apprentice. Although this move to Berlin was intended to enable Erich to follow in his father's professional footsteps—a career path the young man deeply resented—the imperial capital was also a center of arts and letters, an environment in which he could realize his dream of becoming a writer.

The most significant acquaintances Mühsam made in Berlin early on were members of the bohemian writers' and artists' group known as *Die Neue Gemeinschaft* (The New Community). This urban commune was

founded by the writers Heinrich and Julius Hart in 1900, and was an outgrowth of the group of naturalist writers known as the *Friedrichshagener Dichterkreis* (Friedrichshagen Writers' Circle). Members of the New Community saw themselves as outsiders to middle-class society. They tried to live in a style unfettered by social conventions, in an environment of equality and free artistic expression. One of Mühsam's closest friends in the New Community was Gustav Landauer, one of the leading anarchist philosophers in Germany and a student of Pierre Proudhon. Landauer became Mühsam's political mentor during the time of their association with the commune. The two friends eventually became disillusioned with what they perceived as the group's elitism and isolation from social concerns. Landauer left the New Community in 1902, and Mühsam left in 1904.

The next four years were a period of wandering for Mühsam. During this time he settled for a while in a vegetarian-anarchist commune in Switzerland known as Ascona. Although he was ambivalent about the Ascona vegetarians' apparent subordination of free thought to a vegetarian dogma, he admired their commitment to an idealistic alternative to mainstream society. In a memoir-essay on the commune, he proposed that Ascona be converted to a kind of rehabilitation center and refuge for convicted criminals. In such a supportive community, he believed, these outcasts from society could flourish as human beings.[1] Mühsam's sympathy for the rejects of society was a direct outgrowth of the anarchist philosophy he learned from Gustav Landauer.

After a few years of travel through Europe, Mühsam settled in Munich in 1908. There he began to realize both his artistic and his political ambitions. He became a well-known figure of the bohemian subculture in Munich's Schwabing quarter, frequenting bars, coffeehouses, and cabarets and writing and reading poetry. A present-day visitor to Schwabing is reminded of Mühsam's strong identification with the neighborhood when passing street signs for the Erich-Mühsam-Platz, a small square surrounded by cafés. In Schwabing Mühsam became acquainted with the writer Frank Wedekind, one of the best-known cabaret lyricists and performers of that period. Mühsam wrote a large number of cabaret songs in Munich, including his most famous poem, "Der Revoluzzer," a satire of a lower-middle-class streetlamp cleaner who played at being a revolutionary on the weekend. Like Wedekind, Mühsam regarded his cabaret lyrics as somewhat second-rate, inferior to

what he regarded as his serious writing: plays and essays. Indeed, he felt
that the cabaret environment was not worthy of serious art.[2] Yet the
humor and incisive wit of his cabaret work is an unmistakable trademark
of his best writing, and would strongly influence his last full-length text,
Alle Wetter.

At the same time that Mühsam became established as a prominent (if
never prosperous) fixture in the Schwabing cabaret scene, his anarchist
ideology continued to take shape. Under the influence of his political
mentor Gustav Landauer, Mühsam attempted to mobilize the
subproletariat of Munich into a revolutionary movement. The two
anarchist groups he organized, the *Gruppe Anarchist* (Anarchist Group)
and *Gruppe Tat* (Action Group), failed, since the marginalized and partly
criminal underclass of Munich refused to be organized. However, these
failures taught him the perseverance he would later need as an organizer
of the leftist revolution in Munich after the First World War. During the
World War, Mühsam quickly became a committed anti-war activist.[3]
Throughout the war years of 1914–18 he sought to forge coalitions with
Social Democrats, anarchists, and liberal pacifists to bring an end to
Germany's pursuit of the war. He was jailed for his oppositional
activities in April of 1918, and remained imprisoned until the end of
October of that year. Upon his release and return to Schwabing, Mühsam
found the former coffeehouse quarter transformed into a center for
revolutionary organizing in the war's aftermath.

The Munich revolution of 1918–19 was the turning point in Mühsam's
political life. For several years leading up to the end of the war, Mühsam
had written and agitated for just such a revolution. With the fall of the
Hohenzollerns in Berlin and the Wittelsbachs in Munich, Mühsam and
his activist colleagues rushed to fill the power vacuum. Mühsam was
centrally involved in all stages of the revolution, from initial attempts to
forge a revolutionary coalition out of the chaos of late 1918, to the
bloody crushing of Bavaria's second soviet republic in April 1919. When
Mühsam was arrested for high treason after the failed revolution, he
escaped the fate of his mentor Landauer, who was executed by
government troops sent from Berlin to restore order.[4] Mühsam was tried
and convicted of treason and sentenced to fifteen years in prison. He had
served five years of those fifteen when the German government issued a
general amnesty. As Constanze Eisenbart has noted,

while the right-wing putschist Adolf Hitler was able to write his propaganda piece *Mein Kampf* in comparatively comfortable circumstances in the Landsberg jail, Erich Mühsam, the leftist humanitarian revolutionary, ended up in some of the worst prisons of which the state of Bavaria could boast.[5]

Most of Mühsam's confinement was spent in the prison at Niederschönenfeld, where his comrade in the Munich revolution, writer Ernst Toller, was also imprisoned.

Mühsam's literary activity in jail was even more vigorous and focused than it had been previously. Before the revolution, he had published numerous articles and poems in newspapers and literary journals. His own political-literary journal, *Kain. Zeitschrift für Menschlichkeit* appeared regularly from April of 1911 until the outbreak of World War I in 1914. The start of the war presented Mühsam with the choice either to remain silent or to state opinions that were now illegal. He chose to suspend publication of *Kain* during the war. In contrast to the prewar version, which had featured poems and philosophical essays almost exclusively by Mühsam, the postwar *Kain* was a de facto organ for the Munich revolution. The postwar version contained articles rooted in revolutionary practice rather than political theory and philosophy. After his arrest in 1919, and during his imprisonment for treason, Mühsam was a regular contributor to other radical magazines, primarily Franz Pfemfert's *Die Aktion* (Action).

Mühsam also wrote his first significant revolutionary drama in jail. This play, *Judas* (1920), was Mühsam's third full-length play. His earlier efforts at playwriting did not have a particularly political focus. *Die Hochstapler* (The Con Men, 1906) is a comedy whose leading characters swindle a wealthy Jewish investor out of a large sum of money, and in so doing demonstrate to the investor's young son the harshness of capitalism. *Die Freivermählten* (The Open Marriage, 1914) is a domestic drama about free love and bourgeois sexual morality, with roots in Frank Wedekind's *Lulu* plays and Henrik Ibsen's family dramas. Whereas these earlier plays of Mühsam's were generalized critiques of middle-class society, they lacked the political focus he would articulate in *Judas*. This tragedy, depicting a failed workers' uprising in Munich during the war, became a standard number in the repertoire of German workers' theaters in the 1920s. It was first performed in 1921 in the *Mannheimer Volkstheater* (Mannheim People's Theater), and was very well received.

The critic for the Communist Party newspaper *Die Rote Fahne* (The Red Flag) called the play "the truly brilliant fanfare of the age, the voice of the people's longings, the manifestation of the spirit of the times."[6] A Nuremberg production of *Judas* in 1922 enjoyed the same success as the Mannheim staging, selling out two weeks before opening night.[7] The first Berlin performance was staged by Erwin Piscator, the leading practitioner of revolutionary modernism in the Berlin theater, in 1928.

Mühsam wrote one other play in the spirit of revolutionary agitation-propaganda, *Staatsräson* (Statesmanship, 1928). This was a documentary tribute to the Italian-American anarchists Sacco and Vanzetti, whose executions in August 1927 became a cause célèbre for anarchist movements worldwide. Mühsam's was only one voice among many protesting these executions. According to one account, no fewer than one hundred forty-four poems, five plays, seven short stories, and several radio and television plays have been written or produced on the Sacco and Vanzetti case.[8] Mühsam's play was constructed as a documentary drama, using actual quotations from the public record. Yet in contrast to the objective, reportorial tone of the soviet documentary theater troup known as the Blue Blouse, Mühsam's play appealed to the audience's emotions, in the manner of a classical tragedy. *Staatsräson*, like *Judas*, became very popular among workers' theaters, and was produced in Berlin in 1929.

While Mühsam's name was becoming more widely known among radical workers' groups throughout Germany as the author of these plays, his profile as a revolutionary activist was declining. During the years of his imprisonment for treason, the possibilities for revolutionary change blossomed and faded. The stabilization of German currency after the explosion of hyperinflation in 1923 was accompanied by the stabilization and entrenchment of the republican German government under the Weimar constitution. Activists of the radical left, whose revolutionary uprisings had been crushed in 1919–20, and whose politics of spontaneity put them increasingly at odds with the Communist Party, became disillusioned as the Weimar Republic wore on. Mühsam himself had been a relatively young and vigorous forty-one-year-old when he was tried for treason in 1919. Despite ideological differences, he had always sought to cooperate with the leaders of the revolutionary workers' movement. He even joined the Communist Party of Germany (*Kommunistische Partei Deutschlands*) briefly in September of 1919, in

spite of his rejection of Marxist materialist theory. But when he emerged from prison at the end of 1924 he had aged more than a mere five years. There was now no war against which to organize; middle-class culture, against which he had struggled all his life, had become firmly established as the dominant social structure. Even some of those who befriended him, such as Erwin Piscator, perceived him as a relic of a bygone stage of the movement.[9] His finances were hand-to-mouth, his main income being from occasional writings in newspapers and magazines. His two most famous works, the revolutionary plays, were popular in workers' theaters, but these financially strapped companies, of course, were in no position to make him wealthy.

Moreover, Mühsam was well aware of the dire possibilities for social disaster in the wake of the world economic crisis of 1929–30. He had expressed nervousness about the racist and nationalist rantings of Hitler and the National Socialists as early as 1922, before Hitler's ill-fated "beer hall *Putsch*."[10] As disquieting as Mühsam found the rise of the far right, however, he did not shy away from repeated bold attacks on the bourgeoisie and the parliamentary democracy of the Weimar Republic, nor indeed on right-wing politicians. His own new journal, *Fanal* (Torch), was the main outlet for his anarchist political philosophy between 1926 and 1931. After 1931, he published poems and short essays in such periodicals as *Berliner Tageblatt* (Berlin Daily), *Die Welt am Montag* (The World on Monday), and *Ulk* (Funny Mischief). Mühsam's satirical poems in these periodicals were as scornful of the German right wing as "Der Revoluzzer" had been of the Social Democrats in 1905. In a recent edition of some of these poems, Heinz Hug notes that Mühsam wrote many of them under a pseudonym, reluctant to be associated with what he felt was second-rate doggerel.[11] His deprecation of these satirical "forced rhymes" (*abgezwungene Reimerei*) recalls his arm's-length relationship to his prewar cabaret lyrics. As with those early cabaret songs, however, the poems of Mühsam's last years contain a satirical impulse whose vigor bespeaks fearlessness.

It was undoubtedly this public fearlessness in the face of a rising Nazi ideology that led to Mühsam's arrest quite early in the Third Reich. He was apprehended on 28 February 1933, the same night the *Reichstag* building was set on fire at the behest of the Nazis. This fire was Hitler's pretext for the suspension of civil liberties. Mühsam was planning to flee

Germany the next morning, and had borrowed money from friends for that purpose.[12] After a series of transfers from prison to prison, Mühsam was finally moved to the Oranienburg concentration camp, where he was tortured and murdered by Nazi strongmen in a restroom sometime before 10 July 1934. Since he was an anarchist of Jewish ancestry, the deck was stacked against Mühsam as soon as the Nazis came to power. As an unrepentant and tireless public critic of injustice and despotism, he occupied a position near the top of the Nazis' list of targeted enemies, and his arrest immediately after the *Reichstag* fire is the ultimate proof of this.

Alle Wetter: A "Lost" Play

Alle Wetter (Thunderation) is one of the least-known texts in Mühsam's rather neglected literary corpus. Written in 1930, it was not published during the author's lifetime, nor was it ever staged. Mühsam is known to have read part or all of the play at private occasions and at workers' gatherings.[13] Until the 1970s, in fact, it never appeared in print. A paperback version was published by the Klaus Guhl Verlag in (West) Berlin in 1977, but it was later disowned by its editor, Gerd W. Jungblut, as unreliable. In the German Democratic Republic the play was included in a limited anthology edited by Chris Hirte and published in 1984.[14] The only part of the play published during Mühsam's lifetime was the "Alle-Wetter-Lied" (Thunderation Song) from the first and third acts, which appeared in Mühsam's literary-political journal *Fanal* in December 1930. This song is also included in a collection of Mühsam's plays edited by Günther Emig and published in 1977.[15]

Relatively little scholarly attention has been paid to this play. Biographers and scholars of Mühsam in both parts of the formerly divided Germany have long known of the play's existence, yet in spite of the editions by Hirte in the east and Jungblut in the west, *Alle Wetter* has not been extensively discussed in studies of Mühsam's works. Rolf Kauffeldt's 1983 study of anarchism in Mühsam's writing does include a brief discussion of this play. However, Diana Köhnen's 1988 book on Mühsam's conception of utopia does not include any analysis of *Alle Wetter*, which has a stronger utopian focus than any of Mühsam's other works.[16] Perhaps the most striking oversight concerning this text is the

absence of any extensive consideration of *Alle Wetter* in a recent collection of essays published by the *Erich-Mühsam-Gesellschaft* (Erich Mühsam Society) in Lübeck. The society's 1994 publication *Der "späte" Erich Mühsam* (The "Later" Erich Mühsam) surveys the final ten years of Mühsam's life, 1925–34. *Alle Wetter* was written in 1930, but is not examined extensively in that publication.

This apparent neglect of one of Mühsam's most significant works is consistent with the very limited access to original source manuscripts. Both the 1977 edition and a political biography written by American scholar Lawrence Baron in 1976 refer to a copy in the Library of Congress in Washington, D.C., part of a collection of German documents and manuscripts captured by American forces in the Second World War. However, this collection was copied to microfilm and reclassified in the mid-1980s, which effectively hid the collection from the public.

More significant, perhaps, was the restricted access to the Mühsam literary estate in the German Democratic Republic and the Soviet Union. Mühsam's widow, Zenzl, escaped Nazi Germany shortly after her husband was murdered, fleeing to Prague with his papers and manuscripts. She was convinced to move to Moscow in 1935 by the promise that Erich's works would finally be published there. However, Zenzl fell victim to Stalin's purges, and was imprisoned for several months in 1936.[17] After she returned to (East) Berlin in 1955, her husband's papers were sent to the *Deutsche Akademie der Künste zu Berlin* (German Academy of Arts in Berlin, formerly GDR), not directly to Zenzl. In an article in the German weekly newspaper *Die Zeit* in January 1996, Chris Hirte argues that the claim laid on Mühsam's estate by the *Akademie der Künste* is shadowy and questionable. According to Hirte, the East German government, through its institution, the *Akademie,* based its claim on a last will and testament allegedly dictated by Zenzl eight days before her death. This will, which was never officially notarized, bequeathed ownership and royalty rights to the *Akademie* and the government of the GDR. Hirte suggests that the will was faked by the East German government in order to shut Mühsam's legitimate heirs out of any royalty participation in Mühsam's work.[18]

Although Mühsam was officially acknowledged in the GDR as one of the first victims of the Nazis and one of the earliest warning voices against the rise of fascism, his anarchism was anathema to official East German Marxism. As late as December 1988, a query in an East Berlin

bookstore about books by or about Mühsam was met with a brusque and very nervous "We don't have anything here!" The target of Mühsam's satire in *Alle Wetter*, a strong central government dominated by socialists, is clearly the government of the late Weimar Republic. But the nationalization of the weather works and the construction of massive, lifeless government buildings foreshadows in an uncanny way the central planning and nationalization of industry that took place both in National Socialist Germany and later in the German Democratic Republic. Mühsam had always detested dominant central government, whether led by the left or the right. It is thus not surprising that the literature of this self-described "communist anarchist" would be suppressed by a Marxist regime.[19]

The "message" of *Alle Wetter* is a purely anarchist one. Indeed, in a different historical context it might be something that an American libertarian could embrace. In the world of this play, ultimate political power rests in the hands of the workers and farmers; in the final analysis, the buffoonish government proves completely irrelevant. The politicians are loyal to nothing—not to their parties' ideologies, nor to democratic principles, nor to their lovers. On the other hand, the workers stand by their principles with patience and forbearance. The decisive moment in their uprising at the end of the play is the thunderstorm, which restores nature's cycle and brings the world once again into equilibrium—and in so doing eliminates the government from the picture.

The German title of this play, *Alle Wetter*, is a slightly archaic expletive of surprise and astonishment, generally translatable in English as "My goodness!" "By Jove!" or "Thunderation!" Translated word-for-word it means "all weathers." The literal meaning is never used in German conversation. Yet Mühsam has taken not only the interjection, but also the literal meaning of these words as the theme of this play. The workers are gathered together in an intentional agrarian community in which they live simply and share the fruits of their labors. In order for the community to thrive, the workers must accept the vicissitudes of the weather. They all instinctively understand this; as Hantke, one of the villagers, observes in the opening scene, "They can let us farmers have a day here and there, and the brickyard can have a Sunday. But the weather goes on like it's supposed to" (page 43). The weather tower, built for the farmers by the engineer Niedermaier, is a powerful tool for the workers, simply because they understand that it must not be used in exclusive

service to any one interest group. If "all weathers" are put into the hands of the working class, it is because the working class accepts all forms of weather. Indeed, the reader might with reason infer that the weather tower is actually a forecasting station. Rather than exercise brute control over meteorological forces, the farmers carefully attend to the weather cycles and plan accordingly.

In the third act, the politicians gather around the tower to celebrate the nationalization of the weather works as well as the birthday of the state president, Wimmerzahn. The centerpiece of the festivities is a crude pageant in which allegorical qualities of "pretty" weather are heroes, and wind and rain are villains. This celebration takes place in the dry, sunny weather that has been the ruin of the agricultural community. The villagers are frustrated, as the farmers are unable to grow a crop. During the president's birthday celebration, the villagers are pushed to the margins, away from their creation. As a desperate last gesture, Niedermaier occupies the tower and arranges a terrible thunderstorm, which literally washes the politicians away one-by-one. This storm is strongly reminiscent of the penultimate scene in the novel *Der Untertan* (The Subject, published 1918) by Mühsam's fellow Lübecker Heinrich Mann. Mann describes the scene of a patriotic gathering around a statue of Kaiser Wilhelm I. As the leading character of the novel makes a speech, a cataclysmic thunderstorm sweeps the hillside clean of the Kaiser-worshippers.[20] In Mann's novel the ruling class re-emerges from the storm to continue the imperial order. In contrast to Mann's cautionary tone, Mühsam's storm in *Alle Wetter* has a cleansing efffect that is enduring, as the workers reclaim their place in the village.

The unbridgeable gap between the workers and the governmental "big-shots" (*Bonzen*) is evident from the very beginning of act 1 of *Alle Wetter*. The politicans' concern with appearances, which finds its ultimate manifestation in their obsession with "beautiful" weather, contrasts with the workers' practicality and simplicity. The workers see rain as an element of life; the politicos regard it as a messy nuisance. When Mühsam transports the workers from the farm collective into the provincial parliament in the second act, he puts the working class in charge of the restrooms, "the only place in the building where [the politicians] are sometimes honest" (page 177). While the the parliament is filled with scheming, dissembling, even physical violence, in the

restrooms, where the working class presides, the truly smelly business of party politics is limited by the attendants' strict rules of behavior.

Alle Wetter's central government is composed of a grand coalition of widely disparate parties. This reflects the partisan landscape of the government of the later Weimar Republic, which on more than one occasion was made up of a grand coalition. The ten different parties of *Alle Wetter* stand for at least that many in the German parliament in the late 1920s. In addition to the Social Democrats (represented in *Alle Wetter* by the Socialists), parties such as the German People's Party, the German National Party, the Bavarian People's Party, and even a German Racialist Party, held seats in the Weimar parliament. The disdain Mühsam expresses for such a fractured party landscape is apt, since the political rise of the National Socialists can be attributed at least in part to Hitler's ability to exploit fractionalism in the *Reichstag*. The state president of *Alle Wetter*, Wimmerzahn, is a very thinly veiled depiction of the ancient President von Hindenburg, whose impotence in the face of Hitler's machinations also contributed to the Nazi rise to power.

Mühsam's distaste for party politics informs his fascinatingly ambivalent portrayal of the Intransigents *(die Unversöhnlichen)*, who represent the Communist Party. While the party and its fortunes are central to the plot, its representative, Widerborst, appears only very briefly in the second act, to threaten a vote of no-confidence and later to attempt to share the spoils of good weather. One of the most interesting lines of the play is almost a throwaway, when Widerborst interjects that "the first of May has to be a legal nice-weather day too" (page 173). Even this party of the working class fails to understand the importance of the weather cycle. The Communists/Intransigents neither receive the unrelenting ridicule Mühsam reserves for the other parliamentarians, nor do they appear in solidarity with the workers of the collective. Rather, they are spoken of, in absentia, as the closest thing to a people's party as could participate in a parliament—assuming that participation in parliament could ever work to the advantage of the working class. Mühsam, of course, would probably never have accepted that assumption. When in the third act the Intransigents are shut out of control of the weather, despite their newly-won absolute majority in parliament, this development is regarded by the workers as a shame, but not a catastrophe.

The ambivalent position of the Intransigents in *Alle Wetter* reflects Mühsam's own frustrations with the Communists during the revolution of 1919. In the crucial hours of the Munich revolution, the Communist Party demanded sole leadership of the movement without conceding anything to the other factions who had paved the way toward a revolution.[21] In Mühsam's view such hegemony doomed the revolution. Notwithstanding his disdain for the Communists, Mühsam's impulse toward coalition-building that characterized his activism from 1914 to 1919 is evident in his intensely engaged but brief association with a series of political advocacy organizations in the last years of his life.[22] Mühsam's suspicion of the Communist Party's strong centralization led to his resignation in 1929 from the multipartisan advocacy organization for political prisoners, *Rote Hilfe* (Red Aid), because the group had come to be dominated by the Communists. As if ever longing for a group whose work could somehow transcend a narrow set of political interests, Mühsam constantly sought an organizational home base. In *Alle Wetter* the Intransigents are suggested, and then rejected, as such a home; and the true home turns out to be the commune, which is self-regulating and not dominated from the outside.

Mühsam is aware of the emotional resonance of a rural farming community to a German audience. The appeal of *Heimat*, the peculiarly German concept of "hometown" or "homeland," was as strong for the political left as it was for the far right. In *Alle Wetter*, Mühsam maintains a distinction between his concept of inclusive *Heimat* and the xenophobic image of rural German life through his portrayal of the Nazis. The boorish representative of the Workers' Race Party, Barde, is ready to "slug it out" with anyone who dares criticize his leader, Kajetan Teutsch (obviously meant to represent Adolf Hitler). As with many of the character names in this play, the name of the unseen Teutsch has a resonance in German that is impossible to translate. "Teutsch" is an antiquated spelling of *deutsch* (German), and thus invokes a sense of primeval Germanness, a quality the Nazis tried to assert as they ostracized all "foreign elements" from German society. At the same time, the given name Kajetan does not sound German at all, but rather vaguely oriental, exotic, and foreign. Thus Mühsam seems to lampoon Hitler, the rabidly German leader of the Nazis who was born outside the borders of Germany, in Austria.

Mühsam also attacks the hypocrisy of the Nazi assertion of a "true German people" who were contingently connected by language and culture far more than intrinsically by genetics. In act 2, Barde spews racist utterings and threatens the Socialist Hustenreiz with physical violence. Mühsam's attack on the Nazis in this play is remarkably—indeed, naively—unflinching; yet in the last analysis it tends to be somewhat undercut by the silly bluster of the character Barde. Apart from his bullying attack on Hustenreiz, Barde is never an actual threat, either to the workers or to the government. To be sure, Barde's proposal late in the play of a dictatorship under his party's leader is an uncanny foreshadowing of the Nazis' actual rise to parliamentary leadership; but this reflects less Mühsam's clairvoyance than the widespread circulation of such proposals in German political discourse in 1930.

The working-class protagonists are led by the engineer Niedermaier (whose class origins are never clear, although his sympathies are) and his assistant Otti. Otti is the one character who has made a transition from the unschooled proletariat to an emerging technocracy. She embodies both sensitive solidarity with the working class and advanced technological know-how. In the second act she proves more than able to ward off the unwelcome advances of several male politicians and thus to assert her personal dignity. Such a strong leading female character is quite a leap forward for Mühsam. In earlier writings, particularly before 1920, his attitude toward women ranged from mildly sexist to outright misogynist. Apart from Otti, however, *Alle Wetter's* workers are not easily identifiable by name or personality traits, unlike the antagonistic politicians. Moreover, the switch in character roles over the three acts is potentially confusing, although thematically connected with the message of the play. The workers/farmers/parliament servants represent the eternal downtrodden, the forgotten class, those whose labor is used not merely to serve capitalism, but also to serve the basest needs of the rest of society. In depicting the restroom attendants as sages of the parliament building, Mühsam transcends Marxian notions of what constitutes a revolutionary proletariat. While Marx-Engels (and the Marxist parties) felt that only the industrial working class could be organized into a revolutionary movement, Mühsam puts the subproletariat front and center. He suggests that even these lowest of the low, the restroom attendants, are able to join together in an organized labor movement,

having fought successfully for a wage increase (page 187). Furthermore, by making the members of the working class essentially nameless, Mühsam makes a subtle comment on the invisibility of the *Lumpenproletariat*, whom he had tried to organize long before he became a revolutionary. In spite of the workers' apparent lack of individuality, they are the inheritors of the new ideal order after the final storm. The workers are the survivors whose dignity is preserved after the noisy and self-centered politicians are washed away from the scene.

Notes on the Translation

This edition of *Thunderation/Alle Wetter* is the first English-language translation of any of Mühsam's works. The source for this edition is the microform copy of a typed manuscript in the Rehse Collection, part of the Captured German Documents Collection of the Library of Congress. This set of documents is held by the Library's Manuscript Division. According to the Library, the documents were held by the Library in paper form until the mid-1980s, when they were copied to microfilm and recataloged. As a result of this reclassification, prior references to this manuscript in the 1977 edition edited by Gerd W. Jungblut, and in Lawrence Baron's 1976 political biography of Mühsam, are now invalid.[23] The Library of Congress shipped the original documents to the *Bundesarchiv* (Federal Archives) of the Federal Republic of Germany, where they are held today. It is not completely clear whether Jungblut used this manuscript or the original, held in the archives of the Maxim Gorki Institute in Moscow, as the basis of his 1977 edition. In any event, Jungblut protests in two different places that the publisher arbitrarily altered the text of that edition before publication.[24] Access to the Mühsam collection in the Gorki Institute was difficult during the cold war, and the Library of Congress manuscript is the only original version of *Alle Wetter* that was generally available to western scholars prior to German unification.

A cover page on the Library of Congress typescript identifies the text as *Alle Wetter. Volksstück mit Gesang und Tanz, von Erich Mühsam.* No date is given. It is clear from Mühsam's correspondence that he completed work on this play in the early autumn of 1930. From August through October of that year he resided at Burg Weißenstein, a Bavarian

mountain retreat owned by the Munich writer Siegfried von Vegesack.[25] Mühsam's letters indicate that he worked on *Alle Wetter* during this period to the exclusion of everything else, including his journal *Fanal*: "It goes without saying that the constant mental concentration on my play, which uses up every possible working moment, does not allow me to think of *Fanal* production."[26] Although Mühsam was not able to find a publisher or producer willing to accept the play, he did read from it publicly and privately several times.

The Library of Congress typescript is apparently not a finished final draft. At least two different typewriters were used to produce it. (The typeface obviously changes between pages 36 and 37 of the typescript, again between pages 47 and 48, and once again between pages 75 and 76.) Occasional strikeovers and misspellings remind the reader that this text was a work in progress. Among the most significant differences between the present edition of the German text and Jungblut's 1977 version is the spelling of character names. The Jungblut edition spells "Niedermaier" with a "y" ("Niedermayer"). In the typescript the spelling varies from "Niedermeier" early in the text, to "Niedermaier" later, with the latter form prevailing. The Jungblut edition spells the name "Berta" without an "h," while the typescript varies from "Bertha" to "Berta," the latter prevailing. In the list of characters in the typescript, the name of the delegate of the Intransigent Party (*die Unversöhnlichen*) is given as "Wiederborst," which means "brush again." However, everywhere else in the text it is spelled "Widerborst," which means "stubbornness" or "obstinacy." Since the latter spelling makes more sense for the character, and it predominates in the typescript, that is the version used here. The former spelling appears to be a typographical error.

Two other character names are somewhat more problematic. In Jungblut's edition, Niedermaier's assistant is named Otti Jungbleib (Jungbleib means "stay young"). In the typescript, Otti's surname is consistently given as "Jungleib" ("young body"). Although an argument can be made that the former spelling makes sense within the play, that spelling appears nowhere in the Library of Congress manuscript. Therefore the name is spelled here as "Jungleib." Similarly, the Jungblut edition spells the name of the Socialist ministerial adviser as "Tankhafen" ("tanker's harbor" or "tank harbor"). Although that spelling appears in the first few pages of Mühsam's typescript, in the middle of page 7 it changes abruptly (within six lines) to "Trankhafen" ("drink

harbor"), and is consistently spelled that way for the rest of the play. Since neither spelling reflects a theatrically essential element of the play, I have chosen to use the form that predominates in Mühsam's manuscript, "Trankhafen."

It should be clear by now that many of the German character names are more than merely names; they have either a satirical impulse or a descriptive function. Such a use of descriptive names has precedents in German and English literature, for example in the works of Grimmelshausen (the title character in *Simplicissimus*), in English restoration comedy (Mrs. Pinchwife in Wycherly's *The Country Wife*), and occasionally in Shakespeare (Mistress Quickly in *The Merry Wives of Windsor*). In some cases Mühsam seems to comment directly on character traits, as in the case of General Stiefengrat ("stiff backbone") or Delegate Widerborst ("obstinacy"). Other times more general positive or negative associations are invoked, as with Schönbrod ("good bread") or Krampf ("cramp").

One of the most daunting challenges in the translation process was deciding whether to translate these names into English. They are all plausible German surnames, and any attempt to transliterate them into English would sound forced and artificial. On the other hand, a freer translation into plausible English surnames would abandon Mühsam's whimsy and satirical thrust. After long consideration, I have decided to leave these names unchanged. In order that the non-German-speaking reader can appreciate the resonance of Mühsam's character names, I offer here a list of morphological translations:

Barde	bard
Biederhold	honest and kind
Blödel	dullard
Hornbriller	wearer of horn-rim glasses
Hustenreiz	cough irritation
Jungleib	young body
Krachhahn	noisy rooster
Krampf	cramp
Möhre	carrot
Niedermaier	humble man
Schönbrod	good bread

Selters	seltzer
Speicherer	warehouse man
Stechbein	sting leg
Stiefengrat	stiff backbone
Trankhafen	drink harbor
Wachtel	quail
Widerborst	obstinacy
Wimmerzahn	whimper tooth

These character names are actually not often uttered by other characters in the play. Mühsam's satiric intention in his use of this device is somewhat clearer to a reader of the text than it would be to an audience of a stage performance. In any event, to ignore the satirical resonance of these names would be to miss out on a significant element of humor in *Thunderation/Alle Wetter*, a quality present in this play more than in any other of Mühsam's dramas.

Any translation is in part a retelling through the translator's own voice. Mühsam's stage directions place the play "in a German country" (*in einem deutschen Lande*), a vague instruction. Although I have tried to resist the urge to transport the workers' and farmers' speech into any particular regional dialect, inevitably my own roots in rural, western North Carolina will come through in the workers' speech patterns. (Indeed, my rendition of the title as "Thunderation" is a typically Southern Appalachian interjection.) The suggestion of regional dialect is strongest in the speeches of the village mayor, Schönbrod, who wears his age and simple upbringing as a badge of honor. The workers' and farmers' speeches are marked above all by an easy, conversational informality in the German original, and this is the quality I have tried to convey.

In undertaking this translation I have attempted to maintain a clear separation in the registers of language used by the politicians and the workers. In contrast to the down-to-earth speech of the villagers, the speech of the politicians is filled with the conventions of parliamentary debate. This is true not only when they are speaking officially, but also from time to time in personal conversation. Mühsam seems to suggest that these characters are incapable of spontaneity—a quality, according to anarchist ideology, that would drive any true people's revolution. A particular challenge was the character Hornbriller, the government

assessor, who is fond of using as many French, Latin, Italian, and English expressions as possible. Much of Hornbriller's speech in the original German text consists of Germanized borrowings from Latin roots. Fortunately for an American reader, this habit has a parallel in American speech, particularly in the language of bureaucracy and the discourse of the political class (such as the words "prioritize" and "utilize"). Wherever Hornbriller uses such Latin borrowings and coinages, I have translated them as self-consciously polysyllabic words. Where he simply utters French, Latin, or Italian phrases I have, by and large, left these alone.

With one exception, the stage directions appear here as Mühsam wrote them in the typescript. The exception is in act 2, which takes place in the restrooms and staff room of the provincial parliament. Throughout the act, the scenes in which the workers are the primary characters occur in the staff room, the men's scenes in the men's restroom, and the women's scenes in the women's restroom. Although Mühsam does not give any indication as to where characters are onstage when they are speaking, I have added, in both the German text and the English translation, an indication of those areas for clarity.

Through this translation edition I hope to bring an awareness of Mühsam, and especially his last, "lost" play, to an English-speaking audience that has not had previous access to him. If the translation succeeds, it is due to Mühsam's own passion and wit, as will be evident to a reader of the German text. Any weaknesses in the English version are my own.

Notes

1. Erich Mühsam, *Ascona* (1905; reprint in *Erich Mühsam Gesamtausgabe*, vol. 3, *Prosaschriften I*, ed. Günther Emig, Berlin: Verlag europäische ideen, 1978), 103–04.

2. "In the many years that I have appeared as a cabaret performer for longer or shorter periods, I have never presented anything but puns and indifferent trifles. I have always refused to recite my serious literary works before a paying audience that had come to be amused." Mühsam, Namen und Menschen: Unpolitische Erinnerungen, translated David A. Shepherd (Leipzig: Volk und Buch Verlag, 1949), 69.

3. At the very outset of the war Mühsam published a statement that hinted at patriotic enthusiasm, but he later regretted his rashness. He was at the time concerned that his fiancée was caught behind enemy lines. For a more detailed discussion of the context of this statement see David A. Shepherd, *From Bohemia to the Barricades: Erich Mühsam and the Development of a Revolutionary Drama* (New York: Peter Lang, 1993), 33–34.

4. Mühsam's own first-person account of the revolution in Munich can be found in his *Von Eisner bis Leviné: Die Entstehung der bayerischen Ræterepublik* (1929; reprint, Berlin: Klaus Guhl Verlag, n.d.).

5. Constanze Eisenbart, "Erich Mühsam. Anarchismus als Traum von Menschlichkeit und Gerechtichkeit," trans. Shepherd, in *Anarchismus. Zur Geschichte und Idee einer herrschaftsfreien Gesellschaft*, ed. Hans Diefenbacher (Darmstadt: Primus Verlag, 1996), 183.

6. Stefan J. Klein, "'Judas': Arbeiter-Drama in fünf Akten von Erich Mühsam," trans. Shepherd, *Die Rote Fahne*, 16 March 1921 (M).

7. Alexander Abusch, "'Judas' von Erich Mühsam in der Proletarischen Tribüne Nürnberg," *Die Rote Fahne*, 10 February 1922 (M).

8. Heinz Hug, *Erich Mühsam. Untersuchungen zu Leben und Werk* (Glashütten im Taunus: Verlag Detlev Auvermann KG, 1974), 220 n. 589.

9. In his 1929 memoir, *Das politische Theater*, Piscator twice overstates Mühsam's age by ten years when mentioning the 1928 production of *Judas*. Referring to this staging, which was meant to celebrate Mühsam's fiftieth birthday, Piscator writes: "Next came...Erich Mühsam's *Judas*, the staging of which coincided with its author's sixtieth birthday." Erwin Piscator, *Das politische Theater*, trans. Shepherd (Reinbeck bei Hamburg: Rowohlt, 1929), 209. Referring elsewhere to a later staging of the play Piscator writes: "The actors' emergency committee decided to stage *Judas* by Erich Mühsam, which we had originally produced to celebrate his sixtieth birthday" (Piscator, 216). Mühsam was murdered by the Nazis when he was 56 years old, and thus did not live to see his sixtieth birthday.

10. In a letter from prison to the Bavarian Justice Ministry, Mühsam wrote: "Among the prisoners in Niederschönenfeld [the prison where he served most of his sentence], and particularly among their family members, some concern has arisen about the statements of Herr Hitler, who is said to have threatened in a meeting to eliminate the soviet republicans in Niederschönenfeld." Heinz Hug, introduction to *Berliner Feuilleton. Ein poetischer Kommentar auf die mißratene Zähmung des Adolf Hitler*, by Mühsam, trans. Shepherd (München: Boer, 1992), 11.

11. Ibid., 14.

12. Gerd W. Jungblut, afterword to *Alle Wetter. Volksstück mit Gesang und Tanz*, by Mühsam (Berlin: Klaus Guhl Verlag, 1977), 96.

13. One such reading in Vienna was reported in the *Arbeiter Zeitung* (28 January 1931); cited in Jungblut, foreword to Mühsam, *Alle Wetter* (1977), 98.

14. Mühsam, *Streitschriften. Literarischer Nachlaß*, ed. Chris Hirte (Berlin, German Democratic Republic: Verlag Volk und Welt, 1984). Since *Alle Wetter* had been neither published nor produced during Mühsam's lifetime, unlike his other plays, the manuscript was considered part of his literary estate (*literarischer Nachlaß*). The play's omission from any collection headed "Dramas" has undoubtedly tended to obscure awareness of its existence.

15. Mühsam, *Dramen*, vol. 2 of *Erich Mühsam Gesamtausgabe*, ed. Günther Emig (Berlin: Verlag europäische ideen, 1977), 446.

16. Rolf Kauffeldt, *Erich Mühsam: Literatur und Anarchie* (München: Wilhelm Fink Verlag, 1983); Diana Köhnen, *Das literarische Werk Erich Mühsams. Kritik und utopische Antizipation* (Würzburg: Königshausen & Neumann, 1988).

17. For an overview of Zenzl Mühsam's years in exile and her return to the GDR, see Uschi Otten, "Ein Vermächtnis und seine Erfüllung," in *Zenzl Mühsam. Eine Auswahl aus ihren Briefen* (Lübeck: Erich-Mühsam-Gesellschaft, 1995), 92–99.

18. Hirte, "Ärger mit der Beute. Streit um die Werke Erich Mühsams. Neue Akten dokumentieren einen brisanten Fall von Nachlaß-Kriminalität," *Die Zeit* (19 January 1996). As mentioned on the acknowledgments page of this volume, the current director of the archives at the *Akademie*, Volker Kahl, graciously granted the translator permission to publish the present edition without any conditions or demands. Such permission was also generously granted by Sabine Kruse of the *Erich-Mühsam-Gesellschaft* in Lübeck, the organization that Hirte regards as the sole legitimate holder and administrator of these rights. The translator is grateful to both of these institutions for their cooperation.

19. A reader of the German newsmagazine *Der Spiegel* invoked the memory of Mühsam in a letter to the editor immediately after the fall of the Berlin Wall: "Freedom and self-determination are inseparable, whether in capitalism or in socialism. Many anarchists, such as Emma Goldmann, Erich Mühsam, and Gustav Landauer fought against party-socialism. They were just too far ahead of their time." Thomas Schupp, letter, trans. Shepherd, *Der Spiegel* 43, no. 46 (13 November 1989): 10.

20. Heinrich Mann, *Der Untertan* (Munich: Deutscher Taschenbuch Verlag, 1984), 360.

21. See Mühsam, *Von Eisner bis Leviné*. Kurt Eisner was the leader of the Independent Socialists who took control in Munich after the First World War. Eugen Leviné was the Communist functionary sent by the party from Berlin to establish Communist control over the revolution in its last weeks.

22. Hug, "'Er war in erster Linie Literat.' Erich Mühsam in Berlin (1925–1934)," in *Der "späte" Erich Mühsam. Dritte Erich-Mühsam-Tagung in Malente, 15.–17. Mai 1992* (Lübeck: Erich-Mühsam-Gesellschaft, 1994), 31, 34–35.

23. Lawrence Baron, *The Eclectic Anarchism of Erich Mühsam* (New York: Revisionist Press, 1976), 178; Jungblut, foreword to *Alle Wetter. Volksstück mit Gesang und Tanz*, by Mühsam (Berlin: Verlag Klaus Guhl, 1977), 98.

24. In Mühsam, *In meiner Posaune muß ein Sandkorn sein. Briefe 1900–1934*, ed. Jungblut, trans. Shepherd (Vaduz: Topos Verlag, 1984), 2:642, Jungblut writes, "The reader is warned against purchasing this play, which was distorted through arbitrary text alterations by the publishers' editor!" In his own survey chronology of Mühsam's career, *Erich Mühsam. Notizen eines politischen Werdeganges*, trans. Shepherd (Schlitz: Verlag der Slitese, 1984), xiii, n. 20, Jungblut writes, "The text was in parts considerably falsified by the publisher's reader!!!" Jungblut's vigorous protestations notwithstanding, the alterations in the Guhl edition, while at times arbitrary and inexplicable, are not fundamental, and the edition remains by and large true to the Library of Congress typescript.

25. Jungblut, note in Mühsam, *Posaune*, 2:642, n. 1.

26. Mühsam to Rudolf Rocker, 16 August 1930, *Posaune*, trans. Shepherd, 2:649.

Selected Bibliography

This is only a partial bibliography of works by and about Erich Mühsam, with particular relevance to *Alle Wetter* and the last years of Mühsam's life. More complete bibliographies may be found in Hug, *Erich Mühsam*; Hug and Jungblut, *Erich Mühsam (1878–1934). Bibliographie*; Köhnen, *Das literarische Werk Erich Mühsams*; and Shepherd, *From Bohemia to the Barricades*, all listed below.

Abusch, Alexander. "'Judas' von Erich Mühsam in der Proletarischen Tribüne Nürnberg." *Die Rote Fahne*, 10 February 1922 (M).

Baron, Lawrence. *The Eclectic Anarchism of Erich Mühsam*. New York: Revisionist Press, 1976.

Eisenbart, Constanze. "Erich Mühsam. Anarchismus als Traum von Menschlichkeit und Gerechtichkeit." In *Anarchismus. Zur Geschichte und Idee einer herrschaftsfreien Gesellschaft*, edited by Hans Diefenbacher. Darmstadt: Primus Verlag, 1996, 169–91.

Erich-Mühsam-Gesellschaft. *Allein mit dem Wort: Erich Mühsam, Carl von Ossietzky, Kurt Tucholsky. Schriftstellerprozesse in der Weimarer Republik*. Lübeck: Erich-Mühsam-Gesellschaft, 1996.

——. *Anarchismus im Umkreis Erich Mühsams*. Lübeck: Erich-Mühsam-Gesellschaft, 1994.

——. *Erich Mühsam—Revolution und Schriftsteller*. Lübeck: Erich-Mühsam-Gesellschaft, 1990.

——. *Erich Mühsam—Thomas Mann—Heinrich Mann. Berührungspunkte dreier Lübecker*. Lübeck: Erich-Mühsam-Gesellschaft, 1996.

——. *Erich Mühsam und... der Anarchismus und Expressionismus, die "Frauenfrage," Ludwig Thoma*. Lübeck: Erich-Mühsam-Gesellschaft, 1991.

——. *Frauen um Erich Mühsam: Zenzl Mühsam und Franziska zu Reventlow*. Lübeck: Erich-Mühsam-Gesellschaft, 1996.

——. *Musik und Politik bei Erich Mühsam und Bertolt Brecht*. Lübeck: Erich-Mühsam-Gesellschaft, 1995.

——. *Der "späte" Erich Mühsam*. Lübeck: Erich- Mühsam-Gesellschaft, 1994.

Hirte, Chris. "Ärger mit der Beute. Streit um die Werke Erich Mühsams. Neue Akten dokumentieren einen Brisanten Fall von Nachlaß-Kriminalität." *Die Zeit* (19 January 1996): 14.

———. *Wege zu Erich Mühsam.* Lübeck: Erich-Mühsam-Gesellschaft, 1989.

Hirte, Chris and Uschi Otten. *Zenzl Mühsam. Eine Auswahl aus ihren Briefen.* Lübeck: Erich-Mühsam-Gesellschaft, 1995.

Hug, Heinz. "'Er war in erster Linie Literat.' Erich Mühsam in Berlin (1925–1934)." In *Der "späte" Erich Mühsam. Dritte Erich-Mühsam-Tagung in Malente, 15.-17. Mai 1992.* Lübeck: Erich-Mühsam-Gesellschaft, 1994, 27–41.

———. *Erich Mühsam. Untersuchungen zu Leben und Werk.* Glashütten im Taunus: Verlag Detlev Auvermann KG, 1974.

———. Introduction to *Berliner Feuilleton. Ein poetischer Kommentar auf die mißratene Zähmung des Adolf Hitler,* by Erich Mühsam. München: Boer, 1992.

Hug, Heinz and Gerd W. Jungblut. *Erich Mühsam (1878–1934). Bibliographie.* Vaduz: Topos Verlag, 1991.

Jungblut, Gerd W. Afterword to *Alle Wetter. Volksstück mit Gesang und Tanz,* by Erich Mühsam. Berlin: Klaus Guhl Verlag, 1977.

———. *Erich Mühsam. Notizen eines politischen Werdeganges.* Schlitz: Verlag der Slitese, 1984.

Kauffeldt, Rolf. *Erich Mühsam: Literatur und Anarchie.* Munich: Wilhelm Fink Verlag, 1983.

Klein, Stefan J. "'Judas': Arbeiter-Drama in fünf Akten von Erich Mühsam." *Die Rote Fahne,* 16 March 1921 (M).

Köhnen, Diana. *Das literarische Werk Erich Mühsams. Kritik und utopische Antizipation.* Würzburg: Königshausen & Neumann, 1988.

Kreiler, Kurt. *Erich Mühsam—Leben und Tod eines deutschen Anarchisten.* Lübeck: Erich-Mühsam-Gesellschaft, 1994.

Mann, Heinrich. *Der Untertan.* Munich: Deutscher Taschenbuch Verlag, 1984.

Möckel, Birgit. *Das Ende der Menschlichkeit. George Grosz' Zeichnungen, Lithographien und Aquarelle aus Anlaß der Ermordung Erich Mühsams.* Lübeck: Erich-Mühsam-Gesellschaft, 1997.

Mühsam, Erich. *Alle Wetter. Volksstück mit Gesang und Tanz.* TMs, Manuscript Division, German Captured Documents Collection 1844–1945, cont. 233, shelf no 18,806.2, Library of Congress, Washington, D.C.

——. *Alle Wetter: Volksstück mit Gesang und Tanz.* Edited by Gerd W. Jungblut. Berlin: Verlag Klaus Guhl, 1977.

——. *Ascona.* 1905. Reprint in *Erich Mühsam Gesamtausgabe,* vol. 3, *Prosaschriften I,* edited by Günther Emig. Berlin: Verlag europäische ideen, 1978, 49–105.

——. *Dramen.* Vol. 2, *Erich Mühsam Gesamtausgabe,* edited by Günther Emig. Berlin: Verlag europäische ideen, 1977.

——. *In meiner Posaune muß ein Sandkorn sein. Briefe 1900–1934.* Edited by Gerd W. Jungblut. Vaduz: Topos Verlag, 1984.

——. *Namen und Menschen: Unpolitische Erinnerungen.* Leipzig: Volk und Buch Verlag, 1949.

——. *Streitschriften. Literarischer Nachlaß.* Edited by Chris Hirte. Berlin, German Democratic Republic: Verlag Volk und Welt, 1984.

——. *Von Eisner bis Leviné: Die Entstehung der bayerischen Ræterepublik.* 1929. Reprint, Berlin: Klaus Guhl Verlag, n.d.

Otten, Uschi. "Ein Vermächtnis und seine Erfüllung." In *Zenzl Mühsam. Eine Auswahl aus ihren Briefen.* Lübeck: Erich-Mühsam-Gesellschaft, 1995, 92-99.

Piscator, Erwin. *Das politische Theater.* Reinbeck bei Hamburg: Rowohlt, 1929.

Schupp, Thomas. letter, *Der Spiegel* 43, no. 46 (13 November 1989): 10.

Shepherd, David A. *From Bohemia to the Barricades. Erich Mühsam and the Development of a Revolutionary Drama.* New York: Peter Lang, 1993.

Thunderation!/Alle Wetter!

Alle Wetter!
Volksstück mit Gesang und Tanz

von Erich Mühsam

Personen

Schönbrod, Bauer und Dorfschulze
Niedermaier, Ingenieur, Schöpfer des Wetterturms
Otti Jungleib, seine Gehilfin
Peters, Peilmeister im Wetterturm
Fischer, Monteur im Wetterturm
Wimmerzahn, Staatspräsident
Dr. Blödel, Minister für Ruhe, Ordnung und Sicherheit
Stechbein, Geheimrat, später Staatssekretär
Dr. Henriette Trankhafen, Ministerialrätin, Sozialistin
von Stiefengrat, General
Dr. Hornbriller, Regierungsassessor
Krampf, Langtagspräsident
von Krachhahn, Mitglied des Landtages, Grundbesitzer
Speicherer, Mitglied des Landtages, Industriellenpartei
Selters, Mitglied des Landtages, Liberaler
Biederhold, Pfarrer, Mitglied des Landtages, Kirchenpartei
Barde, Mitglied des Landtages, Arbeiterrassenpartei
Hustenreiz, Mitglied des Landtages, Sozialist
Frau Möhre, Mitglied des Landtages, christliche Reformpartei
Frau Wachtel, Mitglied des Landtages, Hausfrauenpartei
Widerborst, Mitglied des Landtages, Partei der Unversöhnlichen
Hantke, Arbeiter, im zweiten Bild Parlamentsdiener
Steinbott, erstes Bild Wursthändler, zweites Bild Arbortwächter, drittes Bild Kleinbauer
Wolff, erstes Bild Jahrmarktangestellter, zweites Bild Parlamentsdiener, drittes Bild Arbeiter

Thunderation!
Folk-Play with Song and Dance

by Erich Mühsam

Cast of characters

Schönbrod, farmer and village mayor
Niedermaier, engineer, inventor of the weather tower
Otti Jungleib, his assistant
Peters, soundings-chief in the weather tower
Fischer, mechanic in the weather tower
Wimmerzahn, state president
Dr. Blödel, minister for law, order, and security
Stechbein, privy councillor, later state secretary
Dr. Henriette Trankhafen, ministerial advisor, Socialist
von Stiefengrat, general
Dr. Hornbriller, government assessor
Krampf, president of the provincial parliament
von Krachhahn, member of provincial parliament, Landowners' Party
Speicherer, member of provincial parliament, Industrialist Party
Selters, member of provincial parliament, Liberal
Biederhold, pastor, member of provincial parliament, Church Party
Barde, member of provincial parliament, Workers' Race Party
Hustenreiz, member of provincial parliament, Socialist
Frau Möhre, member of provincial parliament, Christian Reform Party
Frau Wachtel, member of provincial parliament, Housewives' Party
Widerborst, member of provincial parliament, Intransigent Party
Hantke, worker (parliamentary servant in second act)
Steinbott, (first act sausage vendor, second act toilet attendant, third act peasant)
Wolff, (first act market employee, second act parliamentary servant, third act worker)

Brunner, Arbeiter, zweites Bild Parlamentsdiener
Berta, erstes Bild Jahrmarktangestellte, zweites Bild Abortfrau, drittes Bild Bäuerin
Paula, Gastwirtsgehilfin
Jenny, erstes Bild Buchhalterin, zweites Bild Fraktionssekretärin, drittes Bild Arbeiterin
Annie, Jungarbeiterin, zweites Bild Telefonistin

Personen im Zwischenspiel

Laubfrosch, Gnom, Sonnenscheinchen, Schönwetterchen, Nebel, Regen, Schnee, Sausewind. Ferner: Polizeileutnant, Schutzleute, Landtagsabgeordnete, Beamte, Bauern, Bäuerinnen, Stadt- und Landarbeiter und Arbeiterinnen, Jugendliche, Dorfkinder, Masken, Engel, Feen und Elfen.

Das Stück spielt in einem deutschen Lande in naher Zukunft.

In den Rollen von Hantke, Steinbott, Wolff, Brunner, Berta, Paula, Jenny und Annie sind in den verschiedenen Bildern nicht dieselben Personen gedacht, sondern nur dieselben Charaktere. Die Beibehaltung der Namen geschah der Typesierung wegen. Jede der drei Figuren ist in den drei Bildern von demselben Darsteller zu spielen.

Brunner, worker, second act parliamentary servant
Berta, first act market employee, second act toilet attendant, third act farmer
Paula, waitress
Jenny, first act bookkeeper, second act party secretary, third act worker
Annie, young worker, second act telephone operator

Characters in the interlude-play

Treefrog, Gnome, Little Sunshine, Little Blue-Skies, Fog, Rain, Snow, Gusty Wind.
Police Lieutenant, Police Officers, Provincial Parliament Deputies, Civil Servants, Farmers, Municipal and Provincial Workers, Teenagers, Village Children, Masqueraders, Angels, Elves, and Fairies

The play is set in a German province in the near future.

The actors playing the roles of Hantke, Steinbott, Wolff, Brunner, Berta, Paula, Jenny, and Annie portray different characters in the three acts. Retention of the names is to show that the characters in the three acts are similar types. From act to act the characters should be played by the same actors.

Erstes Bild

Von Buden, Karusell, Jahrmarktständen umrahmter freier, etwas hügeliger Platz vor dem Wetterturm, der mit dem danebenstehenden Windrad die Mitte des Hintergrundes einnimmt. Ein in modernster Architektur ausgeführter, fensterloser, massiver Turm, an dessen Vorderseite eine grosse Windrose mit Zeiger angebracht ist. Das Windrad, dessen Schanzflügel schräg zur Bühne steht und dessen Gerüst die gleiche Höhe hat, wie der Turm, dreht sich anfangs ziemlich langsam, bleibt bald stehen. Zwischen Turm und Rad zu beiden Seiten ist breiter Raum—man sieht im Hintergrund dörfliche Dächer, Bäume und Feld.

Rechts vorn die Schießbude von Berta. Dahinter der Wurststand von Steinbott, links etwas in die Szene hineinragend die Luftschaukel von Wolff. Unmittelbar hinter dem Windrad ein großes Zeltdach, das als Bierzelt kenntlich ist. Vor den Buden rechts stehen im Gespräch Berta, *Frau in den Vierzigern,* Wolff, Steinbott, Paula, *junges Bauernmädchen, das im Bierzelt bedient.* Brunner *und* Hantke *kommen auf die Gruppe zu.*

Berta: Regen gibt's heut nicht? Wie?

Brunner: Das kommt auf's Wetter an.

Steinbott: Die Genossenschaft arbeitet?

Hantke: Die Regierung hat ja Feiertag gewünscht.

Steinbott: Dann wird wohl auch das Wetter schön bleiben.

Paula: Niedermaier wird doch nicht das ganze Fest verderben.

Hantke: Das glaub' ich nicht, daß er viel danach fragt. Uns Landarbeitern kann man wohl mal einen Tag schenken und die Ziegelei kann auch mal Sonntag machen. Aber das Wetter geht so weiter, wie es festgesetzt ist.

Act I

Booths, carrousels, market stands surround an open, somewhat hilly plaza in front of the weather tower, which, along with the windwheel next to it, occupies the middle of the background. A massive tower, in the most modern architectural style, windowless, on the front of which a large weathervane is attached. The windwheel, whose rudder is diagonal to the stage and whose structure is the same height as that of the tower, turns rather slowly at first, then stops. Between the tower and the wheel, on either side, is a broad area. We see in the background village roofs, trees, and a field.

Downstage on the right, Berta's shooting gallery. Behind that, Steinbott's sausage stand. On the left, swinging into the scene, Wolff's swing-boat. Immediately behind the windwheel a large tent, recognizable as a beer tent. In front of the booths several townspeople are chatting: Berta, *a woman in her forties,* Wolff, Steinbott, Paula, *a young farm girl who is waiting tables in the beer tent.* Brunner *and* Hantke *approach the group.*

Berta: No rain today, eh?

Brunner: That depends on the weather.

Steinbott: Is the collective working?

Hantke: The government asked for a holiday.

Steinbott: Well, that'll mean the weather will be nice.

Paula: Niedermaier surely won't mess up the celebration?

Hantke: I don't think he'll worry about it much. They can let us farmers have a day here and there, and the brickyard can have a Sunday. But the weather goes on like it's supposed to.

Berta: Wenn es regnet, kann ich meine Schießbude einfach zumachen.

Wolff: Hätten alle Leute Luftschaukeln, dann wäre jeden Tag Sonnenschein.

Hantke: War Niedermaier noch nicht hier?

Paula: Er muß im Turm sein. Die rote Otti ist schon früh runter.

Berta: Es war ihr garnicht recht, aber sie soll mit dem Jugendchor den Festzug hierauf begleiten.

Brunner: Die hohe Obrigkeit will immer Zirkus haben. Aber andere sollen ihn machen.

Paula: Otti hat es doch bloß getan, weil ja auch das Volksfest ist und nachmittags der ganze Ort herkommt.

Wolff: Dann wird es jedenfalls schön bleiben heute.

Steinbott: Von mir aus kann es den Bonzen ins Maul regnen. Die haben noch nie gefragt, ob bei uns zuhaus das Dach dicht hält oder ob es uns in die Betten tropft.

Brunner: Dir schadet es sowieso nicht. Warme Würstchen schmecken am besten, wenn vom Himmel Dreck fällt.

Aus dem Turm kommen Arbeiter und Arbeiterinnen, darunter Peilmeister Peters, *Monteur* Fischer, Jenny, *Buchhalterin, etwa 30 Jahre, und* Annie, *junge Arbeiterin. Die Mehrzahl verteilt sich zwischen den Buden im Hintergrund. Einige stellen sich zu der Gruppe.*

Wolff: Feierabend!? Gleich morgens?

Fischer: Pause. Niedermaier sagt, die Paragraphenhengste, die nicht wissen, was arbeiten ist, brauchen uns nicht bei der Arbeit zu sehen.

Jenny: Sie müssen doch bald kommen?

Brunner: Sie bürsten erst ihre Zylinder.

Peters: Vielleicht springt für das Werk was raus.

Steinbott: Die gucken doch bloß, ob für sie was rausspringt.

Berta: If it rains, I can just close up my shooting gallery.

Wolff: If everybody had a swing-boat, there would always be nice weather.

Hantke: Hasn't Niedermaier been here yet?

Paula: He must be in the tower. Red Otti came down a while ago.

Berta: She didn't want to, but she's supposed to go with the youth choir when they join the parade.

Brunner: The big authorities always want to have a circus. But I wish they'd let somebody else do it.

Paula: Otti just did it because today's also the people's festival, and the whole village will be here in the afternoon.

Wolff: Then it'll surely stay nice today.

Steinbott: As far as I'm concerned it can rain in the big shots' faces. They never asked us whether our roof's tight or whether it's dripping on our bed.

Brunner: It's not going to hurt you anyway. Warm sausages taste best when it's raining cats and dogs.

Workers *come out of the tower, among them* Peters, *the soundings-chief,* Fischer, *the mechanic,* Jenny, *a bookkeeper about thirty years old, and* Annie, *a young worker. Most mingle among the booths in the background; some come over to the group.*

Wolff: Quitting time? This early in the morning?

Fischer: Break time. Niedermaier says those blockhead lawmakers don't need to see us working. They don't know what it means to work.

Jenny: They must be coming soon.

Brunner: They're brushing off their top hats first.

Peters: Maybe there'll be something in it for the tower.

Steinbott: They're just looking to see if there's something in it for them.

Paula: Ich meine, für Niedermaier wird es viel Ehre geben.

Wolff: Was er sich dafür kauft.

Brunner: Ein Ständchen mit lauter falschen Tönen wird's geben.

Fischer: Denk mal, was sie ihm all die Jahre für Knüppel zwischen die Beine geschmissen haben, bis das Werk im Gang war.

Jenny: Bis die Franzosen sich dafür interessierten; da rückten ein paar Millionäre das nötige Geld heraus.

Hantke: Die Wohltäter? Wir wissen Bescheid.

Peters: Wenn die Genossenschaft nicht wäre, hätten die Kerle aus dem Wetter längst ein Geschäft für Aktionäre gemacht.

Niedermaier kommt aus dem Turm mit kurzer Pfeife und Windjacke.

Annie: Fein, da kommt er.

Berta: Muß er sich denn nicht noch anziehen?

Annie: Das hat der doch nicht nötig.

Niedermaier: So, jetzt ein Glas Bier.

Paula: Ich hol' eins, Herr Niedermaier. *(ab)*

Niedermaier: War gute Arbeit heut Nacht, was, Herr Peters?

Peters: Alles aufgenommen und gepeilt.

Niedermaier: Das Hoch von den Azoren kommt uns gut zu paß. *(blickt auf die Windrose und das Rad, das sich mit Unterbrechungen ganz langsam dreht)* Alles im Lot. Hat sich Fräulein Otti nicht sehen lassen?

Steinbott: Die kommt ja mit dem Besuch.

Niedermaier: Richtig. Kann also nicht mehr lange wegbleiben, sie muß noch die Meldung von der Islandwarte abhören.

Fischer: Schön, Herr Niedermaier. (Paula *mit Bier*)

Paula: Zum Wohl, Herr Niedermaier.

Paula: I mean, it'll be an honor for Niedermaier.

Wolff: He can't buy much with that!

Brunner: It's not going to be very pleasant.

Fischer: Just think of all the monkey wrenches they threw in the works till the tower was working.

Jenny: Until the French got interested in it, then a couple millionaires coughed up the money for it.

Hantke: The benefactors? We know how that goes.

Peters: If it weren't for the collective, those guys would've made the weather a corporation on the stock market.

Niedermaier *comes out of the tower smoking a short pipe and wearing a windbreaker.*

Annie: Ah, good, there he comes.

Berta: Doesn't he need to get dressed?

Annie: No, he doesn't have any use for that.

Niedermaier: Well, now for a glass of beer.

Paula: I'll get you one, Herr Niedermaier. *(She goes off.)*

Niedermaier: That was a good night's work, wasn't it, Herr Peters?

Peters: I've got all the soundings recorded.

Niedermaier: That high in the Azores will be good for us. *(Looks at the weathervane and the wheel, which is sporadically turning very slowly.)* Everything's in order. Have you seen Fräulein Otti?

Steinbott: She's coming with the visitors.

Niedermaier: Right. She can't stay away too long, she still needs to monitor the report from the Iceland station.

Fischer: Okay, Herr Niedermaier. *(Paula enters with beer.)*

Paula: To your health, Herr Niedermaier.

Niedermaier: Aller Wohl! *(trinkt)* Daß der Rummel gnädig vorbeigeht.

Hantke: Im Volksblatt steht, die Regierung wollte heute einen Erlaß verkünden.

Niedermaier: Ich fürchte, sie wollen uns eine Behörde vor die Nase setzen.

Jenny: Wozu denn? Die Genossenschaft hat doch immer genügt, um uns bei der Wetterbestimmung zu beraten.

Fischer: Gerade. Wenn es nicht klappte, hätten sie uns verrecken lassen und gesagt, der Staat hätte ja gleich dagegen gestanden. Jetzt ist alles zufrieden, jetzt besinnen sie sich auf einmal auf die Grundsteinlegung und möchten die Wetterbildung womöglich den Parteibonzen übergeben.

Brunner: Was die fingern, davon wird nicht Tag und nicht Nacht.

Niedermaier: Mir steht dieses von oben gewünschte Fest zum Halse. Mir ist die Arbeit im Turm jeden Tag von neuem eine Feier;plötzlich will die Regierung mitfeiern. Das Ganze ist nur eine Störung, hoffentlich nichts Schlimmeres.

Peters: Ich sprach mit der roten Otti drüber. Die denkt genau so.

Annie: Wir alle, Herr Nidermaier, jeder Arbeiter und jedes Mädel im Turm.

In der Ferne Trommel und Pfeifen

Berta: Sie kommen.

Hantke: Das dauert noch was, bis sie oben sind.

Steinbott: Ich will lieber gleich Feuer unter den Wurstkessel machen.

Die Ministerialrätin Dr. Trankhafen *tritt mit Zeichen hastiger Erregung auf: mit äußerster Geschmacklosigkeit auf jugendlich hergerichtetes welkendes Fräulein mit Kneifer, spitziger und bellender Sprache. Hinter ihr neugierige Dorfkinder.*

Niedermaier: To everyone's health! *(Drinks.)* I hope this whole hullabaloo passes without any problem.

Hantke: In the People's Paper it says that the government wants to make an announcement today.

Niedermaier: I'm afraid they want to put some kind of authority over us.

Jenny: How come? The collective's always been able to give us advice about weather decisions.

Fischer: Exactly. If that hadn't worked so well, they would've let us drop dead and then said the state was against it from the beginning. Now everything's fine, now all of a sudden they're coming to commemorate the groundbreaking, and they'd probably like to turn over the weather planning to the politicos.

Brunner: Whatever they get their hands on will turn into a mess.

Niedermaier: Well, I don't want any part of this festival that the big shots are throwing. As far as I'm concerned, every day of working in the tower is a party; all of a sudden the government wants to join the party. This whole thing is just an interruption, hopefully nothing worse.

Peters: I was talking with Otti about that. She says the same thing.

Annie: We all do, Herr Niedermaier, every worker in the tower.

In the distance a drum and pipes.

Berta: They're coming.

Hantke: It'll be awhile before they get up here.

Steinbott: I think I'll build a fire under the sausage kettle.

Ministerial Advisor Trankhafen *enters, showing signs of hurried excitement. She is a fading spinster dressed in a tastelessly youthful style, with pince-nez and a sharp, bellowing voice. She is followed by curious village children.*

Trankhafen: *(fuhrwerkt auf die Gruppe los)* Aha, hier ist der Festplatz. Der berühmte Wetterturm—so! Der ist ja nicht beflaggt! Wer ist hier verantwortlich?

Jenny: Suchen Sie jemanden?

Trankhafen: Ich sehe auch nirgends ein Rednerpult. Der Herr Minister braucht doch eine angemessene Erhöhung.

Brunner: Paula, roll' ein Bierfaß her.

Wolff: Meine Luftschaukel wär auch eine ganz schöne Kanzel.

Niedermaier: Was wünschen Sie eingentlich und wer sind Sie überhaupt?

Trankhafen: Mit Ihnen habe ich nichts zu schaffen. Wo ist Herr Diplomingenieur Niedermaier?

Niedermaier: Der bin ich!

Trankhafen: Sie? Aber die hohen Herrschaften sind ja schon auf dem Wege hierher.

Niedermaier: Bittesehr!

Trankhafen: Sie werden sie doch nicht so empfangen wollen, im Arbeitskittel?

Niedermaier: Ich komme eben aus dem Maschinenhaus. Die Herrschaften wollen, denke ich, mein Werk besichtigen und nicht meinen Sonntagsrock.

Trankhafen: Es wird nicht den besten Eindruck machen.

Peters: Wollen Sie uns nicht gefälligst sagen, was Sie hier verloren haben?

Trankhafen: Ich verbitte mir diesen Ton. Mit welchem Recht stellen Sie Fragen an mich?

Peters: Ich bin der Peilmeister im Turm.

Trankhafen: Und ich bin Mitglied der Staatsregierung, Ministerialrätin Dr. Henriette Trankhafen vom Ministerium für Ruhe, Ordnung und Sicherheit.

Brunner: Ich hielt sie für einen weiblichen Verkehrsschutzmann.

Trankhafen: *(Scurries up to the group.)* Aha, here's the site of the festival. The famous weather tower! But there's no flag on it! Who's responsible for this?

Jenny: Are you looking for someone?

Trankhafen: I don't see a podium anywhere, either. The minister will need to be appropriately elevated.

Brunner: Paula, roll a beer keg over here.

Wolff: My swing-boat would be a nice pulpit, too.

Niedermaier: What can we help you with, and who are you?

Trankhafen: I don't have any business with you. Where is Herr Engineer Niedermaier?

Niedermaier: That's me!

Trankhafen: You? But the esteemed gentlemen are already on the way here!

Niedermaier: By all means!

Trankhafen: But you surely won't receive them that way, dressed in your overalls?

Niedermaier: I've just come from the machine house. I expect that the gentlemen want to see my work and not my Sunday clothes.

Trankhafen: It won't make the best impression.

Peters: Won't you please tell us what you're looking for?

Trankhafen: I won't be talked to in that tone. What gives you the right to ask me questions?

Peters: I'm the soundings master in the tower.

Trankhafen: And I am a member of the state government, Ministerial Advisor Henriette Trankhafen from the Ministry of Law, Order, and Security.

Brunner: I thought she was a woman traffic cop.

Trankhafen: Es erweist sich als recht gut, daß ich voraus geeilt bin, um nach dem Rechten zu sehen. Kein Rednerpult und nicht mal eine Fahne auf dem Wetterturm.

Niedermaier: Der Turm ist für meteorologische Zwecke gebaut worden. An die Notwendigkeit, Fahnenstangen anzubringen, hatten wir nicht gedacht.

Trankhafen: Ließe sich nicht die Mühle da noch beflaggen?

Fischer: Das Windrad? Wollen Sie das ganze Werk stillegen? *(Das Trommeln und Pfeifen wird wieder hörbar.)*

Trankhafen: Es ist höchste Zeit. Wo sollen sich denn die Redner hinstellen?

Annie: Geht es nicht von dem Hügel da? *(führt sie zu einer erhöhten Fläche vor dem Windrad)*

Trankhafen: Das wird gehen. *(steigt hinauf, prüft)* Verehrte Festversammlung! *(Die Kinder lachen.)* Törichte Rangen, euch wird man noch zu gesitteten Menschen erziehen müssen.

Berta: Die möchte ich als Figur für meine Schießbude.

Hantke: Hat die Regierung sonst noch was zu bestellen?

Trankhafen: Die Bewölkung gefällt mir nicht. Läßt sich das nicht ändern? Sie haben doch das Telegramm von Geheimrat Stechbein erhalten, Herr Ingenieur?

Niedermaier: Hab' ich bekommen.

Trankhafen: Da war doch wolkenlose Klarheit für den ganzen Tag erbeten?

Niedermaier: Der Wind weht, wie er wehen muß und der Regen fällt, wie er fallen muß.

Trankhafen: Was soll das heißen?

Niedermaier: Um 12 Uhr 7 Minuten setzt Sprühregen ein.

Trankhafen: Das ist unmöglich. Knipsen Sie sofort die Sonne an, Herr Peilmeister. *(steuert auf den Turm zu)*

Trankhafen: It was lucky I hurried on ahead to make sure everything was ready. No podium and not even a flag on the weather tower!

Niedermaier: The tower was built for meteorological purposes. We didn't even think about the need to put a flagpole on it.

Trankhafen: Couldn't we put a flag on the windmill up there?

Fischer: The windwheel? Do you want to stop the whole works? *(The drums and pipes are audible once again.)*

Trankhafen: It's time. Where should the speakers stand, then?

Annie: Couldn't they just stand on that hill over there? *(Leads her to an elevated area in front of the windwheel.)*

Trankhafen: That will work. *(Climbs up, tests the area.)* Honored guests of the festival! *(The children laugh.)* Foolish rascals, someone ought to teach you some manners!

Berta: I'd love to have her as a figure in my shooting gallery.

Hantke: Does the goverment require something else?

Trankhafen: I don't like those clouds. Can't that be changed? Didn't you receive the telegram from Privy Councillor Stechbein, Herr Engineer?

Niedermaier: I certainly did.

Trankhafen: Wasn't a cloudless sky requested for the whole day?

Niedermaier: The wind blows and the rain falls where they must.

Trankhafen: What's that supposed to mean?

Niedermaier: At 12:07 it will start to drizzle.

Trankhafen: That's impossible! Please switch on the sun immediately, Herr Soundings- Chief! *(Turns to the tower.)*

Fischer: *(stellt sich vor den Eingang)* Bleiben Sie bei der Politik, vom Wetter verstehen Sie nichts.

Brunner: Das ist kaum 11 Uhr. In einer Stunde können ein paar Minister und Abgeordnete mehr zusammenreden, als ein ganzes Volk bezahlen kann.

Trankhafen: Es ist empörend. Und kein Mensch hat einen Regenschirm bei sich. *(stapft der jetzt nahe einsetzenden Musik entgegen)*

Berta: Soll das Fest denn wirklich verregnen?

Niedermaier: Es dauert nur anderthalb Stunden; das haben die Tomaten- und Gurkenzüchter zu verlangen. Nachher ist bis in die Nacht trockener Westwind.

Hantke: Der kleine Schauer wird uns wohl nicht weh tun.

Jenny: Wenn er uns die lieben Ehrengäste wegschwemmt, wird's erst ein Volksfest.

Wolff: Schade bloß, daß mir die Trankhafen als Kundschaft mit wegläuft. Die hätt' ich gern mal in der Schaukel strampeln lassen.

Der Festzug tritt auf. Voran der Jugendchor, junge Männer und Mädchen aus dem Arbeiter- und Bauernstand. Am Flügel der ersten Reihe Otti Jungleib, *einfach und sehr kleidsam angezogen, dunkle Augen, rote Haare. Dr.* Trankhafen, *neben dem Zug herlaufend, spricht auf sie ein. Es folgt das Trommler- und Pfeiferchor, dessen Musik während des Aufmarsches alles andere übertönt. Hierauf die Regierungs- und Parlamentsmitglieder in loser Gruppe. Minister Dr.* Blödel *neben dem sozialistischen Abgeordneten* Hustenreiz, *einem dürren Schulmeister. Geheimrat* Stechbein, *etwa 50jähriger Lebemann, mit dem behäbigen Abgeordneten Pfarrer* Biederhold *von der Kirchenpartei und der Abgeordneten Frau* Möhre *von der christlichen Reformpartei, einer altmodisch aufgemachten Frömmlerin, deren Blicke fortwährend zum Regierungsassessor Dr.* Hornbriller *schweifen, der stark gestikulierend und mit der Aktentasche fuchtelnd auf den achtzigjährigen Dorfschulzen* Schönbrod *einspricht, dessen zerfurchtes Bauernangesicht gänzlich unbewegt bleibt. Er gibt nur manchmal mit einem Achselzucken zu verstehen, daß er kein Wort versteht. Der General* von Stiefengrat *in Uniform, bildet mit dem Abgeordneten* Krachhahn *von der*

Fischer: *(Stands in front of the entrance.)* You keep to politics. You don't understand anything about the weather.

Brunner: It's just barely 11:00. In one hour a couple of ministers and parliament deputies can talk their way into the people's pockets just fine.

Trankhafen: This is terrible! And no one has an umbrella! *(Trudges toward the approaching music.)*

Berta: Is the festival really going to be rained out?

Niedermaier: It'll just last an hour and a half; the tomato and cucumber farmers asked for it. When it's done there'll be dry west wind into the evening.

Hantke: That little shower won't hurt us.

Jenny: If it washes away the honored guests, then it'll really be a people's festival.

Wolff: It's just a shame that Fräulein Trankhafen ran away. I'd like to have seen her fidgeting around in that swing.

The procession enters. In the front is the youth choir, *young* men *and* women *of the working class, dressed in their Sunday best. On the end of the first row is* Otti Jungleib, *dressed simply, with dark eyes and red hair. Dr.* Trankhafen, *running along next to the procession, is talking to her. The drum and fife corps follows; during the parade their music overwhelms everything else. Then come the government and parliament members in a loose group. Minister* Blödel *walks next to the socialist delegate* Hustenreiz, *a thin schoolmaster. Privy Councillor* Stechbein, *a fifty-year-old man of the world, walks with the corpulent delegate Pastor* Biederhold *of the Church Party and then Frau* Möhre *of the Christian Reform Party, a pious woman dressed in an old-fashioned way, who tosses glances over to the government assessor, Dr.* Hornbriller; *he is gesticulating and waving his briefcase about as he speaks with the eighty-year-old village mayor,* Schönbrod, *whose wrinkled farmer's face remains absolutely unmoved. He simply makes clear from time to time with a shrug of his shoulders that he doesn't understand a single word. General* von Stiefengrat *in uniform is in a group with delegate*

Grundbesitzerpartei und dem Abgeordneten Barde *von der rassischen Erneuerungspartei eine Gruppe. Eine andere setzt sich zusammen aus dem liberalen* Selters, *dem Industriellen* Speicherer *und der Abgeordneten Frau* Wachtel *von der Hausfrauenpartei, einer rundlichen Dame, die etliche Tücher über dem Arm trägt, die sie fröstelnd immer wieder abwechselnd umlegt. Der Landtagspräsident* Krampf *läuft zwischen den Gruppen hin und her. Den Schluß des Zuges bildet ein Verein mit blauer Fahne, bestehend aus* Kleinbürgern, Beamten, Kriegsveteranen *und ähnlichen. Der Zug wird von* Männern *und* Frauen *aus dem Ort begleitet, teilweise in ländlicher Tracht. Besonders neben* Schönbrod *und* Hornbriller *gehen Dorfbewohner, die gespannt den Dorfschulzen beobachten. Der Zug umschreitet den Festplatz. Auf ein Zeichen des* Tambourmajors *bricht die Musik ab. Der Zug bleibt stehen und löst sich auf. Die Ehrengäste werden von* Trankhafen *zur Erhebung geleitet, die sich nun wie eine Art Feldherrnhügel ausnimmt. Die anderen* Teilnehmer *des Zuges zerstreuen sich im Hintergrund zwischen den Zelten.* Niedermaier, *mit* Peters *und* Fischer, *geht in den Turm. Die Übrigen stehen in losen Gruppen in der Nähe der Wurstbude.* Steinbott *verteilt Würstchen unter sie—das Windrad ist in ziemlich rasche Bewegung übergegangen.*

Trankhafen: (*vom Hügel herunter auf* Otti *zu, die links vorn den Jugendchor aufgestellt hat*) Ich bringe es nicht fertig, es dem Herrn Minister mitzuteilen. Er wird außer sich sein. Sie sind doch aber die Gehilfin des Herrn Niedermaier. Haben Sie denn so wenig Einfluß, daß Sie nicht die Anordnungen eines Regengusses an diesem Festtage entgegen dem ausdrücklichen Wünsche der Regierung hätten verhindern können?

Otti: Ich finde die Feldbestellung wichtiger, als das Fest.

Trankhafen: Wenn Ihr Chor in der kurzen Zeit jetzt keine Gelegenheit findet, den Lenkern unseres Staates seine Künste vorzuführen, wird er ja wissen, bei wem er sich zu bedanken hat.

Otti: Annie!

Annie: (*kommt gelaufen*) Ja, Otti?

Otti: Du bist Arbeiterin im Werk und singst und tanzt im Chor. Was tust du lieber?

Krachhahn *of the Landowners' Party and delegate* Barde *of the Workers'*
Race Party. Another group is composed of the Liberal delegate, Selters,
the Industrialist Speicherer, *and Frau* Wachtel *of the Housewives'*
Party, a rather round woman who carries several pieces of cloth under
her arm, which she wraps around her shoulders now and again as if she
were chilly. Provincial Parliament President Krampf *runs back and forth*
among the groups. At the end of the parade a club composed of petit
bourgeois, civil servants, war veterans, *etc., marches with a blue flag.*
The parade is accompanied by men *and* women *from the village, some*
dressed in traditional costumes. A large group of villagers *walk next to*
Schönbrod *and* Hornbriller *and watch the village mayor intently. The*
parade wraps around the festival plaza. At a signal from the drum major
the music stops. The honored guests are led by Trankhafen *to a high spot*
of ground; the group becomes "king of the hill." The other members *of*
the procession spread out in the background among the tents.
Niedermaier *goes into the tower with* Peters *and* Fischer. *The others*
stand in loose groups near the sausage stand. Steinbott *gives them*
sausages. The windwheel has started to move rather quickly.

Trankhafen: (*coming down the hill toward* Otti, *who stands to the left in*
  front of the youth choir) I simply will not be able to tell the minister.
  He will be beside himself. You are, after all, Herr Niedermaier's
  assistant. Do you have such small influence that you couldn't have
  prevented this rain shower, which comes contrary to the express wishes
  of the government?

Otti: I consider the needs of the farmers more important than the
  festival.

Trankhafen: If the members of your choir lose the opportunity to
  perform before the leaders of our state, they will know whom to thank!

Otti: Annie!

Annie: (*Comes running over.*) Yes, Otti?

Otti: You're a worker in the weather works, and you sing and dance
  with the choir. Which do you like more?

Annie: Das ist Beides wunderschön.

Otti: Fräulein Ministerialrat meint, wenn ihr wegen des Regens heut mittag nicht mehr dazu kommt, vor den Geheimraten und Abgeordneten zu singen, würdet ihr auf Herrn Niedermaier böse sein.

Annie: Wir brauchen doch die Regierung nicht zum Zuschauen, wenn wir uns freuen wollen.

Otti: (zum Chor) Wollt ihr, daß ich Herrn Niedermaier bitte, er soll den Wetterkalender umstoßen? den wir mit der Gemeinde und der Genossenschaft zusammen aufgestellt haben? damit die Regierung euch tanzen sieht?

Alle: Nein!

Otti: Dann lauft jetzt auf dem Festplatz herum. Wenn wir noch gewünscht werden sollten, lasse ich Signal blasen.

Trankhafen: Hier scheint ja alles zusammenzuhalten.

Otti: Das ist allerdings richtig.

Hornbriller: (kommt vom Hügel) Pardon, Fräulein Doktor, ich muß konstatieren, daß die Honorationen peu à peu indigniert scheinen. Die Organisation hier ist ja total direktionslos. Wer ist überhaupt maître de plaisir? Der senile Ortskommandant manifestiert sich als kompletter Abderite. Sein naives Desinteressement an der Festivität ist direkt katastrophal. Und der Jubilar fand es selbst nicht einmal opportun, die Honeurs zu machen.

Otti: Herr Niedermaier hat im Turm zu tun. Ihm geht die Pflicht immer über die Höflichkeit.

Trankhafen: Es bedarf keiner Belehrung, Fräulein. Ich bin selbst Sozialistin.

Otti: Da kommt er schon aus dem Turm. *(geht ihm entgegen)*

Hornbriller: Wie? Der Mann in dem legeren Habit? Der so nonchalant auf uns zukommt?

Trankhafen: Jawohl, der Mensch in der geben Windjacke. Was sagen Sie dazu?

Annie: They're both really nice.

Otti: Fräulein Trankhafen, the ministerial advisor, thinks that if you all don't get the chance to sing for the councillors and delegates today because of the rain, you'll be angry at Herr Niedermaier.

Annie: We don't need for the government to watch us if we want to have fun.

Otti: *(to the choir)* Do you all want me to ask Herr Niedermaier to forget about the weather calendar? The one we put together with the village and the collective? So that the government can watch you dance?

Everyone: No!

Otti: Then run around the festival plaza. If we're still wanted, I'll sound a signal.

Trankhafen: Well, here is finally something that's working properly.

Otti: That's certainly right.

Hornbriller: *(Comes from the hill.)* Pardon me, Doctor Trankhafen, I must point out that the honorees seem to be *peu à peu* indignant. The organization here is totally without direction. Just who is the *maître de plaisir*? The senile village commandant manifests himself as a complete simpleton. His naive disinterest in the festivities is absolutely disastrous. And the celebrant himself found it inconvenient to participate in the honors.

Otti: Herr Niedermaier has work to do in the tower. For him duty always goes before manners.

Trankhafen: There's no need to lecture me, young woman. I myself am a socialist.

Otti: There he comes from the tower now. *(Goes toward him.)*

Hornbriller: What? That man in the relaxed *couture*? The one coming so nonchalantly toward us?

Trankhafen: Yes indeed, the person in the yellow windbreaker. What do you say to that?

Hornbriller: Dieses saloppe Individuum, der Repräsentant des epochalen Mirakels! Tableau!

Trankhafen: Sie kommt mit ihm hierher.

Hornbriller: Tant mieux!

Niedermaier: *(auf dem Wege)* Wenn du dann die Meldung von Island aufgenommen hast, gib' die letzten Sendungen zur Neufundlandstation weiter.

Otti: Hast du die neuen Funksprüche oben?

Trankhafen: Sie duzen sich. Hören Sie?

Hornbriller: Ostentativ und coram publico. Es kann irrelevant sein.

Trankhafen: Es ist bezeichnend.

Niedermaier: Ostfriesland verlangt Südwind wegen der Versuche mit Kokospflanzen.

Otti: Haben die Lofoten Anweisung?

Niedermaier: Die Berichte über die letzten Peilungen im Golfstrom erwarte ich noch diese Woche.

Hornbriller: Pardon, Herr, wenn ich Sie aus dem Konzept bringe. Ließe sich Ihr interessanter Dialog nach Absolvierung der pressanten Formalitäten fortsetzen? — Regierungsassessor Hornbriller!

Niedermaier: Angenehm! Mein Name ist Niedermaier. *(flüchtiger Händedruck)*

Trankhafen: Der Herr Regierungsassessor glaubt, Sie nun unverzüglich dem Herrn Minister und den übrigen Herrschaften vorstellen zu sollen.

Niedermaier: Kommt es denn auf meine Person an? Die Dame hat vorhin schon meine Kleidung bemängelt.

Hornbriller: O, man wird die originellen Usancen einer ingeniuesen Individualität chevaleresk tolerieren.

Niedermaier: Zur Begrüßung ist doch als Vertreter der Gemeinde und der Genossenschaft der alte Herr Schönbrod bei den Herren.

Hornbriller: This sloppy individual, the representative of this miracle of our age! Unbelievable!

Trankhafen: She's coming here with him.

Hornbriller: Tant mieux!

Niedermaier: (while walking) Otti, if you've gotten the report from Iceland, then send along the last transmission to the Newfoundland station.

Otti: Do you have the new messages up there?

Trankhafen: He called her by her first name! Did you hear?

Hornbriller: Ostentatious and for the public. It is probably not relevant.

Trankhafen: But it's telling.

Niedermaier: East Frisia requests a southerly wind on account of the experiments with coconut production.

Otti: Did the Lofoten Islands get the word?

Niedermaier: I'm expecting the reports on the latest soundings in the Gulf Stream this week.

Hornbriller: Pardon me, sir, if I am breaking your train of thought. Could your interesting discussion continue after the dispatch of the pressing formalities? Government Assessor Hornbriller!

Niedermaier: Pleased to meet you. My name is Niedermaier. *(quick handshake)*

Trankhafen: The government assessor thought he should introduce you to the minister and the other ladies and gentlemen right away.

Niedermaier: Do you really need me personally to be there? Earlier the lady was complaining about my clothing.

Hornbriller: Oh, I'm sure everyone will generously tolerate the original idiosyncrasies of a genius.

Niedermaier: As far as the greetings are concerned, Herr Schönbrod is with the gentlemen. I'm sure that he can represent the village and the collective.

Otti: Du wirst schon selbst hinaufgehen müssen. Laß dich wenigstens vorstellen. Ich sehe nach dem Rechten.

Niedermaier: Peters und Fischer sind ja im Turm.

Trankhafen: Die Zeit vergeht. Man kann nicht länger warten lassen.

Hornbriller: Also sans phrase, Herr Diplomingenieur. Allons! Excellenz von Stiefengrat hält auf akkurate Präzision. Und wir dürfen auch die anderen illustren Persönlichekeiten nicht quasi antichambrieren lassen. Es wäre ja fast ein Affront.

Niedermaier: Ich verlasse mich auf dich, Otti. *(mit* Hornbriller *zum Hügel)*

Krampf: Mit wem kommt denn da der Herr Regiergunsassessor?

Stiefengrat: Wahrscheinlich ein Arbeiter, der unsere Befehle betreffs der Windrichtung entgegennehmen soll.

Möhre: Eine wunderbare Errungenschaft mit Gottes Hilfe!

Stechbein: Ein Wunder der Technik!

Selters: Der menschliche Geist vollbringt immer Erstaunlicheres!

Speicherer: Wir leben im Zeitalter der Kultur und Zivilisation.

Blödel: Es ist das Zeitalter der Demokratie.

Hustenreiz: Und des sozialen Aufschwungs.

Krachhahn: Die nationalen Belange nicht zu vergessen.

Barde: Und die völkische Erneuerung!

Biederhold: Amen!

Hornbriller: *(bleibt mit* Niedermaier *unter der Anhöhe stehen)* Herr Minister, Herr Landtagspräsident, verehrte Delegierte, Herren und Damen! Endlich gelang es mir, den genialen Konstrukteur des atmosphärologischen Institutes zu eruieren. Hier präsentiere ich Ihnen Herrn Diplomingenieur Niedermaier.

Niedermaier: Guten Tag. *(allgemeine Verblüffung, vielsagende Blicke)*

Krampf: *(geht auf ihn zu, die anderen folgen zögernd, das Weitere spielt sich auf der Mitte der Bühne ab.* Otti, *die* Budenbesitzer *und*

Otti: You'll have to go up yourself. Just let them introduce you. I'll keep everything in order.

Niedermaier: Well, yes, and Peters and Fischer are in the tower.

Trankhafen: It's getting late. We can't keep them waiting any longer.

Hornbriller: So, *sans phrase*, Herr Engineer. *Allons*! His Excellency von Stiefengrat insists on exact precision. And we mustn't leave the other illustrious personages waiting. That would almost be an affront.

Niedermaier: I'll count on you, Otti. *(Goes with* Hornbriller *to the hill.)*

Krampf: Who is that coming with the government assessor?

Stiefengrat: Probably a worker, to tell us something about our order for a change in the wind.

Möhre: A wonderful achievement, with the help of God!

Stechbein: A miracle of technology!

Selters: The human mind keeps creating more and more astounding things!

Speicherer: We are living in an age of culture and civilization.

Blödel: It is an age of democracy.

Hustenreiz: And of a social upswing.

Krachhahn: Don't forget national interests!

Barde: And ethnic renewal.

Biederhold: Amen!

Hornbriller: *(Remains standing with* Niedermaier *below the hill.)* Herr Minister, Herr Provincial President, honored delegates, ladies and gentlemen! I finally succeeded in locating the ingenious constructor of this atmospherological institute. Please allow me to introduce Herr Engineer Niedermaier!

Niedermaier: Good day. *(general perplexity, knowing glances)*

Krampf: *(Goes over to him, the others follow hesitantly. The rest of the scene takes place mid-stage.* Otti, *the* owners *of the booths, and the*

Arbeiter *ziehen sich in den Hintergrund der Buden zurück.*) Nach der parlamentarischen Ordnung heiße ich Sie in unserer Mitte willkommen. Wir verstehen, daß Ihnen die gesellschaftlichen Gebräuche bei festlichen Anlässen, zu denen die Parteien des Landtags ihre Vertreter entsenden, nicht geläufig sind.

Möhre: Aber das macht ja nicht viel aus.

Niedermaier: Ach so, meine Kleidung. Das Wetterwerk erlaubt mir keine Feieretage.

Selters: Wir freuen uns trotzdem.

Blödel: Natürlich—sehr!

Stechbein: Außerordentlich!

Speicherer: Gewiß doch. Vielleicht übernimmt aber doch die mir vom Landtag zugedachte Begrüßung des Herrn einer der mehr dem Volkstümlichen zuneigenden Kollegen.

Krachhahn: Wen haben wir denn da?

Stiefengrat: Für solchen Fall wäre schließlich der Herr Abgeordnete Hustenreiz der gegebene Mann.

Barde: Sehr richtig!

Krampf: Es erhebt sich kein Widerspruch. Dann darf ich Sie bitten, Herr Abgeordneter, sich als Beauftragten des Landtags zu betrachten.

Hustenreiz: Sehr ehrenvoll! Unvorbereiteterweise, verehrter Herr Diplomingenieur, entledige ich mich dennoch gern der Aufgabe, Ihnen im Namen der gesetzgebenden Körperschaften unseres Heimats- und Vaterlandes Gruß und Glückwunsch zu entbieten. Selbst durch das Vertrauen des Werktätigen Volkes ins Parlament erwählt und von der sozialistischen Fraktion desselben heute zu ihrer Vertretung hierher entsandt, glaube ich mich umsomehr berufen, Ihnen an dem Tage, an welchem vor nunmehr fünf Jahren der Grundstein zu Ihrer umwalzenden Kulturschöpfung gelegt wurde, Dank und Anerkennung des ganzen wahlberechtigten Volkes zu übermitteln. Wie hoch unser republikanischer Freistaat Ihre Verdienste schätzt, bewies Ihnen die Regierung bereits vor Jahresfrist als sie Ihnen trotz mangelnder Vorbildung auf Anregung des Vorstandes des Allgemeinen

workers *withdraw to the booths in the background.)* According to parliamentary procedure I welcome you into our midst. We understand that the customs of ceremonies, such as this one to which the parties of the provincial parliament have sent their representatives, are somewhat unfamiliar to you.

Möhre: But that doesn't really matter.

Niedermaier: Ah, I see, my clothes. The weather works don't permit me any holidays.

Selters: Nevertheless we are happy to meet you.

Blödel: Of course, very happy.

Stechbein: Extraordinarily so!

Speicherer: Certainly. But perhaps one of my more popularly oriented colleagues would like to take over my assignment of greeting the gentleman on behalf of the parliament.

Krachhahn: Whom do we have here who could do that?

Stiefengrat: In such a situation Herr Delegate Hustenreiz would probably be the right man.

Barde: Quite right!

Krampf: Hearing no objection, may I ask you, Herr Delegate, to consider yourself the representative of the provincial parliament?

Hustenreiz: I'd be honored. Although I am totally unprepared, Herr Engineer, I nevertheless gladly accept the task of offering you greetings and congratulations on behalf of the legislative bodies of our home and fatherland. I myself, having been elected to parliament with the confidence of the working class, and sent here today by the Socialist faction of that body as its representative, believe it is all the more appropriate that I should convey to you, on this day on which we commemorate the fifth anniversary of the laying of the cornerstone of your revolutionary cultural achievement, the thanks and acknowledgment of all the electorate. The high esteem in which the government of our republican state holds your achievements was shown one year ago, when it granted you, at the suggestion of the board of trustees of the amalgamated labor unions, and in spite of the lack of a prototype, the

Gewerkschaftstrustes den Titel eines Diplomingenieures unter Erlaß der Fachprüfung ehrenhalber verlieh. Sie, der den Menschen die Zügel in die Hand gab, um Wolken, Wind und Wellen zu lenken, stehen heute im schlichten Gewande der Arbeit vor den höchsten Vertretern der Nation. Der Herr Minister für Ruhe, Ordnung und Sicherheit selber ist herbeigeeilt, und mit ihm, unter Führung ihres Präsidenten, die Abgesandten des Langdages—(Stiefengrat *hustet und rasselt mit dem Säbel.*)—auch ein hervorragender Führer unserer vaterländischen Wehrmacht, hat es sich nicht nehmen lassen, an der Feier teilzunehmen. Wenn Sie selber auch den Sinn lediglich auf Nutz und Frommen Ihrer arbeitenden Mitmenschen gerichtet, dem Empfang der Spitzen unseres Staates fernblieben und den greisen Landmann hier ihre Begrüßung überließen, so denkt doch unsere Regierung, gebildet aus Parteien verschiedener Denkart—und auch wir Sozialisten sind in dieser Koalition vertreten—sozial genug, um Ihnen nicht zu grollen. Arbeit kann auch dann noch ehren, wenn sie die Anforderungen des Taktes einmal zu kurz kommen läßt. Ja, ungeachtet alles dessen beabsichtigt der Herr Minister Dr. Blödel heute noch eine besondere Überraschung—

Krampf: Ich möchte Sie doch bitten, Herr Kollege Hustenreiz, dem offiziellen Regierungsakt nicht vorzugreifen. Ihre Aufgabe erstreckt sich allein darauf, dem Herrn Jubilar die vorläufigen Empfindungen der Ehrengäste zum Ausdruck zu bringen. Dies ist wohl in Ihren Darlegungen mit allgemeiner Zustimmung geschehen, so daß Sie nun gütigst zum Schluß kommen wollen und die Jubelfeier alsdann ohne Verzug abgerollt werden kann.

Stechbein: Sehr wahr!

Hustenreiz: So spreche ich Ihnen denn, verehrter Herr Diplomingenieur noch einmal die hohe Genugtuung des hohen Hauses sowie der hohen Regierung über den hohen Aufschwung aus, dem Sie Ihrer hohen Kunst, das Wetter zu regeln, zu geben vermocht haben. Ich bitte Sie, mir zum Zeichen der innigen und unlösbaren Zusammengehörigkeit von Staat und Volk Ihre schwielige Hand zu reichen.

Krampf: Der Händedruck ist erfolgt. Ich stelle das fest. Herr Regierungsassessor Dr. Hornbriller wird jetzt die Freundlichkeit haben, uns die Reihenfolge des vorgesehenen Festprogramms mitzuteilen.

honorary title of Certified Engineer, exempted from the qualifying examination. You, who placed in human hands the reins by which clouds, wind, and waves are steered, you stand here today in modest work garments before the highest representatives of our nation. The minister for law, order, and security came here himself, and with him, under the leadership of the president, the delegates of the provincial parliament *(*Stiefengrat *coughs and rattles his sabre.)* comes as well one of the leading commanders of our national army, who also insisted on being at these festivities. Even though you thought only of the interests of your working comrades and relegated the role of welcoming delegation to this elderly gentleman here, nevertheless the government—composed as it is of parties of differing ideologies (and even we Socialists are represented in the coalition)—believes enough in socialism not to bear you ill will. Labor is still an honorable thing, even if it sometimes gives shortshrift to tact. Yes, apart from all that, Minister Dr. Blödel intends today to present a special surprise...

Krampf: I beg you, Herr Colleague Hustenreiz, not to anticipate the official government ceremony. Your task is simply to express to our honoree the greetings of the honored guests. You have really done this already in your statement, to the satisfaction of us all, so perhaps you could conclude your remarks and allow the ceremony to continue without delay.

Stechbein: How true!

Hustenreiz: Therefore I express to you, honored Herr Engineer, once again the highest satisfaction of the high house of parliament as well as of the highest reaches of the government with the high achievements you have enabled through your high art of regulating the weather. I ask you to give me your callused hand as a sign of your close and insoluable solidarity with the state and its people.

Krampf: The handshake has taken place. I confirm that. Herr Government Assessor Dr. Hornbriller will now be kind enough to tell us the order of events on the festival program.

Hornbriller: Das kostituierende Kommittee, dem ich präsidiert habe, hat folgende provisorischen Dispositionen skizziert, für deren exakten Verlauf rasantes Tempo freilich conditio sine qua non wäre. Wir haben momentan— *(sieht angestrengt auf die Windrose)* Die Konstruktion des Chronometers da irritiert mich—

Niedermaier: Das ist ein Windzeiger. Es ist jetzt 11 Uhr und 13 Minuten.

Hornbriller: Merci. Das Programm wird also präludiert durch ein Referat des Herrn Geheimrats Dr. Stechbein über die zivilisatorische und kulturelle Mission des atmosphärologischen Instituts. Hierauf werden die Herrn Abgeordneten Selters und Speicherer als Parlamentarier vom Metier die Konsequenzen einer eventuellen Nationalisierung der meteorologischen Etablissements für die Bilanz des Etats sowie die Chancen für die merkantilen resp. finanz-technischen privatökonomischen Interessen ausbalanzieren. Dann ein patriotischer Appell seiner Excellenz, des Herrn Delegierten des Militärministeriums, General von Stiefengrat. Als Clou des rhetorischen Programms erteilt hierauf der Chef der Institute unser Jubilar in Person, prinzipielle Informationen über die funktionellen Prämissen der atmosphärologischen Phänomene.

Niedermaier: Das kann ich nicht.

Hornbriller: Sie brauchen nur in vulgären Explikationen in nuce einen authentischen Kommentar zu geben.

Niedermaier: Ich bin kein Redner.

Hornbriller: Ultra posse nemo obligatur. Auf oratorische Rekorde reflektiert niemand; eventuell dozieren Sie die Details später bei der Inspektion der maschinellen und administrativen Installationen des Institutes und des Laboratoriums; davon können wir den prä-destinierten Mentor, den Inspirator und Organisator der Revolu-tionierung des Kosmos, eo ipso nicht dispensieren. Es folgt die Produktion der gesangsartistischen und choreographischen Piecen, des lokalen Jugendchores unter dem Arrangement der Assistentin des Herrn Diplomingenieurs Mademoiselle Ottilie Jungleib und als Finale des opulenten Programms last not least die Regierungsdemanche, die der Herr Minister Blödel urbi und orbi proklamieren wird und die in der Initiative kulminiert, die Institution unter das Protektorat der

Hornbriller: The constitutive committee, over which I have presided, has sketched out the following provisional disposition. In order for it to proceed exactly, a brisk tempo will of course be *conditio sine qua non.* At the moment it is— *(Strains to look at the weathervane.)* The construction of the chronometer there is strange to me—

Niedermaier: That is a weathervane. It is now 11:13.

Hornbriller: *Merci.* The prelude of the program will consist of a report by Privy Councillor Dr. Stechbein on the civilizational and cultural mission of the atmospherological institute. Next Delegates Selters and Speicherer, as members of parliament, will discuss the consequences of a possible nationalization of this meterological establishment for the state treasury, as well as the outlook for commercial or financial implications for private economic interests. Then there will be a patriotic appeal by his Excellency, the delegate of the military ministry, General von Stiefengrat. At the climax of the rhetorical program the head of the institute, our honoree, will himself give some information about the functional premises of this atmospherological phenomenon.

Niedermaier: I can't do that.

Hornbriller: You only need to give a very vulgar explanation of the way it really works.

Niedermaier: I'm not a public speaker.

Hornbriller: *Ultra posse nemo obligatur.* No one will worry about your oratorical experience; perhaps you can act as a docent later on when we all inspect the mechanical and administrative operation of the institute and the laboratory; we can't pass up the chance to hear from the preordained inventor and organizer of this revolution of the cosmos. After that we will see a presentation of the choreographic and vocal talents of the local youth choir under the direction of Herr Engineer's assistant, Mademoiselle Ottilie Jungleib, and as a finale of this opulent program, last but not least, the government's statement that Minister Blödel will proclaim *urbi et orbi*, and that will culminate in the initiative of the government whereby the institution will be

Republik zu stellen. Ein Souper incl. Fidelitas ist das happy end. Zur Retourfahrt sind Autos reserviert; auch steht auf der Station ein Extrazug parat.

Krampf: Ich danke Herrn Regierungsassessor Dr. Hornbriller für die lichtvolle Erläuterung des Tagesplans. Sind im Anschluß daran noch Ausstände oder Ergänzungen gewünscht?

Biederhold: Für diejenigen Festteilnehmer, welche das Jubiläum zum Anlaß nehmen möchten, den Segen des Allerhöchsten für das Vorhaben der Regierung zu erflehen, ist im Anschluß an die Besichtigung eine Weiheandacht dort hinter dem Würstchenzelt vorgemerkt.

Krachhahn: Selbstverständlich wird sich kein stubereiner Mensch einem solchen Seelenbade entziehen. Aber bei der Vorführung der Anlagen da im Turm, darf ich wohl ersuchen, daß Sie Herr Direktor, vielleicht ein kurzes Gewitter einlegen werden.

Niedermaier: Das ist in wenigen Minuten nicht möglich.

Barde: Donnerwetter, warum haben Sie sich denn auf sowas nicht vorbereitet? Wir wollen doch sehen, wie der Zauber hier vor sich geht.

Stiefengrat: Die Armee legt den größten Wert darauf, Aufschluß zu erhalten, ob und in welcher Zeit im Ernstfalle für die Belange der obersten Heeresleitung ein Erdbeben oder Überschwemmungs-katastrophe auf Anforderung geliefert werden kann.

Niedermaier: Meine Arbeit hat nie anderen Aufgaben gegolten, als den Schäden, die die gemeinnützige Wirtschaft auf dem Lande und in den Städten durch ungünstige Witterung erleidet, durch die künstliche Beeinflußung des Wetters abzuhelfen.

Speicherer: Dann sind also die eigentlichen Nutzaufgaben des Unternehmens noch nicht einmal in Angriff genommen worden.

Wachtel: Ich hätte eine Bitte an den Herrn Diplomwettermacher. Hier ist es so zügig. Ließe sich nicht der Ventilator dort abstellen?

Niedermaier: Das ist ein Windrad. Damit wird der electrische Strom für den Wetterturm erzeugt.

placed under the protectorate of the republic. A statement of allegiance will come at the end. We haveautomobiles ready for the return trip, and an extra train will also be waiting at the station.

Krampf: I would like to thank Herr Government Assessor Dr. Hornbriller for the very edifying explanation of the day's agenda. Does anyone wish to propose any additions or supplements to the program?

Biederhold: In the event that any participants in the festival should wish to take this opportunity to offer a prayer for the blessing of the Almighty on the further work of the government, there will be a devotional service behind the sausage tent immediately after the viewing of the institute.

Krachhahn: Well, naturally, no decent person will want to miss such a chance to get his soul cleansed. But when we get to the tour of the installation there in the tower, could I ask you, Herr Director, to perhaps set up a short thunderstorm?

Niedermaier: That's not possible in just a few minutes.

Barde: Well, hell's bells, man, why didn't you prepare something like that in advance? We want to see how this magic works!

Stiefengrat: The army is most of all interested in learning whether it is possible, and how long it will take, in an emergency determined by the supreme command, for an earthquake or flash flood to be delivered on demand.

Niedermaier: The purpose of my work has never been anything other than this: to artificially help relieve the economic damage to farm communities and cities caused by unfavorable weather.

Speicherer: Well then, the actual benefits of this operation haven't even begun yet.

Wachtel: I have a request for the weather man. It is quite drafty here. Could that fan up there be turned off?

Niedermaier: That is a wind wheel. It's used for generating electricity for the weather tower.

Wachtel: Ach so. Aber können Sie nicht ein bißchen Sonne durchlassen? Wissen Sie, ich bin so empfindlich mit meinem Magen.

Hustenreiz: Wahrscheinlich beabsichtigt unser Herr Gastgeber eine plötzliche Überraschung. Das Gewölk, das in der Tat augenblicklich den Himmel trübt, wird bald mit einem einzigen Hebelgriff verschwunden sein.

Niedermaier: Sie verkennen den Zweck—

Trankhafen: *(plötzlich dazwischentretend)* Worauf warten Sie eigentlich? In einer halben Stunde ist der Regen da.

Blödel: Regen? Wieso Regen?

Trankhafen: Sie wissen immer noch nichts? Der Herr Niedermaier und sein Fräulein Jungleib haben es für richtig befunden, das Jubiläum des Wetterturms trotz telegrafischer Sonnenscheinbestellung verregnen zu lassen. Ich enthalte mich jedes eigenen Urteils über ein solches Verfahren.

Krampf: Im Namen des Ältestenrats des Landtages frage ich Sie, Herr Diplomingenieur, ist das wahr?

Niedermaier: Die mit den Bauern getroffenen Vereinbarungen müssen wir unter allen Umständen einhalten.

Krachhahn: Unglaublich!

Barde: Doll!

Stechbein: An die planmäßige Abwicklung des Programms ist demnach nicht zu denken?

Möhre: Das ist ja ganz furchtbar.

Hornbriller: Die eklatante Sabotage aller unserer Dispositionen.

Selters: Man muß sich an den Kopf fassen.

Hustenreiz: Herr Diplomingenieur Niedermaier, schämen Sich sich!

Wachtel: Jetzt zieht es wirklich ganz entsetzlich. Das ist also Absicht? Pfui!

Speicherer: Hier scheint allerhand im Argen zu liegen.

Wachtel: Oh, I see. But couldn't you let a little bit of sunshine through? You know, I have a very sensitive stomach.

Hustenreiz: Probably our host is planning a sudden surprise. That cloud that is darkening the sky just now will be disappearing soon with the movement of a single switch.

Niedermaier: You misunderstand the purpose...

Trankhafen: *(stepping forward suddenly)* What are you all waiting for? The rain will be here in a half hour!

Blödel: Rain? What rain?

Trankhafen: You mean you still don't know? Herr Niedermaier and his Fräulein Jungleib have decided in their infinite wisdom to allow the dedication of the weather tower to be rained out, in spite of an advance telegram ordering sunshine. I will withhold my own judgment of the whole proceeding.

Krampf: On behalf of the council of elders of the provincial parliament, I must ask you, Herr Engineer, is this true?

Niedermaier: We can't change the arrangements we already made with the farmers.

Krachhahn: Unbelievable!

Barde: This is nutty!

Stechbein: Therefore we are not even going to consider the planned agenda of the program?

Möhre: This is terrible.

Hornbriller: An apparent sabotage of all our plans.

Selters: Absolutely unbelievable!

Hustenreiz: Herr Niedermaier, shame on you!

Wachtel: Now the draft is really getting terrible. And you made it happen on purpose? Bah!

Speicherer: Everything seems to have gone wrong here.

Krampf: Sie haben also die Selbstsucht einiger Bauern über den Volkswillen gestellt? Die Regierung und das Parlament nämlich sind die Träger des Volkswillens.

Niedermaier: Solange ich mit meinen Gehilfen und mit der Genossenschaft der Bauern und Arbeiter hier zu bestimmen habe—

Krachhahn: Das muß jetzt die längste Zeit gedauert haben.

Stechbein: Es scheint allerdings notwendig, daß die Staatsgewalt nach dem Rechten sieht.

Möhre: Ich bin fassungslos. Was soll nur geschehen?

Biederhold: Mein Vorschlag geht dahin, daß wir nach Verrichtung eines stillen Gebetes diese Stätte verlassen sollten.

Trankhafen: Schon um unserer Würde willen, dürfen wir uns nicht dem Unwetter aussetzen.

Wachtel: Und wegen der Erkältungsgefahr. Wenn man darmleidend ist—

Blödel: Andrerseits haben wir doch nach den Weisungen des Ministerrats zu verfahren. Ich muß mich unbedingt meines amtlichen Auftrags entledigen.

Hornbriller: Eine fatale Situation.

Hustenreiz: Zur Geschäftsordnung!

Krampf: Zur Geschäftsordnung, Herr Abgeordneter Hustenreiz.

Hustenreiz: Angesichts der tiefbedauerlichen Wendung, welche die Festveranstaltung bedroht, angesichts auch der vom Vertreter der Kirchenpartei, Herrn Abgeordneten Pfarrer Biederhold begründeten, von der Ministerialrätin Frl. Dr. Trankhafen sowie der Vertreterin der Hausfrauenpartei, der Frau Abgeordneten Wachtel unterstützten Anregung, die ganze Feier kurzerhand abzubrechen, mit Rücksicht jedoch wiederum auf den vom Herrn Minister selbst erhobenen Einwand gegen diese Anregung, erlaube ich mir folgenden Vorschlag zu machen, den ich hiermit zum Antrag erhebe: der Herr Landtagspräsident wolle eine Unterbrechung der gegenwärtigen Erörterungen herbeiführen, damit in vertraulicher Beratung erneut zur Tagesordnung Stellung genommen werde, bzw. deren Neufestsetzung

Krampf: So you place the selfish interests of a few farmers above the will of the people? Because, as you know, the government and the parliament are the representatives of the people's will.

Niedermaier: As long as I am making decisions on behalf of my assistants and the collective of farmers and workers...

Krachhahn: It's high time that we put an end to that.

Stechbein: It certainly seems that the powers of state will be called upon to preserve the law.

Möhre: I don't understand. What's happening now?

Biederhold: I suggest that we leave this place immediately after we bow our heads for a silent prayer.

Trankhafen: We shouldn't expose ourselves to this weather, simply in order to preserve our dignity.

Wachtel: And also in order not to catch cold. If a person has stomach problems...

Blödel: On the other hand, we have to carry out the orders of the ministerial council. I absolutely must fulfill my official duty.

Hornbriller: A fatal situation.

Hustenreiz: Point of order!

Krampf: Point of order, Herr Hustenreiz.

Hustenreiz: In view of the very regrettable turn of events threatening the ceremony, and also in view of the suggestion, presented by Deputy Rev. Biederhold and supported by Minsterial Advisor Dr. Trankhafen and the representative of the Housewives' Party, Deputy Wachtel, to terminate the festivities without further ado, but also bearing in mind the objection against this course of action raised by the minister himself, may I be allowed to make the following suggestion, which I put in the form of a motion: that the president of the provincial parliament call a recess in these present discussions, so that the day's agenda might be further discussed in confidential session and the continuation of the discussion be considered for the time remaining

für die noch verbliebene Frist bis zum Inkrafttreten des Niedermaierschen Niederschlages in Betracht gezogen werden könne.

Krampf: Erhebt sich ein Widerspruch? Herr Regierungsassessor, bitte!

Hornbriller: Um die Explikationen des Herrn Abgeordneten Hustenreiz zu arrondieren, nicht um gegen sie zu polemisieren, appelliere ich an Ihre politische Intelligenz, weitere prekäre Eventualitäten a priori zu eliminieren. Wir stehen unter den Auspizien einer force majeur. Das unqualifizierbare Attentat auf die Souveränität der Regierung unter legislativen Instanzen konterkariert alle Intentionen des Programmkommittees. Akzeptieren Sie nun die Proposition Hustenreiz, so müssen implicite Garantien geschaffen werden, die neue Komplikationen coute que coute unmöglich machen. Affairen wie die aktuelle involvieren die latente Gefahr, im Status der Diskussion Temperamente explodieren zu lassen. Die Debatte über die res agenda gibt sub specie der illoyalen Methoden des Herrn Diplomingenieurs pessimistischen Prognosen Raum. Der Diskussion der Konferenz muß daher die absoluteste Diskretion garantiert werden. So delikat es sein mag, eine solche Resolution zu motivieren, muß ich es doch um unsrer Reputation willen als inopportun charakterisieren, nach den passierten Antecedentien die Assistenz des Jubilars bei dem Konsilium zu koncedieren. Der interne Charakter und die relative Gefahr eines publicwerdens der Kommissionsberatung zwingt mich zu der Proposition: die Spezialkonferenz möge ihre Explosivität durch die expresse Deklaration evident machen, daß Funktionäre des atmosphärologischen Institutes an ihrer Diskussionen generell nicht partizipieren sollen. Ein respektives formelles Votum bitte ich dem Antrag Hustenreiz als Amendment zu substituieren.

Speicherer: Sehr vernünftig.

Barde: So ist es richtig. Das heißt deutsch gesprochen!

Stechbein: Weitere Auseinandersetzungen sind nach den überzeugenden Darlegungen der beiden Vorredner entbehrlich. Ermächtigen Sie den Herrn Präsidenten durch Zuruf, gemäß den Anträgen zu verfahren.

Biederhold: Einverstanden.

until the precipitation arranged by Herr Niedermaier is fully implemented.

Krampf: Is there any objection? Herr Government Assessor, if you please!

Hornbriller: In order to complement the explications of Delegate Hustenreiz, but not to polemicize against them, I appeal to your political intelligence to eliminate any further complications *a priori*. We are under the auspices of a *force majeur*. This unqualified attack against the sovereignty of the government countervails every intention of the program committee. If you accept the proposition of Herr Hustenreiz, you must also insist on implicit guarantees that make new complications *coute que coute* impossible. In affairs such as this present one there is the latent danger that temperaments might explode during the course of the discussion. The debate on the *res agenda* allows for a pessimistic prognosis *sub specie* of the rather disloyal methods of Engineer Niedermaier. We must therefore guarantee that the discussions of the conference committee be handled discreetly. As precarious as it might be to motivate such a resolution, for the sake of our reputation I find it inappropriate to concede any participation of the honoree in the committee session. The internal character and relative danger of making public the committee's proceedings forces me to suggest the following proposition: the special conference shall make clear that, due to the explosivity of the discussions, functionaries of the atmospherological institute not be allowed to participate in the discussions. I would like to substitute a formal vote as an amendment to the motion of Herr Hustenreiz.

Speicherer: Very reasonable.

Barde: That's right. Well spoken, Herr Hornbriller.

Stechbein: Any further discussions may be dispensed with, in view of the cogent arguments of the two previous speakers. Let us empower the president by proclamation to proceed according to the motion.

Biederhold: Agreed.

Krampf: Widerspruch wird nicht erhoben. Es ist indessen meine demokratische Pflicht Herrn Diplomingenieur Niedermaier zu fragen, ob er selbst sich etwa zur Sache äußern will.

Stiefengrat: Das ist wohl eine übertrieben Langmut.

Niedermaier: Fürchten Sie nicht, daß ich mich Ihnen aufdrängen werde. Ich habe nur eine Erklärung abzugeben.

Selters: Hört, hört!

Niedermaier: Die Jubiläumsfeier ist von der Leitung des Wetterwerks weder angeregt noch mit ihrer Befragung in ihrem Verlauf vorbereitet worden. Der Regenfall heute ist nach Verständigung mit der Gemeindevertretung dieses Ortes auf ausdrückliches Verlangen des Allgemeinen Tomaten- und Gurkenzüchterverbandes festgesetzt. Die Veranstalter der Kundgebung hätten durch einfache Anfrage jederzeit Auskunft erhalten, welcher Tag für ihre Absichten die geeignetste Witterung aufweisen würde. Daß das unterblieb, fällt nicht mir zur Last. Der Wetterturm mit allen zugehörigen Anlagen gehört einer Genossenschaft werktätiger Bauern und Arbeiter, die mir das Vertrauen schenkt, mit selbstgewählten Hilfskräften nach freiem Ermessen das von mir erdachte und erschaffene Werk in den Dienst der Allgemeinheit zu stellen. Von anderen Stellen oder von obenher befohlene Sonderfeiertage kann ich in meinen Berechnungen nicht berücksichtigen. Es ist mir nur erwünscht, wenn Sie sich Ihr neues Programm ebenso wie das vorige ohne meine Mitwirkung ausdenken wollen. Da der Ortsschulze, mein Freund Schönbrod, der auch Vorsitzender der Wettergenossenschaft ist, wohl nicht von Ihrer Beratung ausgeschlossen werden wird, sind die Angelegenheiten des Werks und der Gemeinde auch ohne mich gut vertreten.

Trankhafen: So spricht nun ein Mann, dessen Name einmal in die Schullesebücher kommen sollte.

Möhre: Da sei Gott vor!

Blödel: Der Ton schien auch mir recht ungehörig zu sein.

Krampf: Gegen die Teilnahme des Herrn Ortsschulzen besteht wohl keine Erinnerung?

Krampf: Hearing no objection, so ordered. It is now my democratic duty to ask Herr Niedermaier whether he wishes to make a statement on this matter.

Stiefengrat: That really shows an excess of patience.

Niedermaier: Please don't worry that I will try to force my opinions on you. I simply want to give an explanation.

Selters: Hear, hear.

Niedermaier: This commemorative ceremony was neither planned by us who work in the weather works, nor were we asked about it. Today's rainfall was agreed on by the communal representatives of this village at the request of the Tomato and Cucumber Growers' Association. If we had only been asked, we would have told the people who organized this event which day might be the best for their plans. It's not my fault that you didn't do that. The weather tower and everything attached to it belongs to a collective of farmers and workers who have placed their trust in me, that I would use this equipment—equipment that I designed and built—for the service of the community. I can't consider requests for sunny days that come from outside the collective or from somebody in the government. I am only asking that you rework your new program for today just like the one before, but without my participation. Since my friend, Village Mayor Schönbrod, who is also chair of the weather collective, will surely be included in your discussions, I'm sure the concerns of the weather works and of the village will be well represented.

Trankhafen: And this is the way a man speaks whose name should one day appear in school books!

Möhre: God help us!

Blödel: His tone seemed quite inappropriate to me.

Krampf: I don't suppose there is any objection to having the mayor participate?

Schönbrod: Doch. In ihren Konventikel oder wie Sie dazu sagen, wir auf dem Lande nennen das man einfach einen Verein—da wüßt' ich nicht, was ich da reinzuschnabeln hätte. Ich bin all über achtzig, und das können Sie sich man sagen lassen: seit daß wir hier den Turm zu stehen haben, kriegen unsere Bauern Jahr für Jahr gute Ernte. Und die Arbeiter kriegen davon zu tun, und da sind wir mit zufrieden. Die letzten zwei Jahr haben wir von der Regierung keinen roten Heller mehr für die Gemeinde verlangt, bloß daß die Regierung von uns immer mehr Steuern und Abgaben verlangt. Das sag' ich Ihnen, und wenn Sie noch so große Herrschaften sind, wenn Sie hier sonst nichts wollen als Unfrieden machen und das Wetterwerk aus dem richtigen Gang bringen, dann hätten Sie man getrost zuhaus bleiben können.

Stiefengrat: Unglaublich!

Schönbrod: Bei uns, da bestimmen vorerst wir selber, das merken Sie sich man. Und wir, das heißt die Genossenschaft und die Gemeinde, wir stehen wie ein Mann zu unserm Freund Niedermaier und zu unserer roten Otti und zu Peilmeister Peters und der ganzen Belegschaft im Turm. Die wissen, was für die Bauern und Arbeiter nottut. Und Sie wissen das nicht, daß Sie das man wissen.

Speicherer: Das sind tatsächlich sehr bedenkliche Zustände hier.

Selters: Sie scheinen ja nicht einmal einen ordnungmäßigen Aufsichtsrat zu haben.

Stechbein: Die Regierung wird sich um die Dinge kümmern müssen.

Speicherer: Sagen Sie, Herr Schulze, was schüttet denn Ihre Genossenschaft eigentlich für eine Dividende aus?

Schönbrod: Da verstehe ich nichts von.

Niedermaier: Das Wesen der Genossenschaft beruht darauf, daß der Gesamtertrag des Werkes den Arbeitenden Genossen selbst zugute kommt.

Selters: Das ist reinste Anarchie.

Krachhahn: Da muß mit eisernem Besen zwischengefahren werden.

Hustenreiz: Wir wollen das, was Sie gesagt haben, nicht auf die Goldwaage legen, Herr Schönbrod. Sie sind ein alter Mann, andernfalls

Schönbrod: Oh yes there is. I wouldn't have any idea what I have to toss into your little convocation, or whatever you call it. Out here in the country we'd call it a club. I am over eighty years old, and so you can listen to me when I say this: since we've had this tower standing here, our farmers have had good harvests every year. And the workers have plenty to do, and so we're happy with it. In the last two years we haven't asked the government for one red penny for our village, and for that the government charges us taxes and payments and such. And I'll tell you this, you important ladies and gentlemen, if you don't want to do anything here except get everybody worked up and mess up the way the weather tower works, then you should have just stayed home.

Stiefengrat: Unbelievable!

Schönbrod: Out here, we make our own decisions. You can see that for yourself. And we—I'm talking about the collective and the village—we are all behind our friend Niedermaier and Otti and Peters the soundings man and everybody who works in the tower. They know what we need for our farmers and workers. And you all don't, and anybody can see that.

Speicherer: This really is a delicate situation here.

Selters: It looks as though they don't even have a real board of directors here!

Stechbein: The government will have to deal with this.

Speicherer: Tell me, Herr Mayor, what sort of dividends is your weather collective paying?

Schönbrod: I don't know anything about that.

Niedermaier: The basic idea of the collective is that everything the tower produces is used for the good of the workers themselves.

Selters: That's nothing but anarchy.

Krachhahn: Someone needs to clean house around here.

Hustenreiz: We are not going to put great weight on your comments, Herr Schönbrod. You are an old man. In other circumstances a speech

könnte eine solche Sprache vor den Spitzen des Staates und der Behörden in keiner Weise geduldet werden.

Schönbrod: Das ist mir einerlei.

Hornbriller: Charmant, à la bonheur. Haben Sie denn keinen Respekt vor Autorität und Staatsräson?

Schönbrod: Sie gehen mich nichts an. Mich geht die Gemeinde und die Genossenschaft was an. Und was die angeht, geht Sie nichts an.

Stiefengrat: Mit solchen Hetzern im Hinterland sollen wir den nächsten Krieg gewinnen—

Biederhold: Möge der Allmächtige die Verblendeten auf den Weg der Demut geleiten.

Möhre: Wenn es nur nicht schon zu spät ist.

Trankhafen: Wir werden mit dem Alten noch solange die Zeit vertrödeln, bis der Wolkenbruch uns hier wegspült.

Blödel Ich muß unbedingt vorher den Auftrag der Regierung vollziehen.

Wachtel: Dabei zieht es immer gräßlicher.

Krampf: Wohin kann man sich denn eigentlich hier zurückziehen?

Schönbrod: Da treten Sie man einfach hinter eine Bude. Das machen wir alle so.

Krampf: Ich meine, wo die Beratung ungestört stattfinden kann.

Niedermaier: Das Bierzelt steht hinter dem Windrad. Da stört Sie jetzt niemand.

Krampf: Dann bitte ich die Herren und Damen, mir zum Bierzelt zu folgen.

Krachhahn: Endlich ein Lichtblick.

Selters: Sie sollten vielleicht doch mitkommen, Herr Ortsvorsteher.

Stechbein: Ihre unpassenden Bemerkungen wollen wir gern Ihren weißen Haaren zugute halten.

Schönbrod: Wo Niedermaier bleibt, bleib' ich auch.

like yours in front of the leaders of the state and the authorities would not be permitted.

Schönbrod: Makes no difference to me.

Hornbriller: *Charmant, à la bonheur.* So I take it you have no respect for authority and matters of state?

Schönbrod: Those things don't matter to me at all. I'm just concerned with the village and the collective. And what happens to them is no concern of yours.

Stiefengrat: And with rabble-rousers like this out in the provinces we are supposed to win the next war...

Biederhold: May the Almighty lead the blind in the path to humility.

Möhre: If it's not already too late.

Trankhafen: We will stand here wasting time with this old man until the cloudburst washes us all away.

Blödel: First I absolutely have to carry out the mission of the government.

Wachtel: And the wind is getting nastier.

Krampf: Where can we retire to around here?

Schönbrod: Why don't you just step behind one of the booths? That's what we do.

Krampf: I mean, where can our meeting take place undisturbed?

Niedermaier: The beer tent is over their behind the wind wheel. No one will bother you there.

Krampf: Then may I ask that the ladies and gentlemen follow me over to the beer tent.

Krachhahn: Finally a break in the clouds.

Selters: Perhaps you should come with us, Herr Mayor.

Stechbein: We can excuse your inappropriate remarks on account of your white hair.

Schönbrod: I'll stay wherever Niedermaier stays.

Trankhafen: Sie werden Ihren Eigensinn noch einmal bereuen müssen.

Schönbrod: Denn man zu.

Die Regierungsvertreter *und* Parlamentarier *setzen sich in Bewegung.*

Wachtel: Wo ist denn das Zelt, Ach, dort. Gott sei dank! *(Eilt voraus.)*

Schönbrod und Niedermaier *kommen in den Vordergrund und brechen gleichzeitig in lautes Gelächter aus. Die Anderen verschwinden im Hintergrund. Als Letzte folgen* Hornbriller *mit Frau* Möhre *und im Abstand* Stechbein *mit* Trankhafen.

Trankhafen: *(laut)* Hören Sie nur, Herr Geheimrat, Sie wagen es noch, uns zu verhöhnen. *(leise)* Theodor!

Stechbein: *(laut)* Es muß durchgegriffen werden. *(leise)* Henriette!

Möhre: *(laut)* Ich hätte nicht geglaubt, daß die Landbevölkerung so verdorben wäre. *(leise)* Norbert!

Hornbriller: *(laut)* Ihre Renitenz wird mit Repressalien quittiert werden. *(leise)* Malvine!

Er geht, sie am Hintern tätschelnd, mit ihr den andern nach.

Niedermaier: *(legt die Hand um den Mund, ruft in die Richtung hinter der Luftschaukel)* Otti! Otti!

Otti: *(unsichtbar)* Hallo! Was ist los?

Niedermaier: Komm doch her!

Otti: *(kommt zum Vorschein.)* Keiner mehr da? Wo sind sie denn alle geblieben?

Niedermaier: Die ganze Obrigkeit sitzt bei Paula im Bierzelt.

Otti: Unsinn!

Niedermaier: Ich durfte nicht mit, weil ich unartig war.

Schönbrod: Und ich hab' ihnen den Buckel hingehalten.

Otti: Was heißt denn das?

Trankhafen: You will regret your obstinacy.

Schönbrod: Maybe so.

Government representatives *and* parliamentarians *begin to move.*

Wachtel: So where is this tent? Ah, there it is, thank God! *(Hurries out.)*

Schönbrod *and* Niedermaier *come down to the foreground and simultaneously break into loud laughter. The others disappear into the background. At the back of the group* Hornbriller *follows with Frau* Möhre, *and then after a bit* Stechbein *with* Trankhafen.

Trankhafen: *(loudly)* Look, Herr Privy Councillor, they dare to still mock us! *(quietly)* Theodore!

Stechbein: *(loudly)* Someone needs to do something about that. *(quietly)* Henriette!

Möhre: *(loudly)* I never would have believed that the people out here in the country were so corrupted! *(quietly)* Norbert!

Hornbriller: *(loudly)* Their obstreperousness will be answered with repression. *(quietly)* Malvine!

He follows the others, patting Möhre *on the rear end.*

Niedermaier: *(Puts his hand to his mouth and calls out behind the swing-boat.)* Otti! Otti!

Otti: *(off)* Hello! What's up?

Niedermaier: Come over here.

Otti: *(Comes forward.)* Is nobody here? Where did they all go?

Niedermaier: The whole government is sitting in Paula's beer tent.

Otti: How crazy!

Niedermaier: I wasn't allowed to go, because I didn't behave myself.

Schönbrod: And I turned my back on them.

Otti: What's that mean?

Niedermaier: Die Trankhafen hat sie geängstigt, daß ihnen ihr wunderschönes Festprogramm verregnen würde.

Otti: Es gibt doch bloß Sprühregen und nur kurze Zeit.

Niedermaier: Das würde ich ihnen doch nicht sagen. Sie wollten uns den ganzen Tag versauen. Jetzt bauen sie ein neues Programm, das noch bei gutem Wetter runtergeleiert werden kann.

Otti: Dann müssen sie sich beeilen.

Niedermaier: Den Minister drückt die Regierungserklärung. Sonst wären sie schon wehklagend abgezogen. Jetzt werden wie wohl noch schnell die mir zugedachten Verbeugungen von der Tagesordnung streichen. Umsobesser.

Otti: Meinen Chor brauche ich ihnen also auch nicht vorzuführen?

Schönbrod: Die freuen sich da doch nicht an. Das ist so schön, daß da bloß die armen Leute und die Kinder was von haben.

Otti: Eine ekelhafte Bande ist das. Nach dem Empfang unten haben die Zierden sämtlicher Parteien und Ministerien mit mir anzubandeln versucht. Je patriotischer einer war, umso deutlicher.

Niedermaier: Ich möchte mal hören, wie der Hornbriller eine Liebeserklärung macht. Der Kerl quasselt einen mit seinen ewigen Fremdwörtern vollkommen besoffen.

Otti: Sowas regiert uns.

Schönbrod: Haben ja den lieben langen Tag sonst nichts zu tun.

Niedermaier: Wenn sie nur ihre Finger von unserm Werk lassen wollten. Das Protektorat dieses Packs fürchte ich mehr alst die Pest.

Schönbrod: Was sollten sie riechen können, wenn sie die Nase darein stecken?

Niedermaier: Haben Sie nicht verstanden, was die Frage nach dem Aufsichtsrat und den Dividenden bedeuten sollte? Sie wollen für das Wetterwerk Gesetze machen, damit sie an der Börse außer mit Giftgas auch mit dem Barometerstand spekulieren können.

Schönbrod: Dann sollen sie es wohl mit der Gemeinde zu tun kriegen.

Niedermaier: Trankhafen scared them into thinking their beautiful ceremony would get rained out.

Otti: But it's just going to drizzle for a little while.

Niedermaier: I wouldn't tell them that. They wanted to spoil our whole day. Now they're putting together a new program that can still be rattled off in good weather.

Otti: Well, they better hurry.

Niedermaier: The minister is feeling pressure from the government decree. Otherwise they would have gone home complaining. Now they'll probably cut the bowing and scraping to me out of the program. All the better.

Otti: So I don't need to bring in my choir to sing for them?

Schönbrod: They wouldn't appreciate it anyway. This is too nice a thing for them, letting the poor people and children be a part of things.

Otti: What a revolting bunch! After the reception down there the dignitaries from all the parties and ministries tried to seduce me. The more patriotic they were, the worse it was.

Niedermaier: I'd really like to hear how Hornbriller makes love to someone. That guy spits out his foreign words as if he were drunk.

Otti: And these characters are our government.

Schönbrod: They don't have anything else to do the whole blessed day.

Niedermaier: As long as they keep their hands off our weather works. I'm more scared of this bunch protecting us than I am of the plague.

Schönbrod: Well what are they going to smell if they stick their noses where they don't belong?

Niedermaier: Didn't you understand what those questions about the board of directors and dividends meant? They want to make laws for the weather works so the stock exchange can speculate on barometric readings instead of on nerve gas.

Schönbrod: Well, they'll have to deal with the village on that.

Annie: *(kommt zögernd vor, hinter ihr andere* Jugendliche*)* Otti, was wird nun mit dem Chor? Sollen wir ins Dorf gehen und nachmittags wiederkommen? wenn der Besuch weg ist? Da ist ja gar keiner mehr?

Otti: Sie kommen wieder. Ja, was machen wir denn jetzt?

Niedermaier: Fangt doch gleich an!

Otti: Aber sie können doch jeden Augenblick wieder hier sein.

Niedermaier: Laß sie doch. Wenn sie ihr Programm ohne uns machen, machen wir unsers ohne sie.

Otti: Du hast recht, ich lasse antreten. Komm, Annie.

Annie: Fein! *(Otti mit den* Jungen *rasch ab.)*

Schönbrod: Die werden kucken!

Niedermaier: Bis die mit ihrer Beratung fertig sind, ist alles vorbei, womöglich auch schon der Regen. Dann hätten wir sie doch den ganzen Tag am Halse.

Schönbrod: Wissen Sie, was ich meine? Ich meine, Sie sollten reden, auch wenn sie das selber garnicht mehr haben wollen.

Niedermaier: Was könnte ich denen groß sagen? Das will immer nur sich selber reden hören und weiß alles besser, am besten das, wovon es garnichts weiß. Wie das Werk arbeitet, kann ich jedem einfachen Menschen erklären, aber nicht Leuten, deren geistige Tätigkeit sich in der Frage erschöpft: wie zieht man gemeinschaftlich dem Volk die Haut von den Knochen und betrügt sich dabei gegenseitig?

Schönbrod: Lassen Sie man. Leicht zu begreifen ist ihr Turm für niemand.

Niedermaier: Natürlich nicht. Um zu verstehen, warum die Maschinen die Luftströme in weiter Entfernung beeinflussen, muß man etwas von Physik, Geographie und Astronomie wissen. Denken Sie, daß von den aufgeblasenen Verbotsfabrikanten ein einziger davon mehr Ahnung hätte als Sie? Oder irgendeine Kuhmelkerin aus dem Dorf?

Annie: *(Comes forward hesitantly, behind her other* young people.*)* Otti, what's going on with the choir? Should we go into the village and come back in the afternoon? If the visitors are gone? I don't see anybody here.

Otti: They'll be back. So, what do we do now?

Niedermaier: Go ahead and start!

Otti: But they could be back any minute.

Niedermaier: Don't worry about that. If they're going to have their program without us, we'll have ours without them.

Otti: You're right. I'll have the choir come over. Come on, Annie.

Annie: Great! *(Otti goes quickly off with the teenagers.)*

Schönbrod: Give them something to look at.

Niedermaier: By the time they're finished with their meeting everything will be over, maybe even the rain. If that happens we'll have them on our backs the whole day.

Schönbrod: Know what I think? I think you ought to speak, even if they don't want you to anymore.

Niedermaier: What grand things could I say to them? That kind of person just wants to hear himself talk, and tries to sound like he knows everything, even when he doesn't know anything. I can explain to any simple person how the operation works, but not to people whose only concern is: how can they all cheat the people without cheating themselves at the same time?

Schönbrod: Ah, don't worry about it. Your tower isn't easy for anybody to understand.

Niedermaier: Of course not. In order to understand how this machine can influence airstreams by long distance, you have to know something about physics, geography, and astronomy. But do you think that a single one of those lawmakers has more of a clue than you do? Or than any milkmaid in the village?

Schönbrod: Das nicht. Aber wüßte unsereiner nicht vom Zusehen, daß im Turm Wetter gemacht wird, dann wär' es für uns schwer, es zu glauben.

Niedermaier: Das stimmt. Die da glauben an alles, wenn sie zugleich glauben können, daß es was einbringt. Weiter wollen sie auch von mir garnichts erfahren. Aber Sie möchten mehr wissen, daher können Sie auch mehr begreifen.

Schönbrod: Ich will gern zuhören.

Niedermaier: Sehen Sie, die künstliche Wetterbildung ist so wenig etwas Unnatürliches wie die Ausnutzung der Sonnenkraft und der Elektrizität der Blitze, die längst gelungen ist. Ich habe mich gefragt, welche Kraft in der Natur selber am stärksten auf die Wetterbildung einwirkt. Das ist dieselbe Kraft, die Ebbe und Flut schafft, die Meereskraft, eine unerschöpfliche Energiemenge, die den ganzen Erdball umkreist.

Schönbrod: Das versteh' ich.

Niedermaier: Sie haben vom Golfstrom gehört. Das ist der Wärmespender der Weltmeere. Gelang es, diese ungeheure Wärmequelle in unsre Gewalt zu bekommen und zugleich die Meereskraft freizumachen, so war die Aufgabe gelöst. Das ist das Geheimnis des Turms, der als erster seiner Art freilich erst in beschränktem Umkreis uns die Atmosphäre gefügig macht.

Schönbrod: Können Sie außer Regen und Sonne noch jede andere Witterung mit der Maschine zuwege bringen? Der General wollte das ja wissen.

Niedermaier: Alle Wetter sind in unsre Hand gegeben.

Schönbrod: Alle Wetter! Da könnt' einer schön was mit anrichten.

Niedermaier: Wir haben Wetterwarten in allen Weltgegenden, besonders auf den hohen Bergen. Die zeigen uns die natürlichen Wetterbildungen nach den Beobachtungen der Himmelserscheinungen und der Luftfeuchtigkeit an. Unsere Funkapparate und Peilvorrichtungen erlauben uns, den Wellen- und Windbewegungen nach unsern Wünschen die erforderliche Richtung zu geben.

Schönbrod: Well, no. But if any of us didn't know from having seen it that the tower makes weather, I think it would be hard for us to believe it.

Niedermaier: That's true. Those guys believe in anything as long as they can also believe that it will earn something. They don't want to hear anything else from me, either. But you want to know more, and so therefore you can understand more.

Schönbrod: I sure do want to hear about it.

Niedermaier: You see, artificial weather control is no more unnatural than taking advantage of solar power, or using the electricity of lightning, and these things have been around for a long time. I asked myself which natural power has the strongest influence on the formation of weather. That would be the same power that makes ebbs and floods, the power of tides, an inexhaustible amount of energy that surrounds the entire globe.

Schönbrod: I understand that.

Niedermaier: You've heard of the gulfstream. That's the source of warmth for the world's oceans. When we were successful in gaining control of that huge source of warmth and at the same time releasing the power of tides, then we solved the problem. That's the secret of the tower, and it's the first of its kind to be able to make the atmosphere available to us, even if it is in just a limited area.

Schönbrod: Can you make any kind of weather with your machine other than rain and sunshine? The general wanted to know.

Niedermaier: All the weather is put into our hands.

Schönbrod: Thunderation! Boy, you could really do something with that!

Niedermaier: We have weather watchers all around the world, especially on the high mountains. They report to us the natural weather formations according to observations of heavenly phenomena and humidity. Our radios and soundings devices enable us to guide the waves and wind movements in the direction we want.

Schönbrod: Wir auf dem Lande wissen, was das wert ist. Sowas zu erfinden!

Niedermaier: Das denken Sie sich. Die Behörden denken sich, daß man dazu nicht schnell genug einen Paragraphenschraubstock erfinden kann.

Trompetensignal. Der Platz füllt sich schnell. Steinbott *aus seiner Bude vortretend.*

Steinbott: Geht's los? Warme Würstchen!

Wolff: Nanu, der Hügel ist leer.

Berta: Feiern wir allein Jubiläum? Ist ja viel schöner.

Otti: Hört mal zu. Unsre hohen Gönner sind böse, weil wir die liebe Sonne nicht den ganzen Tag auf ihre weisen Häupter scheinen lassen wollen. Jetzt beratschlagen sie beim Glase Bier, wie man im Reden Weihesprüche ableiern kann, ohne naß zu werden. Bis sie das entdeckt haben, wollen wir das Fest feiern, wie es uns gefällt. Einverstanden?

Viele: Ja! Anfangen.

Otti: Also! *(erneutes Signal, Schalmeienkapelle stellt sich auf)* Seid ihr alle fertig? *(ordnet die Reihen des* Jugendchors*)*

Jenny: Vater Schönbrod muß sich auf den Hügel stellen.

Hantke: Niedermaier auch.

Niedermaier: Sollen wir Bonzen spielen?

Brunner: Nein, bloß Kegelkönige.

Schönbrod: Das geht ja noch. *(mit* Niedermaier *auf die Erhöhung)*

Otti: Still jetzt! Kapellmeister! *(*Kapellmeister *hebt den Taktstock.* Musiker *setzen die Instrumente an. Um das Windrad herum kommt in aufgeregter Eile* Trankhafen.*)*

Trankhafen: Was haben die Tromptetensignale zu bedeuten? *(Auf ein Zeichen des* Kapellmeisters *werden die Instrumente abgesetzt.)*

Brunner: Die wollten Ihnen bloß zum Frühschoppen aufspielen.

Schönbrod: We country people know how important that is. What an invention!

Niedermaier: That's the way you see it. The way the authorities see it, they can't work fast enough to invent some legal battering ram to control it.

Trumpet signal. The plaza fills up quickly. Steinbott *steps out of his booth.*

Steinbott: Is it time now? Get your warm sausages here!

Wolff: Nah, the hill is empty.

Berta: Are we the only ones celebrating? That would be a lot nicer.

Otti: Listen: our great patrons are angry, because we aren't making the sun shine on their heads all day long. Now they are having a meeting over a glass of beer as to how they can rattle off their dedication speeches without getting wet. Until they decide that, we can have our own festival the way we want it. What do you say?

Several: Yeah! Let's get started!

Otti: Okay! *(Another signal. The* band *arranges itself.)* Are you all ready? *(Arranges the rows of the* youth choir.*)*

Jenny: Mayor Schönbrod should stand on the hilltop.

Hantke: Niedermaier too.

Niedermaier: Are we supposed to act like bigwigs?

Brunner: No, just like kings of the bowling alley.

Schönbrod: That we can do. *(Goes with* Niedermaier *up the hill.)*

Otti: Everyone quiet now. Maestro? *(*Band director *raises his baton. The* musicians *raise their instruments.* Trankhafen *rushes on from around the wind wheel.)*

Trankhafen: What are these trumpet signals supposed to mean? *(At a signal from the* band director *the* musicians *put down their instruments.)*

Brunner: They just wanted to call you to the bar.

Otti: Wir haben uns mit dem Festprogramm selbstständig gemacht.

Trankhafen: Das ist unverantwortlich. Wenn Sie auf mich hören wollen, kann noch alles gut werden.

Annie: Am besten wird es, wenn wir unter uns bleiben.

Niedermaier: Nicht ausfällig werden. Bitte. Die Dame scheint uns eine Mitteilung machen zu wollen, bitte sprechen Sie, Fräulein Ministerialrat.

Trankhafen: Sehr gütig. Die Besprechung dauert zwar noch an, aber Sie dürfen überzeugt sein, daß sie von durchaus versöhnlichem Geiste getragen ist. Herrn Geheimrat Stechbein ist es gelungen, den Herrn Minister zu verständnisvollen Entgegenkommen zu bewegen. Außer Herrn Abgeordneten Hustenreiz habe auch ich selbst für das allerdings recht unpassende Verhalten der Orts- und Werkleitung die Entschuldigung ins Feld geführt, daß den beiden Herren im Verkehr mit den Spitzen unseres Staatswesens offenbar jede Erfahrung mangelt. So besteht nun erfreulicherweise die Geneigtheit, über das Geschehene den Mantel des Verzeihens zu breiten, und der Herr Minister ließ sich sogar dafür gewinnen, seine Genugtuung über das Gedeihen des Werkes in Herzlicher Form zum Ausdruck zu bringen.

Steinbott: Und das alles ganz umsonst?

Trankhafen: Voraussetzung ist nur, das Sie, Herr Diplomingenieur, auch Ihrerseits einlenken und in letzter Minute das Wetter doch noch dem festlichen Anlaß entsprechend aufhellen werden. *(Gelächter)*

Berta: Nein, sind Sie ulkig.

Trankhafen: Helfen Sie der Sonne zum Durchbruch, dann werden Sie das häßliche Gewölk nicht nur vom Himmel, sondern auch aus unsern Herzen vertreiben.

Schönbrod: Da schlag' einer lang hin!

Peters: Die Wolken sind doch kein Ministerrat, daß sie sich auf einen Pfiff ins Bierzelt jagen lassen.

Otti: We went ahead with our own festival program.

Trankhafen: That was irresponsible of you. If you will listen to me, we can set everything right again.

Annie: It's best if we just stay here among ourselves.

Niedermaier: Let's not make a scene, please. The lady apparently wants to tell us something; please go ahead, Frau Minsterial Advisor.

Trankhafen: Very kind of you. The meeting is lasting a bit longer than planned, but you can rest assured that the mood is one of reconciliation. Privy Councillor Stechbein succeeded in convincing the minister to respond sympathetically. In addition to Delegate Hustenreiz I too suggested, as an excuse for the very inappropriate behavior of the the leaders of the village and the works, that the two gentlemen apparently had very little experience in dealing with the leaders of the state. Now, fortunately, there is an inclination toward forgiving these unfortunate occurrences, and even the minister was convinced that he should express his happiness with the way the weather works have developed.

Steinbott: And you don't want anything from us?

Trankhafen: The only precondition is that you, Herr Engineer, also compromise and at the last minute brighten up the weather appropriately for the ceremony. *(laughter)*

Berta: Boy, aren't you funny!

Trankhafen: If you help the sun come out, then you will not only drive the clouds away from the sky, but also from our hearts.

Schönbrod: Well, you can try till you turn blue in the face.

Peters: The clouds aren't like some ministerial advisor who runs into a beer tent whenever someone blows a whistle.

Trankhafen: Das ist ja eine beispiellose Aufsäßigkeit. Doch habe ich nicht nach der unmaßgeblichen Meinung der untergeordneten Stellen zu fragen. Herr Diplomingenieur Niedermaier, ich erwarte Ihre Äußerung.

Niedermaier: Los, Otti!

Otti: Musik!

Die Musik setzt ein, Trankhafen *fluchtartig ab.* Chor *führt Bewegungsspiele auf und singt:*

> Wem der Sinn der Natur ergeben ist,
> Dem gibt die Natur sich zu Braut.
> Wem das Wunder der Erde sein Leben ist,
> Der hat ihr Geheimnis erschaut.
> O Mensch, verlaß nicht der Schöpfung Spur.
> Die Erde bleibt Erde—Natur bleibt Natur.
> Nur im Bund mit der Sonne, im Bund mit dem Meer
> Lenkst die Winde Du, ziehst die Wolken her.
>
> Ob die Sonne scheinen soll, ob der Regen weinen soll,
> Frage Saat und Herde.
> Deiner Hände Meisterschaft,
> Alles was dein Geist erschafft,
> Bringe dar, der Erde.

Beifall, Gruppentanz

Paula: (tritt auf, einen großen Regenschirm in der Hand, wartet, haltlos lachend, bis die Musik aufhört) Kinder, ich kann nicht mehr.

Jenny: Was ist denn mit dir los, Paula?

Paula: Ich hab' mein Lebtag nicht so gelacht! *(schüttelt sich)*

Berta: Erzähl' doch!

Paula: Der Schirm ist für den Minister. Er hat Angst, ihm würde das Ehrendiplom für Herrn Niedermaier vollpladdern.

Trankhafen: That is unheard of impertinence. But I am not here to ask about the opinions of humble subordinates. Herr Niedermaier, I await your answer.

Niedermaier: Go ahead, Otti.

Otti: Music!

The music begins, Trankhafen *runs off as if escaping. The* choir *sings and moves to the music.*

> Whoever understands Nature's story,
> Nature gives herself as his bride.
> Whoever gives himself to Nature's glory,
> From him has Nature nothing more to hide.
> O children, don't forget the lesson of creation's birth:
> Nature is Nature and the Earth is the Earth.
> If, and only if, you listen to the sun and sea
> Can you guide the winds and know just where the clouds will be.
>
> If the sun beams down, or the rains fall on the ground,
> It's for the wheat and barley.
> All of your hands' mastery,
> Everything your mind can see,
> Give the Earth entirely.

Applause, group dance

Paula: *(Enters with a large umbrella in her hand, waits, laughs uncontrollably, until the music stops.)* Oh my gosh, I can't stand it!

Jenny: What's wrong with you, Paula?

Paula: I have never laughed so hard in my whole life! *(Shakes herself.)*

Berta: What? Tell us!

Paula: The umbrella is for the minister. He's afraid he'll get the honorary diploma for Herr Niedermaier all wet.

Niedermaier: Das wollen sie mir immer noch nicht ersparen?

Paula: Es war zum schießen.

Steinbott: Konkurrenz für Berta.

Paula: So eine Fatzkerei. Zuerst hatten sie es mit der Würde des Staates und den vaterländischen Belangen. Bis der lange Sozialist mit seinen unausweichlichen Notwendigkeiten und sozialen Gesichtspunkten kam. Dann der Kerl mit der verrückten Sprache. Den kann man ja nicht nachmachen. Alle zogen gegen Herrn Niedermaier los. Darf ich sagen, was sie Sie genannt haben?

Niedermaier: Nur zu. Sollen doch alle wissen, was ich für ein Monstrum bin.

Paula: Also größenwahnsinniger Rüpel und kleiner Techniker, dem ein Erfolg zu Kopf gestiegen wär, na und Lümmel und frecher Bursche und noch viel dergleichen. Und der Regierungsassessor schrie immer fort Parvenu, Ignorant, Arrivist—ich hab' mir das nicht alles merken können.

Hantke: Wir sind ja nun auch im Bilde.

Paula: Wegen des Programms konnten sie ewig nicht einig werden. Schließlich stellten sie sich in kleinen Gruppen in die Ecken, und bei mir hinten bei den Bierfässern erschien mit einem Mal die komische alte Jungfer mit dem Kneifer.

Otti: Die Trankhafen.

Paula: Die. Und hinterher, was meint ihr? Der Geck, den sie Geheimrat nennen. Die hatten in ihrem Versteck nett was zu politisieren. Wißt ihr, was die taten? Ich konnt ja alles vom Ausschank hören. Die haben geknutscht, was das Zeug hielt.

Fischer: Guten Appetit!

Paula: "Mein Theodor, meine Henriette," und "meine Heinriette, mein Theodor" ging das immerzu.

Wolff: Wie in meiner Luftschaukel.

Paula: Das Schönste kommt noch. Ich denk' garnichts, kommt die Dicke angesetzt, die sich all die Tücher um den Bauch wickelt und

Niedermaier: So they're not going to let me out of that?

Paula: It was hilarious, really entertaining.

Steinbott: Competition for Berta's shooting gallery.

Paula: What a bunch of fools. First they were all worried about the dignity of the state and the good of the fatherland. That lasted until that tall Socialist piped up with his "unavoidable necessities" and social points of view. Then that guy who talks funny. I can't imitate him. Everybody ganged up against Herr Niedermaier. May I say what they called you?

Niedermaier: Sure. Everybody should know what kind of monster I am.

Paula: All right: a boor with delusions of grandeur, and little technician whose success has gone to his head, a lout, a cheeky rascal, and more things like that. And the government assessor keep shouting *parvenu*, ignoramus, *arriviste*—I couldn't get all of it.

Hantke: They probably had something to say about us, too.

Paula: They kept disagreeing about the program. Finally they gathered in small groups in the corners, and over by me, behind the beer kegs, all of a sudden I saw that funny old spinster with the pince-nez.

Otti: That's Trankhafen.

Paula: Yeah, that's her. And behind her, who do you think? That dandy they call the privy councillor. They were making some nice politics in their little corner! You know what they were doing? They were groping each other!

Fischer: Bon appetit!

Paula: "My Theodore, my Henriette, my Henriette, my Theodore," over and over again.

Wolff: Just like in my swing-boat.

Paula: Wait, the best is coming. I didn't think anything about it, then the fat lady comes over, the one who has all the cloths wrapped around

sucht den stillen Ort. Rennt sie doch grade hinter die Bierfässer, wo die beiden Konferenz haben. Quitscht natürlich und stolpert zu mir zurück. Ich zeig' ihr das Häuschen hinten und seh' ihr nach, daß sie auch findet. Grad will sie rein, wer kommt raus? Das Fremdwörterlexikon. Aber auch nicht allein, sondern mit der frommen Ziege, mit dem keuschen Augenaufschlag.

Schönbrod: Kiek mal an.

Paula: Jetzt kommen ja nun die Beiden aus dem Versteck bei mir, weil es klingelte und die Sitzung weitergehen sollte. Erst sie. Was die geschnauft hat. Und danach der Herr Geheimrat und will mich doch im Vorbeigehen in den Hintern kneifen. Ich hab' ihm schön eine gelangt.

Peters: Gut gemacht, Paula.

Brunner: Schlankweg ins Antlitz der Obrigkeit?

Paula: Mitten vors Maul. Das fiese, alte Ferkel.

Fischer: Scheint aber noch gut bei Kräften zu sein.

Niedermaier: Und was weiter?

Paula: Dann schickten sie, als geblasen wurde, die Person hierauf. Na, als die wiederkam, das Geplärr. Skandal und Frechheit und Gesindel und einer wollte gleich den Kriegerverein alarmieren und den Turm kaputtschlagen.

Jenny: Das könnte ja ein lustiges Fest werden.

Paula: Die haben mehr Angst vor dem bißchen Regen, als meine Großmutter vorm Gewitter. Bloß der Minister—Blödian heißt er ja wohl—jammerte immerfort: "ich muß doch den Staatsakt vollziehen" und der Pfarrer salmte was von Sünde und Frevel und die Dicke quakte dazwischen, daß sie durch die Rücksichtslosigkeit hier wieder ihren Darmkatarrh kriegen würde.

Brunner: Daher der Name Kabinettssitzung.

Paula: Dann mußte ich zum Minister kommen und der fragte mich, ob ich einen Regenschirm besorgen könnte, weil er doch keine feuchte

her, and she's looking for the privies. She runs over behind the beer kegs where those two were having their conference. Of course she shrieks and stumbles back over to me. I show her wherethe little house is out back and I look to make sure she finds it. Just as she's going in, who do you think comes out? The guy with the dictionary in his head. But not by himself; he comes out with that pious nanny-goat who always hides her eyes.

Schönbrod: You don't say!

Paula: And now the two come out of their little hiding place over by me because the bell rang and they were supposed to get back to the meeting. She came first, huffing and puffing. And then the privy councillor, and as he's going past me he grabs my rear end. I whacked him a good one.

Peters: Good for you, Paula.

Brunner: Right in the face of authority?

Paula: Right in the chops. That disgusting old pig.

Fischer: But he seems to have recovered.

Niedermaier: And then what?

Paula: Then they sent that woman up here, just when the trumpet sounded. And when she came back the howling started. All about scandal and impudence and rabble, and somebody wanted to call in the reserves and demolish the tower.

Jenny: That would've been some festival.

Paula: They were more scared of a little shower than my grandmother is of a thunderstorm. But the minister—I think he's called Bloated—kept yammering: "I have to complete the ceremony" and the preacher mumbled something about sin and evil, and the fat lady was quacking that she was going to get another intestinal infection from all this rudeness.

Brunner: She needs to take her seat on the cabinet.

Paula: Then I was called over to the minister, and he asked me if I could get him an umbrella, because he didn't want to present a wet

Urkunde übergeben möchte, und dabei buckelte der Assessor mit seinem Kauderwelsch um ihn rum, daß ich bald geplatzt wäre.

Steinbott: Was ist denn nun bei dem ganzen Gequatsch rausgekommen?

Paula: Ich mußte ja weg, den Schirm holen. Als ich rausging, redete grade der schneidige General was von Niedermaiers Dolchstoß von hinten.

Niedermaier: Jetzt bringen Sie aber dem Minister den Regenschirm, Fräulein Paula, daß wir die Staatsaktion bald überstanden haben.

Annie: Meint ihr, daß der Chor noch Zeit hat, bis sie wiederkommen?

Otti: Die kümmern uns garnicht. Wir tanzen, solange es noch trocken ist. Alle fertig? *(klatscht in die Hände) Musik! (Chor führt Bewegungsspiele aus, singt.)*

> Nur der Mensch, der nicht Herr noch Knecht sein will,
> Soll das Feld, soll den Acker bestellen.
> Nur wer Gleicher in gleichem Recht sein will,
> Dem fügen sich Winde und Wellen.
> Der Erste, der Boden sein Erbgut hieß,
> Der machte die Erde zum Knechtverließ.
> Weh der Macht, die den Himmel zu eigen begehrt,
> Sie trifft unser Fluch, sie fällt unser Schwert.
>
> Was der Menschengeist erschafft, was der Hände Meister-
> schaft
> Wachsen läßt aus Erden,
> Ob der Regen weinen soll, ob die Sonne scheinen soll,—
> Freiheit soll draus werden!

Während das Lied gesungen wird, steigen Blödel, Stechbein, Trankhafen, Stiefengrat, Krampf, Biederhold, *und* Hornbriller, *der den Regenschirm trägt, zum Hügel herauf und stellen sich ohne Gruß zu* Niedermaier *und* Schönbrod. *Entrüstete Blicke auf den* Chor *und fragende Gebärden.*

Krampf: Die Volksbelustigung da ist durchaus geschäftsordnungs-widrig.

certificate, and the assessor kept running around yapping in his pig Latin and I thought I was going to burst!

Steinbott: So what came out of all this nonsense?

Paula: I had to leave to get the umbrella. When I went out the general was saying something about Niedermaier sticking a knife in his back.

Niedermaier: Well, go ahead and take the minister his umbrella, Fräulein Paula, so that we can get this state ceremony over with.

Annie: Do you think the choir still has some time until they come back?

Otti: They don't care about us anyway. Let's dance, as long as it's still dry. Everybody ready? *(Claps her hands.)* Music! *(Choir sings and moves with the music.)*

> Whoever wants not to be lord or vassal
> May have a say in how to plant the field.
> Whoever wants no more than to be equal
> The wind and waves to his desires must yield.
> Whoever first did say the Earth was his domain,
> He put the Earth in prison, and bound it up with chains.
> But he who arrogantly claims dominion o'er the sky
> Will hear the people's curse and feel our fury by and by.
>
> Everything your mind can see, all of your hands' mastery
> Is Nature's cultivation.
> If the rain falls down, if the sun shines on the ground,
> It means our liberation.

While the song is being sung, Blödel, Stechbein, Trankhafen, Stiefengrat, Krampf, Biederhold *and* Hornbriller, *who carries an umbrella, climb up the hill to* Niedermaier *and* Schönbrod, *without greeting them. Indignant glances at the* choir, *inquiring gestures.*

Krampf: That little folk entertainment there is not on the agenda.

Hornbriller: (winkt vergeblich mit dem Schirm dem Kapellmeister zu)
Das ist die pure Renitenz, Herr Diplomingenieur, dieser deplacierte
Spektakel muß inhibiert werden.

Niedermaier: (wartet den Schluß des Liedes ab, dann) Otti, bitte! (Auf
Ottis Zeichen setzt Musik und Tanz unvermittelt ab.)

Berta: Wo haben sie denn die andern alle gelassen?

Fischer: Die sind zur Strafe in der Kneipe sitzen geblieben.

Wolff: Trauerfeier in engsten Kreise.

Krampf: Verehrte Anwesende! Ich bitte un größte Ruhe!

Hornbriller: Silentium!

Krampf: Wir treten in den Weiheakt ein. Das Wort zu einer Erklärung
hat Herr Regierungsassessor Hornbriller.

Hornbriller: Wertes Auditorium! Das konstituierende Festkommittee
hat das provisorische Programm dieses Meetings faut de mieux radikal
umdisponieren müssen. Die Intervention der Regierung, es mögen für
die Festivität die simpelsten meteorologischen Prämissen präpariert
werden, wurden von den lokalen Instanzen zynisch ignoriert.

Hantke: Können Sie nicht deutsch sprechen?

Hornbriller: Meine Diktion bedarf keine Korrektur. Der seriöse und
konziliante Appell an den primitivsten Respekt vor der Staatsautorität
begegnete provokatorischer und obstinater Resistenz. Selbst das im
kritischsten Moment noch express durch Fräulein Ministerialrätin Dr.
Trankhafen motivierte Kompromiß, auf der Basis loyalen Pardonierens
der Regierung zu akkordieren, wurde unter frivoler Ironisierung einer
so urbanen Geste in alle konventionellen Usancen desavouierender
Manier als induskutabel refüsiert.

Steinbott: Ihnen haben sie wohl die Schnauze im Schraubstock
verbogen?

Hornbriller: Auf ordinäre Injurien reagiere ich nicht.

Krampf: Mir stehen leider keine geschäftsordnungsmäßigen Mittel zu
Gebote, derartige Ungehörigkeiten gebührend zu rügen. Sonst hätte ich
den Zwischenrufer einen Ordnungsruf erteilen müssen.

Hornbriller: *(Waves the umbrella in vain towards the* band director.*)* This is pure recalcitrance, Herr Engineer; this misplaced spectacle must be stopped.

Niedermaier: *(waits until the end of the song, then)* Otti, please! *(At a sign from* Otti *the music and dance stop immediately.)*

Berta: Where did they leave everybody else?

Fischer: They had to stay in the bar as punishment.

Wolff: They're crying in their beer.

Krampf: Honored guests! May we have quiet, please!

Hornbriller: *Silentium*!

Krampf: We are beginning the dedication ceremony. Government Assessor Hornbriller has the opening remarks.

Hornbriller: Ladies and gentlemen. The constitutive festival committee was forced to radically redispose this rendezvous *faut de mieux*. The preconditions of the government that the simplest meterological premises be prepared for the festivities were cynically ignored by the local instances.

Hantke: Can't you use plain language?

Hornbriller: My diction is not in need of any correction. The earnest and conciliatory appeal to a respect for state authority on the most primitive level was met with a provocative and obstinate *résistance*. Even the compromise that was suggested in the critical moment by Fräulein Government Advisor Dr. Trankhafen, that the government should excuse the disturbance in exchange for a small sign of respect, was refused with a frivolous irony inappropriate to such an urbane gesture.

Steinbott: Somebody must have bent your mouth up in a vise.

Hornbriller: I do not react to such common insults.

Krampf: Unfortunately I do not have any authorized means at my disposal for reprimanding this kind of impropriety. Otherwise I would have imposed on the interrupter a call to order.

Hornbriller: Wir stehen also vis à vis einer irreparablen Diskrepanz
zwischen den Intensionen der gouvernementalen Organe und der
Omnipotenz einer intransigenten lokalen Autokratie. Eine Kapitulation
der Staatsrepräsentanten vor rabiaten Obstruenten kann nicht einmal
ventiliert werden. Rebus sic stantibus ist der Konferenz die zu
observierende Taktik direkt oktroyiert worden: nämlich das präsumtive
Festprogramm ab ovo zu liquidieren und die offiziellen Formalitäten
auf die dem Herrn Minister obligatorisch gemachte Manifestation zu
reduzieren. In Konsequenz dessen, wurde auch die Assistenz bei dem
Akt limitiert auf die designierten Delegierten der respektiven
Ministerien, den Herrn Parlamentspräsidenten und den Repräsentanten
der koalierten Parteien, Herrn Abgeordneten Biederhold, dessen
Mandat zugleich die Ministration der religiösen Zeremonien involviert.
Die in petto gehaltenen Gratulationen und Ovationen, soweit sie nicht
den ex officio zu exekutierenden Funktionen immanent sind, werden
eliminiert. Dixi.

Krampf: Ich erteile nunmehr das Wort zur Verlesung einer
Regierungsverkündigung, dem Herrn Minister für Ruhe, Ordnung und
Sicherheit, Herrn Dr. Blödel.

Blödel: *(kramt Papiere aus seiner Aktentasche)* "In Anbetracht der
bedeutsamen Kulturtat, als welche sich die Meisterung der irdischen
Witterung nach mehrjähriger Erprobung einwandfrei erwiesen hat, in
Anbetracht ferner, der erhebenden Tatsache, daß die erste mit allen
neuzeitlichen Hilfsmitteln der Wissenschaft und Technik ausgestattete
Wetteranlage in unserm geliebten Heimatlande ihre Stätte gefunden
hat; in Anbetracht drittens des Umstandes, daß die Landesregierung
glaubt, sich gegenüber den Belangen des Vaterlandes der
gebieterischen Pflicht nicht entziehen zu dürfen über die bisher
lediglich einer privaten Organisation unterstellten meteorologischen
Einrichtungen ihre schützende Hand auszubreiten; in Erwägung
außerdem, daß der Schöpfer und Leiter des unvergleichlichen
Kulturwerkes Herr Diplomingenieur Niedermaier sich durch seine
vorbildliche Arbeit im Dienst der Allgemeinheit den Anspruch auf die
unverbrüchliche Dankbarkeit der Lebenden wie der künftigen
Geschlechter erworben hat, und daß die Regierung die Stimme des
Volkes wohl zu deuten weiß, welche von ihr amtliche Schritte

Hornbriller: We are therefore standing *vis à vis* an insurmountable discrepancy between the intentions of the governmental organs and the power of an obstinant local autocracy. We cannot allow even the expression of state capitulation to such rabid obstructionism. *Rebus sic stantibus*, the conference agreed on the observance of the following tactic: the presumptive ceremonial program should be liquidated *ab ovo*, and the official formalities should be reduced to the minister's usual duties. As a result, the participation in the ceremony was limited to the designated delegates of the respective ministries, the president of the parliament, and the representative of the coalition parties, Delegate Biederhold, whose mandate also involves the ministration of religious ceremonies. The congratulations and ovations, held *in petto*, to the extent that they are not immanent *ex officio* to the various functions, were eliminated. *Dixi.*

Krampf: I hereby give the floor to the minister for law, order, and security, Dr. Blödel, for the purpose of reading the government decree.

Blödel: (Digs papers out of his briefcase.) "In consideration of the cultural significance of the mastery of the weather, which has proven successful after several years of experimentation; in further consideration of the fact that the first weather station to be constructed with all the scientific and technological means available in the modern age is located here in our beloved homeland; in further consideration of the belief on the part of the provincial government that it is incumbent on it not to evade its commanding duty in light of the needs of the fatherland, to extend its protective hand to this meteorological installation, which has previously been under the supervision merely of a private organization; moreover in consideration of the fact that the creator and director of this incomparable cultural phenomenon, Herr Engineer Niedermaier, through his exemplary work in service of the community, deserves the undying thanks of those living today as well as generations yet to come, and that the government has heard the voice of the people, who have called upon it to take official measures

erheischt, um dem redlichen Manne für sein vorbildliches Walten im
gemeinnützigen Dienste den Dank des Vaterlandes durch besondere
Auszeichnung zum Ausdruck zu bringen,—hat dieselbe die Feier des
fünfjährigen Erinnerungstages der Grundsteinlegung zum Wetterturm
zum erwünschten Anlasse genommen, in öffentlicher Festkundgebung
im Beisein der beglaubigten Vertreter der einschlagigen Ämter und
Behörden sowie der gesetzgebenden Körperschaften und angesichts
der in vaterländischer Begeisterung festlich versammelten örtlichen
Bevölkerung durch den Mund des Ministers für Ruhe, Ordnung und
Sicherheit folgenden Beschluß kund zu tun: A) der Betrieb Wetterturm
eingetragene Genossenschaft wird mit allem baulichen und sonstigem
Zubehör *(ängstlicher Blick zum Himmel, es fallen die ersten Tropfen)*
vorbehaltlich weiterer Entschließung unter den Schirm des Staates
gestellt.

*Hornbriller spannt den Regenschirm auf und hält ihn über Blödel.
Lachen in der Menge.*

"B) Ein unter streng demokratischen Gesichtspunkten eigens zu
schaffendes Wetteramt wird mit der Aufgabe betraut, die Übereinstimmung der Anordnungen, der Werkleitung mit den Belangen des
Vaterlandes und des Volkes zu sichern und der bestehenden
Genossenschaft beratend und helfend zur Seite zu stehen. C) Der den
Wetterturm umgebende Raum einschließlich der Grünflächen bis zu
den Grenzen der nächst gelegenen Ortschaften erhält für alle Zeiten
den Namen Wetterborn und wird somit unter Loslösung von der
bisherigen Zugehörigkeit zum Nachbardorfe zur selbständigen
Gemeinde erhoben."

Schönbrod: *(auffahrend)* Wie? Was? Loslösung vom Nachbardorf? Da
soll doch gleich der Deuwel reinschlagen!

Krampf: Ich ersuche den Zwischenrufer, den Herrn Minister nicht zu
unterbrechen.

Schönbrod: Das ist eine aufgelegte Niedertracht. Da bleib ich nicht
länger bei stehn. *(Steigt vom Hügel herunter, stellt sich zu* Otti.*)*

Steinbott: Das wär schöner, das Werk bleibt beim Dorf.

Peters: Wir lassen uns nicht vom Dorf wegreißen.

to express the thanks of the fatherland for his exemplary achievements in the common interest, by bestowing a special citation—therefore the government has chosen the celebration of the fifth anniversary of the laying of the cornerstone, in a public ceremony in the presence of the legal representatives of the pertinent offices and authorities as well as of the legislative bodies and, in recognition of the local population, here assembled in patriotic enthusiasm, in the voice of the minister for law, order, and security to make the following proclamation: A) The Weathertower, Incorporated, is to be placed, along with all its attendant and peripheral accessories *(Looks nervously at the sky, the first raindrops are beginning to fall.)* under the protection of the state, which reserves the right to make further similar resolutions.

Hornbriller *opens the umbrella and holds it over* Blödel. *Laughter in the crowd.*

"B) A Weather Bureau, expressly created according to strictly democratic principles, will have the responsibility of assuring that the concerns of the fatherland and the people are always followed in the direction of the weather works, and also of serving as an advisory and supporting office for the existing local collective. C) The area immediately surrounding the weather tower, including the land extending to the borders of the neighboring village, will be henceforth named Weatherspring and will be elevated to the status of an independent community by means of its detachment from the neighboring village, to which it previously belonged."

Schönbrod: (with a start) What?! What's that? Detachment from the neighboring village? The devil you say!

Krampf: I will ask the gentleman to refrain from interrupting the minister.

Schönbrod: This is downright meanness. I'm not standing up here a minute longer! *(Walks down the hill and stands next to* Otti.*)*

Steinbott: It would be nicer if the works stayed with the village.

Peters: We won't let ourselves be torn off from the village.

Jenny: Die sollen es bloß wagen!

Wolff: Wir lassen das Werk nicht antippen. *(allgemeiner Lärm)*

Krampf: Sie dürfen den Herrn Minister nicht inmitten eines Staatsaktes stören.

Hantke: Die Friedensstörer sind Sie!

Stechbein: Das ist ja unausstehlich, dieser Lärm.

Trankhafen: *(zu* Niedermaier*)* Greifen doch Sie ein!

Niedermaier: Lassen Sie mich in Ruhe.

Biederhold: *(zur* Masse*)* Wer nicht gehorcht der Obrigkeit, den wird die Obrigkeit richten. *(großer Lärm)*

Berta: Schert euch hier weg! Hier hat keine Obrigkeit was zu suchen.

Stiefengrat: Ich schlage vor, diese Bande unter sich zu lassen und der Polizei das Weitere anheim zu stellen.

Krampf: Wird zu dem Vorschlage seiner Excellenz das Wort gewünscht, Herr Regierungsassessor Hornbriller?

Brunner: Achtung, der dumme August als dressierte Nachtigall. *(Es wird ruhig.)*

Hornbriller: Ohne mich durch Invektiven irritieren zu lassen, gehe ich in medias res. Die turbulenten Szenen während einer offiziellen Proklamation des Mandatars unserer Regierung sabotieren auch unser modifiziertes Programm. Inzwischen hat auch Jupiter pluvius interveniert, sodaß die Demarche faktisch jetzt schon als ein Fiasko kat exochen exklatant ist. Die impulsive Intuition seiner Excellenz ist daher nicht brevi manu ad acta zu legen. Ich will das Votum des Herrn Ministers nicht präjudizieren. Doch scheinen mir die Prämissen des ministeriellen Manifestes kaum mehr existent. Wenn wir daher angesichts der tumultärischen Exzesse und der atmosphärischen Depression die Reputation der Staatsautorität nicht länger diskreditieren lassen und unsre Mission unter Protest quittieren, statt uns ad infinitum koramieren zu lassen, so wird die Regierung tolerant genug sein, uns für die fernere Abstinenz von dieser Orgie impertinenter Provokationen die Indemnität post festum sans phrase zu konzedieren.

Jenny: Just let them try!

Wolff: We won't let you touch our tower! *(general uproar)*

Krampf: You mustn't disturb the minister in the middle of a state ceremony.

Hantke: You are the disturbers of the peace!

Stechbein: This noise is unbearable.

Trankhafen: *(to* Niedermaier*)* Why don't you do something!

Niedermaier: Leave me out of it.

Biederhold: *(to the* crowd*)* Whoever doesn't obey the authorities will be judged by the authorities. *(loud noise)*

Berta: You all get out of here! The authorities don't have any business here!

Stiefengrat: I suggest that we leave this rabble alone and leave the rest to the police.

Krampf: Do you wish to speak to the suggestion of Herr General Stiefengrat, Herr Hornbriller?

Brunner: Listen, the clown is playing the role of a trained bird. *(It becomes quiet.)*

Hornbriller: Without allowing myself to become irritated by invective, I will go directly *in medias res*. The turbulent scenes during the official proclamation of our government's mandate sabotaged also our modified program. In the meantime, *Jupiter pluvius* has also intervened, and this means that the ceremony has *ipso facto* become a fiasco. His Excellency's impulsive intuition can therefore not be rejected *brevi manu ad acta*. I do not wish to prejudice the minister's vote. Nevertheless, I do not believe that the premises of the ministerial manifesto are any longer extant. If we therefore no longer allow the reputation of the state authorities to be discredited by these tumultuous excesses and atmospheric depression, and if we abandon our mission under protest, instead of letting ourselves be criticized *ad infinitum*, then the government should be tolerant enough to concede to us an indemnification from this orgy of provocation *post festum sans phrase*.

Blödel: Nein, das geht nicht. Dem einmütigen Auftrag des Kabinetts muß ich unter allen Umständen entsprechen.

Trankhafen: Dann bleibt nichts übrig, als den Kelch bis zur Neige zu leeren. Ließe sich nicht aber vielleicht jetzt noch der störende Regen wenigstens solange zurückhalten? bis der Herr Minister seine Pflicht erfüllt hat?

Niedermaier: Wenn die Regierungsverkündung nicht mehr lange dauert, werden Sie nicht übermäßig durchnäßt werden. In etwa einer Viertelstunde setzt allerdings kräftiger Regen ein.

Wolff: Am besten wär' ein ordentlicher Hagelschlag, der ihnen Beine macht.

Stechbein: Haben Sie denn nicht soviel Macht, den Mob da zur Ruhe zu bringen?

Niedermaier: Das ist kein Mob. Das sind meine Freunde. Denen habe ich nichts vorzuschreiben.

Stiefengrat: Unverschämtheit!

Krampf: Die Geschäftsordungsdebatte ist erschöpft. Ich bitte den Herrn Minister in der Tagesordnung fortzufahren.

Blödel: Mein Leitstern ist: Pflichterfüllung bis zum Äußersten! *(liest)* "D) Mit Rücksicht auf seine stets bewährte Pflichterfüllung bis zum Äußersten bleibt Herrn Diplomingenieur Niedermaier die Leitung des Werkes bis auf Weiteres auch fernerhin anvertraut. E) Zur Bekräftigung ihrer uneingeschränkten Zufriedenheit mit seinem Wirken und zum Zeichen ihrer Erkenntlichkeit für sein im Verkehr mit den Behörden stets gleichbleibend freundliches, taktvolles, zuvorkommendes, bescheidenes Auftreten und das beispielgebende gute Einvernehmen auch aller seiner Mitarbeiter und der ganzen Bevölkerung mit den amtlichen Stellen wird die Regierung am Turm zum Wetterborn eine Gedenktafel anbringen lassen, welche den Namen Niedermaier, sowie die Erinnerung an den heutigen Jubeltag, Kindern und Kindeskindern in dauerndem Gedächtnis halten soll. An welchem Regierung und Volk in gegenseitiger Liebe und ungetrübter Harmonie zur fünften Jahresfeier der Grundsteinlegung des Wetterturms sich in strahlendem Sonnenglanze zusammenfanden."

Blödel: No, that won't do. I must agree with the unanimous resolution of the cabinet, by all means.

Trankhafen: Then there is nothing left but to see this to the bitter end. But couldn't the rain at least be delayed a bit now? Just until the minister has fulfilled his duty?

Niedermaier: If the government declaration doesn't last much longer then you won't get too wet. But of course in about fifteen minutes the heavier rain will start.

Wolff: The best thing would be a good hailstorm to chase 'em out of here.

Stechbein: So I take it that you are powerless to bring this mob under control?

Niedermaier: This isn't a mob. These are my friends. I am not going to demand anything from them.

Stiefengrat: What impudence!

Krampf: The debate on procedure is now closed. I would ask that the minister please continue with the agenda.

Blödel: My guiding principle is: fulfill your duty to the end! *(Reads.)* "D) In view of Herr Engineer Niedermaier's fulfillment of his duty to the end, the directorship of the weather works shall remain entrusted to him until further notice; E) as a confirmation of its unequivocal satisfaction with the achievements of the weather tower and as a sign of its recognition of the unwavering friendly, courteous, tactful, and modest attitude displayed by the weather collective in its dealings with the government, as well as the exemplary good behavior of its employees and of the entire population, the government shall install at the Weatherspring Tower a plaque to commemorate the name Niedermaier and to remind our children and our children's children of this jubilee day, during which the government and the people, in mutual admiration and umblemished harmony, gathered to celebrate the fifth anniversary of the laying of the cornerstone in glorious

—Halten Sie doch den Schirm ordentlich, Herr Regierungsassessor, die Urkunde weicht ja auf.

Hornbriller: Pardon!

Blödel: "F) Herr Diplomingenieur Niedermaier wird für seine Treue zum Staat der Titel Wetterrat verliehen."

Niedermaier: Das auch noch.

Blödel: "Die näheren Ausführungen der unter Ziffer A) bis F) festgesetzten Bestimmungen ergehen durch die zuständigen Ministerien. Das Vaterland über alles! Gezeichnet: der Staatspräsident: Wimmerzahn; gez. Der Ministerrat: Blödel, Trostreich, Klirrschwert, Schiebling, Schwamm, Funzelmann." —Anschließend obliegt mir noch die Pflicht dem Herrn Jubilar unter Bekundung der Segenswünsche des ganzen Volkes die urkundlichen Dokumente zu überreichen. Hier. Und ihm die warme Gesinnung der Staatsregierung durch auftragsgemäßen Händedruck auszudrücken. Darf ich bitten, Herr Wetterrat. *(reicht ihm die Fingerspitzen, die er rasch wieder zurückzieht.)* Was hiermit geschen ist. *(Gelächter und Lärm.)*

Krampf: Wir wären damit am Ende der Tagesordnung angelangt. Ich schließe die Kundgebung.

Niedermaier: Bitte noch einen Augenblick.

Stechbein: Wir haben hier nichts mehr zu suchen.

Trankhafen: Jetzt gehen wir, Sie haben es selbst nicht anders gewollt.

Biederhold: Auch die Andacht werden wir an einer würdigeren Stelle halten.

Hornbriller: Roma locuta, causa finita.

Blödel: Kommen Sie, Fräulein Doktor, der Schirm wird uns beide vor Nässe schützen.

Schönbrod: Bleiben Sie jetzt mal alle schön stehen. Wenn Herr Niedermaier was sagen will, wird er wohl wissen, warum.

Stiefengrat: Wie weit soll die Frechheit hier noch getrieben werden? Kehrt, marsch!

sunshine"—please hold the umbrella up a bit, Herr Government Assessor, the proclamation is getting soggy.

Hornbriller: Pardon!

Blödel: "F) In recognition of his loyalty to the state, Herr Engineer Niedermaier shall receive the title Weather Councillor."

Niedermaier: That's all I need!

Blödel: "Implementation of points (A) through (F) shall be undertaken by the appropriate ministries. Long live the fatherland! Signed: State President Wimmerzahn, Ministerial Councillors Blödel, Trostreich, Klirrschwert, Schiebling, Schwamm, Funzelmann." Subsequent to the proclamation I am obliged to convey the best wishes of the entire populace and to hand you, Herr Niedermaier, the proclamation document. Here. And to express the warmest wishes of the state government by extending you my hand. May I, Herr Weather Councillor? *(Proffers his fingertips, then pulls them back quickly.)* Which I have now done. *(laughter and noise)*

Krampf: We have reached the end of the agenda. I hereby adjourn the meeting.

Niedermaier: Wait, just a minute, please.

Stechbein: We have nothing more to do here.

Trankhafen: We are leaving now, just as you wanted.

Biederhold: We will also have the prayer service in a more worthy setting.

Hornbriller: Roma locuta, causa finita.

Blödel: Come along, Dr. Trankhafen, the umbrella will keep us both dry.

Schönbrod: Just you all stay put for a minute. If Herr Niedermaier has something to say, then he has a good reason.

Stiefengrat: How much longer must we put up with this insolence. About face, forward march!

Peters: *(mächtig)* Halt—stillgestanden! Unsre Arbeit hat das Wort. *(lautlose Stille)*

Niedermaier: Ich sage der Regierung pflichtschuldigsten Dank. Der Herr Minister hat mir Worte des Lobes gesagt, aber unterlassen, das Lob auf meine Mitarbeiter und Helfer, auf die Genossenschaft, die Gemeinde, vor allem auf unsern alten jugendlichen Dorfschulzen Schönbrod auszudehnen. Ich hole das hiermit nach. Ohne die aufopfernde Unterstützung aller, die mir im gleichen Zielen brüderlich verbunden sind, hätten mir Sonne und Mond, Erde und Meer ihre Hilfe verweigert, das Wetter zu regeln, wie die arbeitenden Menschen es brauchen. Auch unserm Jugendchor danke ich, der für die Freude sorgt, ohne die ein rechtes Werk nicht gedeihen kann. Die Regierung hat die Absicht ausgesprochen, die Turmanlage von der Dorfgemeinde loszulösen.

Schönbrod: Niemals!

Niedermaier: Ort und Werk waren, sind und bleiben verbunden. Dafür werden wir alle sorgen, die wir hier vor fünf Jahren den Grundstein gelegt haben, wir hier und nicht der Staat! Das Werk gehört zum Ort und bleibt beim Ort, mag kommen, was will! *(großer Beifall)*

Stechbein: Das ist stark.

Trankhafen: Es ist die Kriegserklärung gegen den demokratischen Staat.

Otti: Es ist der Treueschwur des guten Kameraden!

Schönbrod: Ja, deern!

Niedermaier: Da ich vorläufig die Leitung des Werkes behalten soll—

Fischer: Immer!

Niedermaier: —so verspreche ich, daß alle Maßnahmen wie bisher ausschließlich von sozialen Notwendigkeiten bestimmt werden sollen. Nie ohne Zustimmung der Gemeinde, denn die Gemeinde, das ist die Genossenschaft, und die Genossenschaft, das ist das Werk. Alle, die am Werk arbeiten, arbeiten mit Begeisterung für unsere Sache, obgleich die Genossenschaft—das sind wir ja selbst—arm ist und keinem von uns den anstrengenden Dienst ausreichend entgelten kann. Aber keiner von uns will mehr als jeder andere. Und wir tragen

Peters: (in a mighty voice) STOP! Stand right where you are! It's time for the working class to speak! *(absolute silence)*

Niedermaier: I am duty bound to say thanks to the government. The minister had words of praise for me, but forgot to offer words of praise to my co-workers and helpers. This should have been extended to the collective, to the community, above all to our old and young village mayor, Herr Schönbrod. I hereby correct that omission. Without the selfless support of everyone who has joined with me in a common goal I would have received no help at all from the sun and the moon, the earth and the seas. I would not have been able to regulate the weather for the needs of the working people. I also thank the youth choir for providing the joy without which real achievement cannot flourish. The government has stated its intention to separate the tower area from the rest of the village.

Schönbrod: Never!

Niedermaier: The town and the weather works were, are, and will remain connected. We will see to that, those of us who laid the cornerstone here five years ago, we who live here, not the state! The works belong to the village and will stay with the village, come what may! *(great applause)*

Stechbein: That is strong language.

Trankhafen: It is a declaration of war against the democratic state.

Otti: It's an oath of loyalty by our good comrade!

Schönbrod: That's right, girl.

Niedermaier: Since I will be the director of the works for the time being—

Fischer: Forever!

Niedermaier: —I promise that all decisions will be made according to social necessity, as they have been up to now. Never without the agreement of the community, because the community is the collective, and the collective, that's the weather works. Everybody who works at the tower works here with enthusiasm for our cause, even though the collective—that's all of us ourselves—even though it's poor and can't pay any of us enough for our hard, tiring work. But no one among us

Entbehrung und Armut gern um der Zukunft derer willen, die ungern und gezwungen Entbehrung und Armut tragen müssen. Jetzt soll unser Werk, was niemand von uns je verlangt hat, gewissermaßen ein staatliches Unternehmen werden. Gut, dann mag das Wetteramt seine Tätigkeit damit beginnen, allen Arbeitern und Angestellten eine ausreichende Lebenshaltung zu sichern.

Hornbriller: Ein Amoklauf der Arroganz.

Niedermaier: Noch eins, Freunde. Ich bin durch die Verleihung eines Titels ausgezeichnet worden. Ich erwarte, daß ihr alle mich weiterhin bei meinem ehrlichen Namen nennt. Statt der Gedächtnistafel am Turm könnten wir besser warme Fußmatten für die Arbeit im Turm brauchen. Hoffen wir, daß das Eingreifen des Staates in die Angelegenheiten des Volkes durch unser kameradschaftliches Zusammenstehen in seinen schlimmsten Gefahren wird abgewehrt werden können. Darin sind wir einig: den Boden, den wir uns gemeinsam geschaffen haben, geben wir nicht wieder preis. Wir werden ihn verteidigen, wenn es sein muß mit unsern Körpern. *(Jubelnder Beifall.* Niedermaier *wird vom Hügel heruntergezogen und von den Jugendlichen fast erdrückt.)*

Blödel: Es ist jetzt in der Tat genug. Ich werde nicht länger Zeuge solcher Vorgänge bleiben.

Krampf: Nicht einmal die äußeren, parlamentarischen Formen sind diesen Leuten geläufig. Darf ich mich Ihnen anschließen, Herr Minister?

Blödel: Sehr erfreut. Doch, Herr Regierungsassessor, mir scheint, der feine Sprühregen macht den Schirm jetzt entbehrlich. Bis dieser Mensch den Landregen strömen läßt, werden wir wohl unter Dach sein. *(mit* Krampf *ab)*

Hornbriller: *(klappt den Schirm zu)* Voilà, es ist noch ganz passabel. Ich werde das parapluie dann en passant der Serviermamsell im Restaurant retournieren.

Stechbein: Was sagen Sie zu der Aufführung des Ingenieurs, Excellenz, an seinem eigenen Ehrentage?

wants any more than anyone else. But we are glad to put up with a bit of want and poverty for the sake of the future, for the future of those who might have to put up with want and poverty. Now they say that our tower should somehow become a state enterprise, something none of us has ever asked for. Well, all right, then let the Weather Bureau begin its work by ensuring that all laborers and employees receive a sufficient wage.

Hornbriller: Arrogance run amok.

Niedermaier: One more thing, friends. I have been recognized by having a title bestowed on me. I expect you all to keep calling me by my own real name. Instead of some plaque on the tower we would have been better off with warm foot mats in the tower for the workers. Let's hope that the most dangerous parts of the state's intervention in the people's business can be held at bay through our own solidarity. Let us be united: we won't give up the ground we have gained with our own collective labor. We will defend it, if need be, with our bodies. *(Thunderous applause.* Niedermaier *is carried down from the hill and almost crushed by the teenagers.)*

Blödel: That really is enough. I don't wish to be a witness to such a spectacle a moment longer.

Krampf: They don't even know the first thing about parliamentary procedure. May I join you, Herr Minister?

Blödel: My pleasure. You know, Herr Assessor, I believe the drizzle is light enough that we can do without the umbrella. By the time this fellow makes it rain hard, we will be inside. *(Goes off with* Krampf.*)*

Hornbriller: *(Closes the umbrella.) Voilà*, it is quite passable. I will return the *paraplui* to the young *mamsell* in the restaurant, *en passant.*

Stechbein: What do you think of this performance by the engineer on the day of his own commemorative ceremony?

Trankhafen: Es ist der Gipfel der Undankbarkeit. Im selben Augenblick, in dem die Regierung die Wohltaten gradezu über ihn ausschüttet.

Stiefengrat: Der Kerl muß unschädlich gemacht werden.

Hornbriller: À tou prix, vorher wird das Etablissement nicht prosperieren *(Stechbein mit Trankhafen ab, Hornbriller folgt ihnen.)*

Stiefengrat: *(laut in der Menge)* Unser wehrhaftes Vaterland, hurra! *(Gelächter)*

Biederhold: Gott schütze es und gebe dieses Werk in die Hände Erleuchteter, die seiner nicht spotten. *(mit Stiefengrat ab)*

Schönbrod: Unser Wetterturm, unsre Genossenschaft, unsre Gemeinde—hoch! *(Alle stimmen ein.)*

Annie: Wird das Wetter noch sehr schlecht?

Otti: Nicht schlechter als jetzt. Davor brauchen wir nicht wegzulaufen.

Hantke: Sagten Sie nicht, es würde noch starken Regen geben?

Niedermaier: Das war nur, um die lieben Gäste zu verscheuchen. Sonst hätte es womöglich noch mehr Ehren gegeben.

Fischer: Laßt uns heute vergnügt sein. Wenn das Wetteramt erst da ist, wird's damit aus sein.

Brunner: Sie werden die Sonne an die Kette legen und einen Polizeihund draus machen.

Berta: Nicht bange machen. Wer will mal schießen?

Wolff: Wer will in die Luftschaukel?

Jenny: Erst soll der Jugendchor noch was singen.

Otti: Wollt ihr? Was denn?

Annie: "Alle Wetter"!

Trankhafen: It is the pinnacle of ingratitude. In the very same moment that the government showers him with praise.

Stiefengrat: We need to make this guy harmless.

Hornbriller: À *tou prix*; until we do, this enterprise won't be able to turn a profit. *(*Stechbein *goes off with* Trankhafen, Hornbriller *follows them.)*

Stiefengrat: *(loudly in the crowd)* Cheers for the defense of our fatherland! Hurrah! *(laughter)*

Biederhold: May God protect it and give this work into the hands of enlightened people who don't mock it. *(Off with* Stiefengrat.*)*

Schönbrod: Let's hear it for our weather tower, our collective, our village! *(Everyone cheers.)*

Annie: Is the weather still going to get bad?

Otti: No worse than it is now. We don't need to run away from it.

Hantke: Didn't you say that the rain was going to get heavier?

Niedermaier: That was just to scare our honored guests away. If I hadn't they might have given out even more honors!

Fischer: Let's have fun today. As soon as the weather office is in place the fun will be over.

Brunner: They'll try to put a leash on the sun and turn it into a guard dog.

Berta: Don't worry. Who wants to take some shots at my shooting gallery?

Wolff: Who wants to ride in the swing-boat?

Jenny: First let's let the youth choir sing something.

Otti: Do you want to? What'll it be?

Annie: "Thunderation"!

Otti: Gut. Stellt euch auf. *(Der* Chor *und die Musik stellen sich auf.)*

Steinbott: Da kommt Paula mit Bier. Die Würstchen sind auch warm.

Niedermaier: Mir gleich ein Glas, Fräulein Paula. Na, ist die feine Kundschaft weg?

Paula: Die meisten sitzen schon im Auto. Sie denken, die Sintflut kommt.

Hantke: Jetzt feiern wir nach unserm Programm.

Brunner: Das Kasperltheater ist schon zu Ende.

Schönbrod: Still jetzt, Ottis Chor ist all aufgestellt.

Otti: *(gibt das Zeichen, Musik, Bewegungsspiele, Gesang)*

> Die Leidenschaften in der Brust,
> Noch niemand war, der sie getrennt.
> Aus einem Herd flammt Schmerz und Lust.
> Haß lodert nur, wo Liebe brennt.
> So mischt die Ebbe sich der Flut,
> Hüllt Goldstaub sich in Asche grau,
> In gleichem Wolkenbette ruht
> Der Schnee bei Hagel und beim Tau.
> Aus der Sonne dunstet Unheil,
> Aus den Blitzen zuckt Erbarmen,
> Alle Wetter, alle Wetter
> Hält der Himmel in den Armen.
>
> Nur wen des Lebens Buntheit schreckt,
> Der fürchtet sich vorm Untergehn.
> Vernichtung ist's, die Leben weckt,
> Und alles Sterben ist Entstehn.
> Im müden Stamme frißt der Wurm.
> Zur Sonne strebt der junge Trieb.
> Feg' ihm die Bahn, Zerstörer Sturm!
> So hat der Tod das Leben lieb.
> Wolkenbruch und Strahlengluten,
> Reif und Frost und Erdenbeben,

Otti: Okay, everyone get in place. *(The* choir *and the* musicians *take their places.)*

Steinbott: Here comes Paula with the beer. The sausages are still warm.

Niedermaier: I'd like a glass, Fräulein Paula. So, have the fine ladies and gentlemen left?

Paula: Most of them are still sitting in their cars. They think a great flood's coming.

Hantke: Now let's go ahead with our program.

Brunner: The puppet theater is over.

Schönbrod: Be quiet, now, Otti's choir is all ready.

Otti: *(Gives the signal, the music begins, the* choir *begins to sway with the music and sings.)*

> The passions in the human breast,
> No one could ever keep apart.
> Both joy and pain dwell in one nest,
> Hate blazes in a loving heart.
> Flood waters mix with the ebbtide.
> Gray ashes hide gold dust from view.
> In the same bed of clouds abide
> The snow, the hail, and morning's dew.
> Disaster streams forth from the sun,
> Compassion from the lightning's blaze
> Thunderation, all the weather
> Dwells in Heaven's realm always.
>
> The ones who fear life's colors bright
> Dread also every life's demise.
> Destruction brings new life to light
> And something's born when something dies.
> The dead branch nourishes the worm
> The young sprout strives toward the sun.
> Sweep clean his way, destroyer storm!
> When death comes, then is life begun.
> Cloudbursts and the glowing sun,
> Rime and frost and earthquakes too,

Alle Wetter, alle Wetter,
Töten und erzeugen Leben.

(Tanz)

Peters: So, jetzt geh' ich in den Turm. Nachmittag wird klarer Himmel.

Otti: Ich geh' mit. Muß den Funkspruch von der Islandwarte abhören.

Jenny: Kommt aber bald wieder.

Niedermaier: Ja, heute machen wir Feiertag. Kein Bonzenfest, sondern Volksfest.

Paula: Bier! Bier!

Wolff: Hierher! Zur Luftschaukel! Hierher!

Berta: Stutzenschießen, Scheibenschießen! Bewegliche Ziele!

Steinbott: Warme Würstchen!

Jahrmarkttreiben—die Luftschaukel ist in Bewegung, ein Karussell dreht sich. Händler *mit Luftballons, Pfauenfedern, usw. Drehorgelmusik.*

Schönbrod: Das kann das Wetteramt nicht!

VORHANG

Thunderation, all the weather
Kills and creates life anew.

(dance)

Peters: Well, I think I'll go into the tower. The sky will be clear this afternoon.

Otti: I'll come too. I need to get the radio report from the Iceland station.

Jenny: But you all come back soon.

Niedermaier: Yes, today we're celebrating. Not for the big shots, for the people!

Paula: Beer! Beer!

Wolff: Step right up to the swing-boat! Step right up!

Berta: Rifle shooting, target shooting! Hit the target!

Steinbott: Warm sausages!

Festival, carnival atcivities. The swing-boat is swinging, a carousel is turning. Vendors *sell balloons, peacock feathers, etc. Music from an* organ grinder.

Schönbrod: I'd like to see the Weather Bureau do that!

CURTAIN

Zweites Bild

Abort im Landtag. Links für Damen, rechts für Herren. Man sieht in beiden Abteilen Kabinentüren und neben den Eingängen die Waschvorrichtung. In der Abteilung für Männer sind die Nischen des Pissoirs so gebaut, daß der Kopf des Benutzers über der Brüstung sichtbar bleibt. Die Zwischenwand zwischen den Abteilungen reicht bis etwa vier Schritte vor der Rampe. Den Vordergrund nimmt ein korridorartiges Zimmer ein, das als Aufenthaltsraum des Landtagpersonals dient. Dieser Raum wird durch eine die Mitte nur in geringer Breite verdeckende tapizierte und gleichgültig ausgeschmückte Rückwand nur angedeutet. Er ist durch besondere Eingänge links und rechts mit den Abtritten verbunden und kann auch beiderseits von den Kulissen aus erreicht werden. In den Szenen, die hier spielen, wird durch Lichtwirkungen der Eindruck eines vom Hintergrunde getrennten Raumes hervorgerufen. Auch die Möblierung des Zimmers ist nur durch ein paar Sitzgelegenheiten angedeutet.

Links wäscht sich Dr. Trankhafen *die Hände. Hinter ihr steht* Berta *mit Handtuch. Rechts wäscht sich* Barde *die Hände, hinter ihm steht* Steinbott *mit Handtuch.*

(in der Herrenabteilung)

Barde: Seife!

Steinbott: Liegt keine da?

Barde: Geben Sie ein andres Stück. Wer weiß, wer das schon benutzt hat.

Steinbott: Nur Abgeordnete. Bitte, hier.

Act II

Restrooms of the provincial parliament. On the left the ladies' room, on the right, the men's. In both sections we see stall doors, and next to the entrances the sinks, soap, and paper towels. In the men's room, the urinals are built so that the user's head can be seen over the privacy wall. The wall between the two restrooms reaches to about four steps from the edge of the stage. The foreground is occupied by a hall-like room that serves as the waiting room for the parliament staff. This room is indicated by a rear wall, covered with wallpaper and decorated, which covers only a small area in the middle. It is connected to the wings with special entrances on the left and right. In the scenes that take place here, the lighting is used to suggest the impression of a room that is separated from the background. The furniture in this room is also merely suggested by a couple of chairs.

On the left Dr. Trankhafen *is washing her hands. Behind her stands* Berta *with a towel. On the right* Barde *is washing his hands, behind him stands* Steinbott *with a towel.*

(in the men's room)

Barde: Soap!

Steinbott: Isn't there any there?

Barde: Give me another piece. Who knows who's used that one?

Steinbott: Only delegates. Here you go.

(in der Damenabteilung)

Trankhafen: Haben Sie Fräulein Jungleib heute schon hier gesehen?

Berta: Ist sie im Landtag?

Trankhafen: Sie nimmt seit einigen Tagen an den Kommissions-
beratungen über das Wetteramt teil.

Berta: Ich kenne nur die Damen vom Landtag selber und die
Sekretärinnen von den Fraktionen und vom Büro.

Trankhafen: Da muß Ihnen doch ein neues Gesicht aufgefallen sein.

Berta: Meinen Sie die blonde Stenotypistin, die sie jetzt bei den
Unversöhnlichen eingestellt haben?

Trankhafen: Nein, Fräulein Jungleib ist rothaarig.

Berta: Ach die, ich glaubte die wär' von der Kunst und vielleicht die
Freundin von jemand.

Trankhafen: Aha, das dachten Sie also. Nein, sie wird als Sachverständige gehört.

Berta: Ist's möglich? Und die ist doch so nett, als ob sie zu uns gehörte
oder eine vom Theater wär.

Trankhafen: Dacht' ich mir doch, daß sie sich gleich mit aller Welt
gemeinmachen würde. *(arbeitet mit dem Lippenstift)*

(Herrenabteilung)

Barde: Sagen Sie mal, Wertgeschätzter, Sie sehen und hören hier in den
Gängen und Treppenhäusern wohl auch so allerhand?

Steinbott: Was grade in mein Fach fällt.

Barde: Na ja, nicht übel. Ich meine—na, sozusagen außeramtliche
Verständigungen zwischen gewissen Herren und Damen—eben—auch
unpolitischer Art.

Steinbott: Abgeordnete sind am Ende auch Menschen.

Barde: Können ja mal ein paar Beobachtungen zum Besten geben?
Was?

(in the women's room)

Trankhafen: Have you seen Fräulein Jungleib here today yet?

Berta: Is she in the parliament?

Trankhafen: She's been taking part in the commission hearings on the Weather Bureau for the past few days.

Berta: I only know the ladies in the parliament, the secretaries of the parties, and the ones from the office.

Trankhafen: Well, then, you must have noticed a new face.

Berta: Do you mean the blonde typist that the Intransigent Party hired?

Trankhafen: No, Fräulein Jungleib has red hair.

Berta: Oh, her. I thought maybe she was an artist and maybe somebody's girlfriend.

Trankhafen: Ah, is that what you thought? No, she is being called as an expert witness.

Berta: Is that possible? But she was so nice, I thought she was one of us, or worked in the theater.

Trankhafen: Just as I thought, she's buddying up to the whole world. *(Works with lipstick.)*

(men's room)

Barde: Say there, my good man, you probably hear and see all kinds of things here in the hallways and stairways, eh?

Steinbott: Whatever I catch in the course of my work.

Barde: Well then, not bad. I mean—well, so to speak, unofficial communications between certain gentlemen and ladies—that is—you might say—of a non-political nature.

Steinbott: Delegates are people too.

Barde: Could you maybe tell a couple of your observations, hmm?

Steinbott: Das gehört nicht zu meinem Dienst, Herr Abgeordneter.

Barde: Ich frage Sie nicht aus Neugier, Mensch.—Kamm!

Steinbott: Bitte.

Barde: Gut gereinigt?

Steinbott: Mit Salmiakgeist. Er wird außer von Ihnen auch höchstens mal von Herrn Regiergunstrat Hornbriller verlangt.

Barde: Schon gut. *(kämmt sich)*

(Damenabteilung)

Trankhafen: Wenn Sie das Fräulein also kennen,—haben Sie vielleicht gesehen, ob sie sich da draußen mal irgendwo mit Herrn Geheimrat Stechbein getroffen hat?

Berta: Die hab' ich noch mit niemanden gesehen. Und das kümmert mich auch garnichts. Ich meine, das sollten Sie selber wissen.

Trankhafen: Sie sind verschwiegen. Ich weiß. Immerhin—wenn Ihnen einmal etwas auffallen sollte—hier haben Sie 50 Pfennig. *(ab)*

(Herrenabteilung)

Barde: Hier haben Sie eine Mark, mein Lieber. Wäre mir lieb zu erfahren, mit wem die rothaarige Wetterhexe schöntut. Sie haben sie doch schon gesehen?

Steinbott: Aber noch mit keinem von den Herren.

Barde: Habe gewisse Brüder von der linken Seite im Verdacht. Können mir ja mal einen Wink geben.

Selters: *(tritt ein, stellt sich in eine Nische)* Das Plenum muß doch bald anfangen, Herr Kollege Barde.

Barde: Wenn die Wetterkommission nicht rechtzeitig fertig wird, wird Krampf wohl später ansetzen.

Selters: Zu einer Einigung über die Vorlage wird die Kommission heute wohl kaum mehr kommen.

Steinbott: That's not part of my duties, Herr Delegate.

Barde: I'm not asking just out of curiosity, man. —Comb!

Steinbott: Here you are.

Barde: Was it well cleaned?

Steinbott: With spirits of ammonia. Apart from you it's really only used by Herr Government Assessor Hornbriller.

Barde: All right. *(Combs his hair.)*

(women's room)

Trankhafen: So if you know who the young lady is—have you perhaps seen whether she has met with Herr Privy Councillor Stechbein out there somewhere?

Berta: I haven't seen her with anybody. And that's not really my business. I would think you would know about that yourself.

Trankhafen: You're being discreet. I understand. Still—if you should notice something—here's fifty pfennigs. *(Exits.)*

(men's room)

Barde: Here's one mark, my dear fellow. I'd really love to know who the red-haired weather vixen has been flirting with. You've surely seen her by now?

Steinbott: But not with any of the gentlemen.

Barde: I suspect certain leftist characters. You can maybe give me a little wave.

Selters: *(Enters, stands in one of the urinal stalls.)* The plenary session will begin soon, Herr Colleague Barde.

Barde: If the weather commission isn't finished on time, Krampf will probably start later.

Selters: I doubt that the commission will come to an agreement on the bill today.

Barde: Ist mir wurscht. *(zu* Steinbott*)* Da, heben Sie die Seife für mich auf. Wer weiß, was für Genossenpfoten sich sonst noch dran verewigen. *(Ab.* Frau Möhre *begibt sich zur Linken in eine Kabine.)*

Widerborst: *(Abgeordneter der Unversöhnlichen, stellt sich in eine Nische neben* Selters*)* Mit der Vorlage wird die Regierung kein Glück haben.

Selters: Ob die Kommission noch lange zu tun hat? Sie gehören ihr doch an.

Widerborst: Die Herren können sich schwer von der hübschen Sachverständigen trennen.

Selters: Ich hab' sie gesehen, ein reizendes Kerlchen.

Widerborst: Hat aber Haare auf den Zähnen. Wie die dem General Stiefengrat über's Maul gefahren ist.

Selters: Was Sie nicht sagen.

Widerborst: Der möchte ja auch am liebsten aus dem Wetteramt einen Kasernenhof machen. Wo man die Wolken Parademarsch exerzieren läßt.

Selters: Nun Herr Kollege Widerborst, als Linksliberaler möchte auch ich dem Militär keine übermäßige Machtfülle im Staate geben. Andrerseits darf doch der Gesichtspunkt der Landesverteidigung niemals unberücksichtigt bleiben.

Widerborst: Wir Unversöhnlichen bewilligen diesem Wetteramt keinen Mann und keinen Groschen.

Selters: Die Schaffung des Amtes ist ja Dank der Einsicht der Sozialisten und der Arbeiterrassenpartei jedenfalls gesichert. Die Schwierigkeit liegt nur noch bei den Verwaltungsfragen.

Widerborst: Ihr Verrat wird diesen sogenannten Arbeiterparteien nichts nützen. Wir verlangen selbstverständlich bei der Verteilung der neuen Ämter die uns nach unserer zahlenmäßigen Stärke zukommende Beteiligung. *(Frau* Möhre *verläßt die Kabine, bleibt aber von* Widerborsts *kräftiger Stimme gefesselt stehen und horcht.)*

Barde: Doesn't matter to me. *(to* Steinbott*)* Here, save this soap for me. Who knows which comrades will stick their paws all over it. *(Off. Frau* Möhre *goes into a stall on the left side.)*

Widerborst: *(Delegate of the Intransigents, stands at a urinal next to* Selters.*)* The government won't have any luck with that bill.

Selters: Will the commission be at it much longer? You're a member of it.

Widerborst: The gentlemen can't bear to part from the pretty expert witness.

Selters: Yes, I saw her, quite a pretty little thing.

Widerborst: But she's got a sharp tongue. You should have seen the way she took on General Stiefengrat!

Selters: You don't mean it!

Widerborst: Of course, he'd like to make the Weather Bureau into a barracks-yard, where he could have the clouds march a close-order drill.

Selters: Well, Herr Colleague Widerborst, as a left-liberal I too would rather not give the military an excess of state power. On the other hand we must never lose sight of the necessity of defending our country.

Widerborst: We Intransigents will not approve a single man nor a single penny for this Weather Bureau.

Selters: The creation of the Bureau is assured in any event, thanks to the agreement of the Socialists and the Workers' Race Party. The only difficulties concern the administration of it.

Widerborst: Your treason won't do these so-called workers' parties any good. Naturally when these new offices are distributed wedemand our just share according to our numerical strength. *(In the women's room, Frau* Möhre *leaves the stall, but she remains standing in place when she hears* Widerborst's *strong voice, and she keeps listening.)*

Selters: So hoch mir der Grundsatz der Verhältnisdemokratie in unsrer Republik steht, so scheint mir doch die Einfügung in die Staatsnotwendigkeiten die unerläßliche Bedingung, um sie für die Zulassung für so wichtige Posten anwendbar zu machen.

Widerborst: So! Das ist die Absicht des Finanzkapitals. Uns, die einzigen Vertreter der Werktätigen, die Beaufsichtigung eurer dunklen Machenschaften zu unterbinden! Nun, wir werden der herrschenden Klasse die Maske vom Gesicht reißen. Unter Führung der Unversöhnlichen Partei—

Selters: Aber, verehrter Herr Kollege, an dieser Stätte ist doch Ihre Eiferung ganz unangebracht.

Widerborst: Sie werden mich im Plenum hören. Wir werden ein Mißtrauensvotum einbringen! *(wütend ab)*

(Damenabteilung)

Möhre: Das war doch der Unversöhnliche Widerborst. Mit wem sprach er denn?

Berta: Das weiß ich nicht, ich hab' nicht hingehört.

Möhre: Kann man das nicht in Erfahrung bringen?

Berta: Dann müssen Sie sich zu den Herren hinüberbemühen.

Möhre: Der Betreffende ist ja noch da. *(Horcht angestrengt.* Speicherer *tritt auf, geht an die Wasserleitung.)*

(Herrenabteilung)

Speicherer: Ah, Herr Kollege Selters, was Neues?

Selters: *(kommt vor)* Ich bin ja nicht in der Kommission.

Speicherer: Hab' mir die Geschichte eben angehört. Die Sozialisten wollen natürlich alle Hauptreferate. Hustenreiz macht die bekannte Rechnung auf: soviel Mandate im Landtag, soviel Posten im Wetteramt.

Selters: Das ist einmal die demokratische Ordnung.

Selters: As important as I consider the principle of proportional democracy in our republic, I do believe that the needs of the state absolutely have to be considered when distributing such important jobs.

Widerborst: I see! So this is what the finance capitalists plan to do: to place us, the only true representatives of the working people, under the control of your own machinations! Well, we will rip the mask from the face of the ruling class. Under the leadership of the Intransigent Party—

Selters: But my dear colleague, this is neither the time nor the place for such an impassioned expression.

Widerborst: You'll see me on the floor! We are going to bring a vote of no-confidence! *(Exits furiously.)*

(women's room)

Möhre: That was the Intransigent Widerborst. But with whom was he speaking?

Berta: I don't know, I wasn't listening.

Möhre: Couldn't we find out?

Berta: Well, you'll have to get over to the gentlemen's side.

Möhre: The gentleman in question is probably still there. *(Strains to eavesdrop.* Speicherer *enters the men's room, goes to the faucet.)*

(men's room)

Speicherer: Ah, Herr Colleague Selters, any news?

Selters: *(Comes forward.)* I'm not a member of the commission.

Speicherer: I just heard the whole story. The Socialists want to make the main speeches, of course. Hustenreiz is counting it up like he always does: however many seats in the parliament, that many jobs in the Weather Bureau.

Selters: That is simply the rule of democracy.

Speicherer: In Ehren. Nur darf die Wirtschaft dabei nicht vor die Hunde gehen. Wollen Sie diese Leute, die doch ihre oppositionelle Vergangenheit immer noch von gewissen Arbeiterströmungen abhängig machen, am Ende gar in den Aufsichtsrat hineinlassen?

Selters: Alles hat natürlich Grenzen. Auf der anderen Seite haben Sie doch ihre sozialistische Lehre in vollkommene Übereinstimmung mit den Erfordernissen der bestehenden Wirtschaftsordung gebracht. Sie bewilligen, was wir brauchen. So können wir sie schwerlich von den rein verwaltungstechnischen Ämtern ausschalten.

Speicherer: In privaten Unternehmungen hat das demokratische Verfahren eher einen Sinn. Nehmen wir eine Zeitung. Da bestimmt der Mehrbesitz an Aktien ohne weiteres die politsche Haltung. In einem lebenswichtigen Staatsbetrieb dagegen—*(zu* Steinbott*)* Bitte ein Handtuch. *(Paula tritt auf.)*

(Damenabteilung)

Paula: Tag Berta. Bin eben abgelöst worden. Ich bleib' ein bißchen bei dir.

Berta: Setz' dich, Paula.

Möhre: Sie sind doch das Büfettfräulein? Ist Herr Regierungsassessor Hornbriller im Erfrischungsraum?

Paula: Nur Herr Geheimrat Stechbein. Er sitzt mit Fräulein Ministerialrätin in der Weinabteilung. Herrn Regierungsassessor sah ich in den Saal gehen, wo die Kommission tagt.

Möhre: Ist Fräulein Dr. Trankhafen schon lange da?

Paula: Nein, Herr Geheimrat wollte schon zahlen.

Möhre: Also, von meiner Fraktion, christliche Reformpartei, niemand. Es ist gut, Fräulein. *(horcht)*

(Herrenabteilung)

Selters: Was hatten Sie übrigens für einen Eindruck von der Person, die der Wetterrat Niedermaier uns da als Vertreterin hergeschickt hat?

Speicherer: Of course. But we can't let the whole economy go to the dogs because of that. Do you really want to let these people onto the board of supervisors, even if their past history as the opposition has made them independent from certain elements of the workers' movement?

Selters: Everything has its limits, to be sure. On the other hand they have adjusted their socialist theory to agree completely with the necessities of the existing economic order. They will approve what we need. So it would be very difficult to shut them out of the purely technical and administrative jobs.

Speicherer: In private enterprises the democratic process makes more sense. Take a newspaper, for example. The majority of the shareholders determine its political stance. But in a vital business of the state—*(to* Steinbott*)*—towel, please! *(Paula enters the women's room.)*

(women's room)

Paula: Hi, Berta. I just got off work. I'll stay here with you for a little while.

Berta: Sit down, Paula.

Möhre: Aren't you the waitress from the dining room? Is Government Assessor Hornbriller there?

Paula: Only Privy Councillor Stechbein. He's sitting with the ministerial advisor in the wine area. I saw Herr Hornbriller go into the hall where the commission is meeting.

Möhre: Has Dr. Trankhafen been there long?

Paula: No, the Privy Councillor wanted to pay the bill.

Möhre: So, no one from my party, the Christian Reformers. Good. *(Eavesdrops.)*

(men's room)

Selters: By the way, what was your impression of that woman Herr Niedermeier sent us as his representative?

Speicherer: Kesses Luder, was? War mir damals beim Turm schon aufgefallen.

Selters: Hat sie wenigstens bessere Manieren, als der unmögliche Ingenieur?

Speicherer: Kühl bis ans Herz. Aber der ganze Landtag macht Schielaugen nach ihr. *(Krachhahn tritt ein.)*

Krachhahn: Natürlich, wo man hinkommt, überall dasselbe Gespräch.

Speicherer: Zum ersten Mal Einstimmigkeit im Landtag: sowas Nettes hat es hier noch nicht gegeben.

Krachhahn: Nur die Weiber stimmen dagegen. Die Trankhafen pürscht unverdrossen hinter ihrem Stechbein her.

Speicherer: Und Möhre hinter ihrem Hornbriller.

Möhre: Gemeinheit!

Selters: Wer hat denn nun das Glück bei der Schönen?

Speicherer: Ich glaube, der große Volkserneuerer Kajetan Teutsch gibt sich mächtige Mühe.

Krachhahn: Das Mädel kommt mir aber nicht so vor, als ob sie in dem Punkt Ähnlichkeit mit unserer Republik hätte.

Selters: Wie meinen Sie das?

Krachhahn: Na, daß sie jedem die Liebe glaubt, der ihr nicht gerade ins Gesicht spuckt.

Selters: Wo steht sie eigentlich politisch?

Krachhahn: Da sieht sie der Republik schon ähnlicher: schwarze Augen, rotes Haar und goldenes Gemüt.

Speicherer: Dabei von rührender Ahnungslosigkeit in allen Dingen, auf die es ankommt.

Krachhahn: *(tritt in eine Nische)* Sie meinen, wie die da oben den Wetterbetrieb befummeln. So geschickt das kleine Aas ihre Sache verteidigt,—lassen wir die Gesellschaft da noch lange murksen, dann ist die Landwirtschaft zum mindesten beim Satan.

Speicherer: Pert little thing, eh? I noticed her that time at the tower.

Selters: Does she at least have better manners than that impossible engineer?

Speicherer: Cool as a cucumber. But the whole parliament is making eyes at her. *(*Krachhahn *enters.)*

Krachhahn: Of course, wherever you go it's the same conversation.

Speicherer: For the first time, a unanimous opinion in the parliament: we've never had anything here that looked as nice as she does.

Krachhahn: Only the women would vote against that. Trankhafen keeps right on tagging along behind Stechbein.

Speicherer: And Möhre is always behind Hornbriller.

Möhre: What vulgarity!

Selters: So who got lucky with that pretty girl?

Speicherer: I think the great racial renewer Kajetan Teutsch is trying his best.

Krachhahn: But the girl doesn't seem to me to have a lot in common with our republic when it comes to one particular point.

Selters: What do you mean by that?

Krachhahn: Well, that she would fall for anyone who didn't spit in her eye.

Selters: Where does she stand politically?

Krachhahn: Well, there is where she looks a little more like the republic: black eyes, red hair, and a golden disposition.

Speicherer: And all the while pitifully dense about the things that matter.

Krachhahn: *(Steps into a niche.)* You mean the way they're kicking the weather works around up there. As well as she knows how to defend her own cause—if we let them mess around with the corporation much longer, then the agricultural economy will go to the devil.

Speicherer: Die gesamte Wirtschaft. Der Schaden ist ja jetzt schon ungeheuer. Dabei könnte der Wetterdienst mit Leichtigkeit zu einem höchst gewinnbringenden Unternehmen gemacht werden.

Selters: Die Hautpsache ist, eine gesunde kaufmännische Leitung einzusetzen.

Speicherer: Das bisherige Verfahren ist einfach kindisch. Man faßt die Wetterlage kurzerhand den Bedürfnissen der im Freien arbeitenden Berufe an. Dabei fragen sie nicht die Unternehmer, die das Risiko mit ihrem Vermögen tragen, sondern die ahnungslosen Arbeitnehmer.

Selters: Das ist freilich mehr als naiv. Immerhin können sie auf glänzende Ernten im ganzen Lande verweisen.

Krachhahn: Eben, das ist der Ruin der Landwirtschaft.

Speicherer: Und vieler anderer Wirtschaftsgebiete. Unsre ganze Zoll- und Steuerpolitik wird durchkreuzt und nun muß man ihre wahnsinnigen Menschheitsduseleien hören. Die großen Stürme hat man über breite Zonen zersteubt und dadurch zu Nutzwinden gemildert. Klingt brav, nicht wahr? Die praktische Wirkung ist, daß es keine Sturmschäden an den Häusern gibt, folglich Arbeitsausfall im Baugewerbe, schwerste Schädigung grade des Industriezwieges, von dessen Belebung in der wärmeren Jahreszeit die Leute das größte Aufheben machen. Machen das Wetter zum Bauen und zerstören den Anlaß der Bautätigkeit. Das ist die glatte Verhöhnung der Arbeiter, meine Herren.

Krachhahn: Es sind gemeingefährliche Narren.

Speicherer: Weiter. Der Hochseefischerei wird während der Fangzeit ein Wetter beschert, das eine Übersättigung des Marktes mit billigen Fischen bewirkt. Folge?

Krachhahn: Die Pleite der Viehzucht. *(Kommt wieder vor.)*

Speicherer: Nicht davon zu reden, daß die Ölmäntelfabrikanten durch Absatzstockung zugrunde geht. Oder, das Fräulein legt eine Statistik vor, die beweist, daß die Schiffsunfälle auf einen winzigen Prozentsatz heruntergegangen sind. Sehr edel, nur an die Versicherungs-gesellschaften denkt kein Mensch.

Selters: Sehr wahr.

Speicherer: You mean the whole economy. The damage is pretty serious already. And the weather service could quite easily be made into a very profitable enterprise.

Selters: The most important thing is to get good, healthy, business-oriented leadership in place.

Speicherer: Up to now the whole operation has been run absolutely childishly. They are only dealing with the weather needs of people who work outdoors. They're not asking the entrepreneurs who take risks with their capital, they're only asking the clueless workers.

Selters: You know, that really is naive. Still, they can point to their great harvests all over the country.

Krachhahn: Exactly: that will be the ruin of the agricultural economy.

Speicherer: And of a lot of other sectors of the economy. Our whole customs and tax policy is being thwarted, and now we have to listen to their crazy rantings about humanity. They've taken huge storms and spread them out over large areas, and turned them into beneficial winds. Sounds good, doesn't it? Of course, the practical effect is that there is no longer any storm damage to houses,consequently a loss of jobs in the construction business. The worst damage happens to just the very industry that the people make a fuss about stimulating in the warm season. They create good weather for building, but at the same time they destroy the very reason for construction activity. That's nothing but a mockery of the working class, gentlemen.

Krachhahn: These fools are a danger to society.

Speicherer: There's more. The deep-sea fisheries are blessed with weather during the catching season that causes a glut of cheap fish on the market. The result?

Krachhahn: The cattle breeders go broke. *(Steps forward.)*

Speicherer: Never mind the fact that the manufacture of rain slickers goes to ruin because of stagnant sales. Or the young lady presented a statistic that proved that shipwrecks declined a tiny percentage point. Very noble, except that nobody is thinking about the insurance companies.

Selters: Very true.

Krachhahn: Noch doller: Hagelschläge gibt es überhaupt nicht mehr. Sämtliche Hagelversicherungen sind kaputt.

Selters: Das sind in der Tat schlimme Auswüchse.

Krachhahn: Für die Preisbildung ist es eine Katastrophe. Die Scheuern bersten und wir müssen das Brotgetreide, um es nicht zu Schleuderpreisen herzugeben, einfach verfaulen lassen.

Speicherer: Es ist Zeit, Kraft zu zeigen. Wir drei, meine Herren, als die berufenen Vertreter von Industrie, Landwirtschaft und Handel, müssen die Richtlinien festlegen, durch die ohne Rücksicht auf humane und soziale Redensarten das Wetteramt der Obhut der leitenden Wirtschaftskräfte unterstellt wird.

Selters: Wenn wir Sorge tragen, daß der Aufsichtsrat ausschließlich aus Vertrauenspersonen unserer Parteien zusammengesetzt wird, so werden wir die übrigen Posten ruhig paritätisch verteilen können.

Speicherer: Ja, dann haben wir den Betrieb in seiner ökonomischen Auswertbarkeit in der Hand. Kommen Sie, wir können hier hinten ganz unauffällig den Geheimvertrag entwerfen, den wir unsern Fraktionen vorlegen.

Selters: Die demokratischen Formen müssen natürlich gewahrt werden.

Krachhahn: Wenn Sie Wert darauf legen. *(verschwinden hinter der Wand)*

(Frauenabteilung)

Trankhafen: *(tritt auf)* Ach, Sie sind hier, liebste Frau Möhre.

Möhre: Denken Sie—aber pst—ich war zufällig Zeugin wichtiger politischer Verabredungen.

Trankhafen: Nicht möglich. Erzählen Sie doch.

Möhre: Wollen Sie denn nicht erst Ihr wertes Bedürfnis verrichten?

Trankhafen: Nein, ich war eigentlich schon hier—ich wollte nur nachsehen—berichten Sie doch, was Sie erlauscht haben.

Möhre: Ob es mir aber mein christliches Gewissen nicht verbieten sollte, es zu verraten?

Krachhahn: It's even crazier. There aren't any more hailstorms. Now the companies that insure against hailstorms are completely done for.

Selters: These really are bad side effects.

Krachhahn: It's really a catastrophe when it comes to setting prices. The grain silos are bursting at the seams. We have to simply let it sit there and rot if we don't want to sell it dirt-cheap.

Speicherer: It is time to show strength. We three, gentlemen, the representatives from industry, agriculture, and trade, have to set some guidelines that stipulate that the weather office be made subject to the leading economic indicators, without regard to humane and social slogans.

Selters: If we make sure that the supervisory board is made up exclusively of agents of our own parties, then we won't have to worry if the other positions are filled by the other parties.

Speicherer: Yes, then we'll have in our hands the full possibilities for exploiting the enterprise. Come, we can step back here and draft a secret agreement without being noticed, and then present it to our factions.

Selters: Of course, we must protect the forms of democracy.

Krachhahn: Well, if you really think that's important. *(They disappear behind the wall.)*

(women's room)

Trankhafen: *(Appears.)* Ah, you are here, my dear Frau Möhre.

Möhre: Yes indeed, but—pssst!—I just happened to be witness to a very important political agreement.

Trankhafen: You don't mean it! Tell me!

Möhre: Don't you want to take care of necessary business first?

Trankhafen: No, I was already here in fact, I just wanted to check—tell me what you overheard.

Möhre: But shouldn't my Christian conscience forbid me from betraying it?

Trankhafen: Ich bitte Sie, Frau Möhre. Ich kann doch schweigen.

Möhre: Die Unversöhnlichen wollen ein Mißtrauensvotum einbringen.

Trankhafen: Was Sie nicht sagen.

Möhre: Aber das ist noch garnichts. Die Industriepartei, die Landwirtschaftler und die Liberalen machen da nebenan gerade einen Geheimvertrag, daß sie den Aufsichtsrat im Wetteramt ganz allein besetzen wollen. Ich hab' alles ganz deutlich gehört: Krachhahn, Speicherer und Selters setzen den Entwurf gerade auf.

Trankhafen: Da muß man natürlich gleich Gegenminen legen.

Möhre: Ich meine doch auch, daß man die Christliche Reformpartei nicht von dem ganzen Gewinn ausschließen darf.

Trankhafen: Ich werde meine Parteifreunde verständigen lassen. Da ich Beamtin bin, muß ich mich selber natürlich zurückhalten. Aber die Mittelparteien müssen ebenfalls benachrichtigt werden. Die Hausfrauenpartei wird eine solche Übervorteilung ja gewiß nicht gleichmütig hinnehmen.

Möhre: Das meine ich eben, niemand wird sich doch in seiner Bedrängnis alle Öffnungen zustopfen lassen.

Wachtel: *(kommt eilends herbei)* Ich kann die Aufregungen nicht vertragen.

Trankhafen: Da ist ja grade Frau Wachtel von der Hausfrauenpartei.

Möhre: Wissen Sie schon, Frau Kollegin Wachtel—

Wachtel: Ja. Es ist ein Skandal. Der Schreck—verzeihen Sie— *(will weiter)*

Trankhafen: Wovon sprechen Sie denn da? Was ist geschehen?

Wachtel: Ich denk, Sie wissen. Die Kommissionssitzung ist aufgeflogen.

Trankhafen: Aufgeflogen? Wieso?

Wachtel: Die Rassischen haben sie gesprengt. Ja, doch.

Möhre: Um Gotteswillen, und das haben wir versäumt! Aber wie ging es denn zu? Laufen Sie uns doch nicht fort!

Trankhafen: I beg you, Frau Möhre—I can keep my mouth shut.

Möhre: The Intransigents want to bring a vote of no-confidence.

Trankhafen: What are you saying!?

Möhre: But that's nothing. The Industrial Party, the Landowners, and the Liberals are drafting a secret agreement next door that they alone will occupy all the seats on the supervisory board of the Weather Bureau. I heard it all quite clearly: Krachhahn, Speicherer, and Selters are writing the thing up even as we speak.

Trankhafen: Well, of course we need to lay some defensive mines.

Möhre: I really do think that the Christian Reform Party shouldn't be excluded from the profits.

Trankhafen: I'll let my party colleagues know what's going on. Since I'm a civil servant I have to keep myself out of the affair. But the center parties need to be informed as well. The Housewives' Party certainly won't sit still for this kind of pre-arrangement.

Möhre: That's exactly what I mean: surely no one will allow all openings to be shut off in such a time of distress.

Wachtel: *(Comes in hurriedly.)* I can't take any more of this excitement.

Trankhafen: There's Frau Wachtel of the Housewives' Party now.

Möhre: Have you heard, Frau Wachtel—?

Wachtel: Yes. It's a scandal. How horrible—forgive me— *(Tries to leave.)*

Trankhafen: What are you talking about? What happened?

Wachtel: I think you know. The meeting of the commission is dissolved.

Trankhafen: Dissolved? What do you mean?

Wachtel: The Racialists broke it up. Yes, they did!

Möhre: Oh my God, and we missed it! But how did it happen? Don't run away.

Wachtel: Der Abgeordnete Hustenreiz und Herr Barde—wegen Herrn Teutsch und der Dame vom Wetteramt—

Trankhafen: Also doch. Und Hustenreiz und Teutsch hat sie in ihre Netze gezogen!

Möhre: Das sind ja furchtbare Verirrungen.

Wachtel: Mein Gott, so ist es ja nicht. Aber—wissen Sie—die Feier am Wetterturm—Zugluft schlägt immer auf den Darm. *(schnell in eine Kabine)*

Trankhafen: Von Hustenreiz hätte ich es ja nicht gedacht! *(Draußen nähert sich Lärm und Geschrei. Speicherer, Selters und Krachhahn kommen zum Vorschein.)*

(Herrenabteilung)

Krachhahn: Was ist denn das für ein mörderliches Getöse?

Steinbott: Da werden wohl wieder die Parteien verschiedener Meinung sein.

Hustenreiz: *(stürzt herein, schmeißt die Tür zu)* Das ist Banditentum! Das ist nicht mehr parlamentarisch.

Barde: *(tobt herein mit geschwungenem Lineal)* Wo ist der Judenlümmel?!

Hustenreiz: Hilfe! Hilfe! *(duckt sich in einer Nische)*

Selters: *(zaghaft)* Doch keine Gewalttätigkeit, Kollege Barde!

Speicherer: Ruche, meine Herren!

Barde: Weg da! *(Hustenreiz entkommt in eine Kabine.)* Feiger Halunke.

Krachhahn: *(hält sich den Bauch vor Lachen)* Das ist ja kostbar. Was hat's denn gegeben, lieber Barde?

Barde: Der Scheißkerl will unsern Führer beleidigen! Dieses Stück Mist von Kajetan Teutsch!

Speicherer: Erzählen Sie schon!

Wachtel: Representative Hustenreiz and Herr Barde got into it—because of Herr Teutsch and the lady from the Weather Bureau—

Trankhafen: Of course. And she pulled Hustenreiz and Teutsch into her net.

Möhre: They're letting themselves be terribly misled.

Wachtel: My God, it's not as bad as that. But—you know—the ceremony at the weather tower—drafts are always hard on the digestive tract. *(Rushes into a stall.)*

Trankhafen: I never would have thought it possible of Hustenreiz! *(Outside noise and shouting are heard approaching.* Speicherer, Selters *and* Krachhahn *come into the men's room.)*

(men's room)

Krachhahn: What kind of murderous din is that?

Steinbott: The parties are probably having another difference of opinion.

Hustenreiz: *(Storms in, slams the door shut.)* That is robbery! That's not parliamentary!

Barde: *(Enters in a rage swinging a ruler.)* Where is that Jewish lout?

Hustenreiz: Help! Help! *(Ducks into a urinal niche.)*

Selters: *(timidly)* Please, no violence, Colleague Barde!

Speicherer: Calm down, gentlemen!

Barde: Step aside! *(*Hustenreiz *escapes into a stall.)* You cowardly wimp!

Krachhahn: *(holding his belly with laughter)* This is great! What's the matter, my dear Barde?

Barde: This son of a bitch is trying to insult our Führer! This little piece of Kajetan Teutsch's crap!

Speicherer: Tell us!

Barde: Sagt doch das Arschloch: gewisse Herren—und meint Kajetan Teutsch —interessierten sich wohl weniger für die Erklärungen des Wetterfräuleins als für ihre weibliche Persönlichkeit!

Selters: Das ist allerdings stark.

Krachhahn: Ha ha ha! Ist wohl dem Häschen zu dicht auf den Leib gerückt!

Barde: Die hysterische Nutte scheint es mit den Linken zu halten. Quitscht plötzlich los, geht hoch wie eine Rakete, erklärt mit keuscher Würde, sie spräche nicht weiter, solange Herr Teutsch sich nicht weggesetzt hätte. Er hätte mit den Beinen nach ihr geangelt.

Krachhahn: Ist ja großartig.

Barde: Und der rötliche Oberkellner da will gleich den Anstandswauwau spielen und läßt die hanebüchene Unverschämtheit vom Stapel. Ich hatte ihn sofort bei der Krawatte.

Speicherer: Die Sitzung also gesprengt?

Barde: Klar. Allgemeine Keilerei.

Selters: Ein bedauerlicher Fall. Im Plenum mag so etwas einmal vorkommen, aber in der Kommission, wo man unter sich ist!

(Damenabteilung)

Trankhafen: Mein Parteifreund Hustenreiz ist also unschuldig. Wir müssen aber hören, was nun beschlossen ist. *(Jenny tritt ein.)* Aha, die Fraktionssekretärin meiner Partei. Kommen Sie aus der Kommissionsitzung? Was gibt's?

Jenny: Sie hauen sich. Das heißt jetzt nur noch die Unversöhnlichen mit den Landwirtschaftlern und den Rasseparteilern.

Möhre: Wie unchristlich.

Wachtel: *(kommt aus der Kabine)* Ach, Frau Wärterin, haben Sie keine Choleratropfen?

Berta: Ich habe nur Abführmittel hier.

Wachtel: Um alles in der Welt! Nein!

Barde: The asshole said: certain gentlemen—and he meant Kajetan Teutsch—were less interested in the young weather lady's explanations than they were in her feminine charms.

Selters: That certainly is strong.

Krachhahn: Ha ha ha! That probably hit close to home!

Barde: The hysterical slut seems to be in with the left wingers. All of a sudden she shrieks, blows up like a rocket, and declares with chaste dignity that she wouldn't speak any more, until Herr Teutsch moved away from her. She said he had tried to grope her with his legs.

Krachhahn: This is terrific!

Barde: And that pinko headwaiter there tries to play all Goody Twoshoes and starts to make a speech about the impertinence of it all. I had him by the necktie in two seconds.

Speicherer: Broke up the meeting?

Barde: Sure. Everybody got into the brawl.

Selters: A regrettable incident. It's one thing if something like this happens in the plenary session, but in the commission, where we are among ourselves!

(women's room)

Trankhafen: So my party colleague Hustenreiz is innocent. We have to find out what's been decided. *(Jenny enters.)* Aha, my party's secretary. Are you coming from the commission meeting? What's new?

Jenny: They're beating each other up. That is, right now it's just the Intransigents against the Landowners and the Racialists.

Möhre: How un-Christian.

Wachtel: *(Comes out of the stall.)* Oh, attendant, do you have anything for diarrhea?

Berta: All I have here is laxative.

Wachtel: Oh, for heaven's sake! No!

Paula: Am Büfett gibt es einen sehr guten Magenbittern, Frau Abgeordnete. Der hilft Herrn Minister Blödel immer.

(Herrenabteilung)

Hornbriller: *(tritt auf)* Sich so zu echauffieren. Eine blamable Affaire. Ich recherchiere nach Herrn Hustenreiz.

Barde: Er erleichtert sein Herz. Sonst fällt es ihm in die Hosen.

Hornbriller: Ist er blessiert?

Krachhahn: Ach wo, blaß aber munter.

Hornbriller: Nur vom Chock derangiert, tant mieux. Hallo! *(klopft an)*

Hustenreiz: *(von innen)* Herr Regierungsassessor?

Hornbriller: Ein Journalist wünscht Sie über die Attacke zu interviewen. Wollen Sie ihn informieren?

Hustenreiz: Solange diese Bedrohung andauert, bleibe ich, wo ich bin.

Krachhahn: Wehren Sie sich doch, Mensch.

Barde: Er soll bloß rauskommen, der Schlappschwanz. Ich werde ihm die Chuzbe schon austreiben.

Speicherer: Es lohnt sich nicht, Kollege Barde.

Selters: Lassen Sie es nun auf sich beruhen.

Hornbriller: Durch kollegiale Intervention ließe sich gewiß eine honorige Satisfaktion entrieren.

Barde: Ich hau' ihn in die Fresse! Dann kann er laufen.

Hustenreiz: Hilfe, Hilfe!

Hornbriller: Er appeliert an Sukkurs. Ich werde den Interviewer selbst instruieren. *(ab)*

Speicherer: Ich habe auch keine Lust, mich in eine Prügelei verwickeln zu lassen. *(ab)*

Selters: Ich schließe mich an. *(ab)*

Paula: At the buffet table in the cafeteria there are some very good bitters, Frau Delegate. They always help Minister Blödel.

(men's room)

Hornbriller: *(Enters.)* Everyone is so upset! A very damaging *affaire*. I am seeking Herr Hustenreiz.

Barde: He's taking a load off his mind. Otherwise it'll fall into his pants.

Hornbriller: Is he wounded?

Krachhahn: Ah, no, he's pale but he's alert.

Hornbriller: Only deranged from the shock, *tant mieux*. Hello! *(Knocks.)*

Hustenreiz: *(from within)* Herr Government Assessor?

Hornbriller: A journalist would like to interview you about the attack. Do you want to speak with him?

Hustenreiz: As long as this threat lasts, I will stay where I am.

Krachhahn: Defend yourself, man!

Barde: Just let him come out, that weakling. I'll knock the chutzpah out of him!

Speicherer: It's not worth it, Colleague Barde.

Selters: Just let it rest.

Hornbriller: Surely an honorable solution can be reached through collegial intervention.

Barde: I'll punch him one in the chops, then he can run.

Hustenreiz: Oh, help! Help!

Hornbriller: He's appealing for *succours*. I will speak with the interviewer myself. *(off)*

Speicherer: I have no desire to get involved in fisticuffs. *(off)*

Selters: I'll join you. *(off)*

Krachhahn: Viel Glück, Kollege Barde. *(ab)*

Barde: So, Brüderchen, jetzt sind wir unter uns. Ich spucke mal in die Hände.

Steinbott: Nun sag' ich Ihnen was, Herr. Wenn Sie sich prügeln wollen, dann tun Sie das im Sitzungssaal. In meinem Abort hat jede Partei gleiches Recht. Wenn hier Sitzung ist, gibt's keinen Krach,der nicht dazu gehört, und wer sich nicht so benimmt, wie sich das auf dem Abort schickt, den schmeiß' ich raus.

Barde: Mischen Sie sich nicht in Dinge ein, die Sie nichts angehen.

Steinbott: Hier bin ich Präsident und hier mach' ich die Geschäftsordnung. Verstanden? Kommen Sie ruhig raus, Herr Abgeordneter. Im Abort ist reine Luft. *(Hustenreiz kommt schlotternd zum Vorschein.)*

Barde: Jammerkerl!

Steinbott: *(stellt sich zwischen beide)* Jetzt setzen Sie sich da man in die Ecke. Da sieht Sie keiner und da faßt Sie keiner an. Und Sie, Herr Barde, wenn Sie hier noch was zu besorgen haben, tun Sie es gleich. Für andere Geschäfte ist dieser Ort nicht da.

Barde: Das will ein deutscher Mann sein! *(ab)*

(Damenabteilung)

Otti: *(tritt auf)* Guten Morgen.

Trankhafen: Jetzt können wir das Fräulein ja selber fragen. Ihretwegen hat also die Kommissionssitzung einen so jähen Abschluß gefunden?

Otti: Ich mußte mir unangenehme Annäherungen vom Leibe halten. Das ist alles.

Trankhafen: In der Regel haben die Herren ein Gefühl dafür, wo sie Annäherungen wagen können.

Möhre: So heißt es.

Otti: Dann will ich Ihren Erfahrungen nicht widersprechen.

Krachhahn: Good luck, Colleague Barde. *(off)*

Barde: So, little boy, it's just you and me now. I'm spitting on my hands.

Steinbott: Listen, sir. If you all want to beat each other up, then do it in the meeting hall. In my restroom each and every party has the same rights. When there's a meeting here there are no fights that aren't part of the meeting. If anybody behaves in a way that's not appropriate for a restroom, then I'll throw him out.

Barde: Don't get involved in things that aren't your business.

Steinbott: I'm the president here and I set the agenda. You understand? You can come out now, Herr Delegate. You're safe in the restroom. *(*Hustenreiz *appears, trembling.)*

Barde: You miserable little—

Steinbott: *(Places himself between the two.)* Now you sit down over there in the corner. No one will see you there and no one will touch you. And you, Herr Barde, if you have anything else to take care of here, then take care of it right now. This is not the place to do other business.

Barde: And you call yourself a German man! *(off)*

(women's room)

Otti: *(Enters.)* Good morning.

Trankhafen: Now we can ask her ourselves. Was it on account of you that the commission meeting was stopped so suddenly?

Otti: I had to put a stop to some inappropriate advances, that's all.

Trankhafen: As a rule the gentlemen have a good sense of when they might dare to make advances.

Möhre: That's what I've heard.

Otti: Well then I certainly don't want to contradict your experience.

Trankhafen: Das ist derselbe Ton, den man schon in Wetterborn beliebte.

Wachtel: Dort habe ich mir die Magenerkältung zugezogen. Ich gehe jetzt und lasse mir einen Bittern geben.

Möhre: Wir gehen wohl lieber gleich mit. *(alle drei ab)*

Otti: Die parlamentarischen Gebräuche sind nicht so leicht zu lernen.

Berta: Wir haben da nicht hineinzureden.

Paula: Wir tun unsre Arbeit und halten den Mund, Fräulein.

Otti: Ach so. *(wäscht sich die Hände, singt)*

> So ist's bei den Menschen bestellt, ja, ja,
> Dem Reichen gehört die Welt, aha,
> Der Arme muß sich beackern,
> Muß sich für den Reichen rackern.
> Der Arme verbringt sein Leben soso,
> Füllt dem Reichen die Truhen und Fässer.
> Der Reiche, der steht daneben, oho!
> Tut nichts, kann nichts und weiß alles besser.
> Das dauert, solang sich der Arme nicht wehrt
> Und hört auf, sobald er sein Recht begehrt.
> Und wenn das geschieht, dann ist's so bestellt:
> Wer die Arbeit tut, dem gehört die Welt.
> Ja, ja, aha—soso, oho—
> Wer heute seufzt, der ist morgen froh!

Paula: Haben Sie aber eine hübsche Stimme!

Otti: Beim Wetterturm singe und tanze ich mit einem ganzen Jugendchor.

Berta: Gibt es da soviele bessere Leute?

Otti: Da gibt es nur die allerbesten Leute, lauter Arbeiter und Bauern.

Jenny: Ach, Sie halten es mit denen?

Otti: Da müssten Sie doch aus meinem Lied gemerkt haben.

Trankhafen: That's the same tone we heard at Weatherspring.

Wachtel: I got my gastrointestinal infection there. I'm going to go get some bitters.

Möhre: Why don't we all go with you. *(all three off)*

Otti: These parliamentary customs aren't easy to learn.

Berta: We aren't supposed to say anything about them.

Paula: We just do our jobs and keep our mouths shut, Fräulein.

Otti: I see. *(Washes her hands and sings.)*

> The world works just like this, aha,
> The rich man thinks the world is his, aha.
> The poor man works and sweats,
> Gives the rich man all that he gets.
> The poor man spends his life just so,
> Carries the rich man's bags, with a bow.
> The rich man stands off to the side, oho,
> Can't do a thing, but he always knows how.
> This while the poor man stands idly by,
> And it ends when he asks for his piece of the pie.
> When he speaks up, things turn in his favor.
> The world belongs to the ones who labor.
> Aha, aha—oho, oho
> Tomorrow things will be better, you know.

Paula: Don't you have a nice voice!

Otti: At the weather tower I sing and dance with a whole youth choir.

Berta: Are there really so many nice people there?

Otti: There are the best people in the world there, all farmers and workers.

Jenny: Oh, so you're on their side?

Otti: You should be able to tell that from my song.

Berta: Sind Sie Kommunistin?

Otti: Sowas Ähnliches werde ich wohl sein. Nur mit dem Parteikram habe ich nichts im Sinn.

Paula: Wir alle nicht. Aber hier im Hause kann man auch ein Lied davon singen.

Jenny: Wenn wir auch keine solche Stimme haben wie Sie.

Paula: Ich bediene nämlich im Erfrischungsraum. Da müssten Sie mal hören, was das für Menschen sind, die Wähler ausschmieren, ohne daß sie es merken—das ist die ganze Regierungskunst.

Otti: Ich habe einen Vorgeschmack davon bekommen: wenn man das Wetter bestimmen soll, kommt es doch darauf an, daß wir die Feldbestellung und die Ernte, die Schiffahrt und die Arbeit überall unter guten Bedingungen schaffen können. Ich habe ihnen unsre Berechnungen erklären wollen, von all dem wollten sie garnicht hören. Gefragt haben sie nach der Geschäftsaufsicht, ob man nicht Arbeiter einsparen, Rücklagen machen, die Arbeitszeit verlängern, gestaffelte Löhne einführen könnte. Die meisten hörten überhaupt nicht hin. Aber alle wollten mal in meine Notizen sehen. In Wirklichkeit schielten sie in meinen Halsausschnitt.

Jenny: Das kennen wir hier zur Genüge.

Paula: Hier bei Berta ist der einzige Ort im Landtag, wo man vor ihnen seine Ruhe hat. *(langgezogenes Klingelzeichen)*

Otti: Was soll das?

Jenny: Das erste Glockenzeichen zehn Minuten vor Beginn der Vollsitzung.

Berta: Müssen Sie da auch wieder dabei sein?

Jenny: Aber Berta, das müßtest du doch wissen, daß bei den Beschlüssen des ganzen Parlaments kein Sachverständiger mehr was zu suchen hat.

Berta: Are you a communist?

Otti: I'm probably something like that. I just can't put up with all that party stuff.

Paula: We can't either. But here in the building we can sing songs about it.

Jenny: Even if we don't have a voice like yours.

Paula: I'm a waitress in the dining room. There you'd get a pretty good idea of what kind of people these are, these characters who cheat the voters without their knowing it. That's how they run the government.

Otti: I already saw a bit of that: if you're going to control the weather, you should do it to create good conditions everywhere for planting and harvest, for shipping and for working. I wanted to explain our calculations to them, but they didn't want to hear a word. They only asked about the business prospects, about things like cutting back on workers, saving here and there, lengthening the workday, introducing staggered wage levels. Most of them didn't even listen. But they all wanted to look at my notes. Actually they were trying to look down my neckline.

Jenny: We know all about that.

Paula: In here with Berta is the only place in the whole parliament building where we can have a break from them. *(long, drawn-out bell signal)*

Otti: What does that mean?

Jenny: The first bell sounds ten minutes before the full session.

Berta: Do you have to be there too?

Jenny: Wait, Berta, you know that when the whole parliament is passing a resolution they don't allow expert witnesses.

(Herrenabteilung)

Hustenreiz: (kommt zum Vorschein) Es hat schon geläutet. Der Mensch wird doch nicht vor der Tür auflauern.

Steinbott: Man keine Angst. Das war doch bloß, daß ihm sein Kajetan in der Parteischule einen raufsetzt. Aber bleiben Sie man lieber noch ein bißchen hier. Der Schreck ist noch nicht verflogen.

Hustenreiz: Mir ist noch ganz schlecht von der Aufregung.

Steinbott: Für solche Fälle habe ich einen Kognac da. Wenn Sie einen Lütten mögen?

Hustenreiz: Ganz gern, aber schenken Sie sich selber auch einen ein.

Steinbott: Alle Mal. *(Wolff und* Brunner, *beide in Livree, treten ein.)*

Wolff: Hier kommen wir grade zur rechten Zeit.

Brunner: Schnaps! Du, Steinbott, bei dir hat es noch nie so gut gerochen.

Steinbott: Herrn Abgeordneten ist nicht recht wohl. Geht man solang ins Botenzimmer. Ich bring' euch einen hin.

Brunner: Brauchst kein Licht anmachen, die innere Beleuchtung genügt. *(mit* Wolff *in den halbdunklen Vorraum)*

Steinbott: Trinken Sie man noch einen? *(Trinkt selbst zweimal.* Hustenreiz *setzt sich wieder.)*

Biederhold: (Aktendeckel unter dem Arm, tritt ein) Alles frei, guter Mann?

Steinbott: Wo Herr Pfarrer belieben. Papier? Was zu lesen?

Biederhold: Ich bin mit allem ausgerüstet. *(verschwindet in einer Kabine)*

(Botenzimmer)

Steinbott: (bringt die Flasche und zwei Gläser nach vorn) Aber Maul halten.

Wolff: Das ist Unterhaltung genug.

(men's room)

Hustenreiz: *(Emerges from stall.)* There's the bell. The man surely won't be waiting outside the door.

Steinbott: Just don't worry. That was all just to win points with his Kajetan Teutsch. But why don't you wait here a few more minutes anyway. The danger hasn't completely passed.

Hustenreiz: I am still sick from the excitement.

Steinbott: I have congac here for situations like these. Would you like a small one?

Hustenreiz: Yes, please, but pour yourself one as well.

Steinbott: You bet. *(*Wolff *and* Brunner, *both in livery, enter.)*

Wolff: Here we come, just in time.

Brunner: You have whisky! Steinbott, it's never smelled this good in here!

Steinbott: The delegate isn't feeling so well. You all go into the staff room. I'll bring you a drink.

Brunner: No need to turn on the light, it's bright enough in here. *(Goes with* Wolff *into the half-darkened staff room in front.)*

Steinbott: Can I pour you another? *(He has another himself.* Hustenreiz *sits down once again.)*

Biederhold: *(Enters with a file folder under his arm.)* Everything clear, my good man?

Steinbott: Wherever you like, Reverend. Paper? Something to read?

Biederhold: I am fully equipped. *(Disappears into a stall.)*

(staff room)

Steinbott: *(Brings the bottle and two glasses to the front.)* Here. But keep your mouth shut.

Wolff: This will pass the time just fine.

(Damenabteilung)

Annie: *(tritt links auf)* Gottseidank, jetzt hab' ich Zeit. Ist hier die Luft rein? *(erblickt* Otti*)* Ach, entschuldigen Sie!

Otti: Meinetwegen brauchen Sie doch nicht verlegen zu sein. Ich bin hier auch nur der Gesellschaft wegen.

Berta: Denk dir, Annie, das Fräulein hat uns schon was vorgesungen.

Otti: Sah ich Sie nicht schon im Postraum?

Annie: Ja, ich bin die Telefonistin, ich weiß auch, wer Sie sind, Fräulein Jungleib von Wetterborn.

Otti: Wetterborn sagt bei uns kein Mensch. Den Namen haben sie uns aufgezwungen. Bei uns spricht man bloß vom Turm, und mich nennen alle die Rote Otti.

Annie: Wißt ihr schon, daß Stechbein Staatssekretär werden soll? Das Wetteramt soll ja eine eigene Behörde werden.

Paula: Darum hat er auch mit der Trankhafen Wein getrunken.

Jenny: Seht doch. Gestern hat er mich auf dem Gang angehalten und gefragt, ob ich mich nicht verbessern möchte. Er könnt' mir vielleicht zu einem schönen Gehalt verhelfen. Ich hab' ihm gesagt, ich wäre für die Arbeit, die er wohl meinte, nicht zu bezahlen.

Berta: Ja, hinter den Blonden ist er ganz besonders her.

Otti: Diese Dinge scheinen beim Regieren eine große Rolle zu spielen.

Paula: Davon machen Sie sich gar keine Vorstellung. Im allgemeinen haben die Republikaner die Blondinen lieber und die Nationalen die Brünetten.

Otti: Ich dachte, die politische Farbe entscheidet. Die Haarfarbe ist also wichtiger?

Jenny: Bei manchen Mädeln kommt die politische Farbe von selbst nach. Aber der Stechbein täuscht sich, wenn er meint, er könnte sich bei mir von seiner Ministerialrätin erholen.

(women's room)

Annie: *(Enters at left.)* Thank God I finally have some time. Is there fresh air in here? *(Sees* Otti.*)* Oh, excuse me!

Otti: You don't need to be embarrassed on my account. I'm just here for some company.

Berta: Guess what, Annie, the young lady sang us a song.

Otti: Didn't I see you in the mailroom?

Annie: Yes, I'm the telephone operator, and I know who you are: Fräulein Jungleib from Weatherspring.

Otti: Nobody says Weatherspring at home. They forced that name on us. At home we just talk about the tower and everyone calls me Red Otti.

Annie: Have you all heard? Stechbein is supposed to become state secretary. The Weather Bureau is going to get its own administration.

Paula: That's why he was drinking wine with Trankhafen.

Jenny: Listen to this. Yesterday he stopped me in the hall and asked me if I didn't want to improve myself. He said he could get me a better paying job. I told him you couldn't pay me to do the kind of work he was talking about.

Berta: Yeah, he really runs after blonde hair.

Otti: This kind of thing seems to be very important in the government.

Paula: You have no idea. In general the republicans prefer blondes and the nationalists prefer brunettes.

Otti: I thought the party colors were what mattered. You mean hair color is more important?

Jenny: A lot of girls choose their party colors later on. But Stechbein is wrong if he thinks he could take time out from his little ministerial advisor with me.

(Herrenabteilung)

Biederhold: *(aus der Kabine)* Die alles berücksichtigt, meine Damen
und Herren— *(Hustenreiz stellt sich vor das Klosett und zieht
Notizbuch und Bleistift vor.)*—kann ich die weittragenden Besorgnisse
nicht verhelen, welche meine Partei erfüllen. Verkennen wir auch nicht
die Bedeutung einer so wertvollen Erfindung—vielmehr
einer—Einrichtung—nein—

(Damenabteilung)

Otti: Wer predigt denn da?

Berta: Das ist der Pfarrer Biederhold von der Kirchenpartei. Der übt
seine Reden immer dort ein.

(Herrenabteilung)

Biederhold: —eines Verfahrens, das die Gestaltung des Wetters dem
Willen der Menschen unterstellt, so liegen doch hierin auch ernstliche
Gefahren für die Seele des Volkes. Meine Herren und Damen! Die
Vorsehung hat sich von Angebinn das Recht vorbehalten, durch weise
Verwendung der Himmelsgewalten den Wandel der Menschen zu
belohnen und zu bestrafen—will sagen—

Stechbein: *(tritt ein, stutzt)* Ach! *(Hustenreiz macht ihm Zeichen.
Stechbein ruft zur Tür hinaus.)* Saaldiener!

Hantke: *(in Livree, wird sichtbar)* Herr Geheimrat?

Stechbein: Einen Augenblick!

Biederhold: Die heiligen Bande der Familie—besser: Wenn wir uns
vermessen, den Maßnahmen des Allerhöchsten vorzugreifen—ver-
dammt! *(blättert)*

Stechbein: Benachrichtigen Sie schnellstens die Fraktionsführer.

Hantke: Alle?

Hustenreiz: *(flüsternd)* Für die Sozialisten bin ich schon zur Stelle.

(men's room)

Biederhold: *(from the stall)* Considering all this, ladies and gentlemen—(Hustenreiz *moves in front of the toilet and pulls out a notebook and pencil.)*—I can no longer conceal the far-reaching apprehensions of my party. We must not overlook the significance of such a valuable invention—rather, installation—no—

(women's room)

Otti: Who's that preaching?

Berta: That's Pastor Biederhold from the Church Party. He always practices his speeches there.

(men's room)

Biederhold: —of a process that subordinates the weather to the human will; for herein are also serious dangers to the soul. Ladies and gentlemen! Providence has from the beginning of time reserved the right of rewarding and punishing the human behavior with wise application of the forces of nature—I mean—

Stechbein: *(Enters, stops short.)* Ah! (Hustenreiz *makes a sign.* Stechbein *calls out the door.)* Messenger!

Hantke: *(Appears, dressed in livery.)* Herr Privy Councillor?

Stechbein: One moment!

Biederhold: The sacred bonds of the family—wait, that is: If we presume to intervene in the measures of the Lord most high—dammit! *(Turns the page.)*

Stechbein: Inform the party leaders immediately.

Hantke: All of them?

Hustenreiz: *(whispering)* I'm here for the Socialists.

Stechbein: Also alle übrigen, außer den Unversöhnlichen. Auch Fräulein Dr. Trankhafen. *(Hantke ab)*

Biederhold: Die Familie zerfällt. Unzucht und Völlerei erheben schamlos ihr Haupt. Der Unglaube bemächtigt sich der unverständigen Massen.

Paula: (von Damenabteilung zuhörend) Paßt auf, jetzt kommen wir Mädel dran.

Biederhold: Frauen und Mädchen, bar aller frommen Scheu—

Jenny: Es ist jedes Mal dasselbe.

Biederhold: —tragen ohne Erröten Haare und Kleider so kurz, daß Lüsternheit und Sünde gradezu herausgefordert werden. Schimpfliche Mittel, um die gerechten Folgen—

Wolff: Das muß schwer auszudrücken sein.

Links und rechts füllt sich der Abort mit Zuhörern, darunter Barde, Widerborst, Krachhahn, Speicherer, Selters; *bei den Damen* Trankhafen, Wachtel, Möhre.

Biederhold: —die gerechten Folgen frevelhafter Begierden—oder gleich: sündiger Handlungen zu verhüten, welche leider zur Fortpflanzung des Menschengeschlechtes unerläßlich sind—, finden reißenden Absatz. Selbst in diesem hohen Hause mehren sich die Stimmen, die das schändliche Laster der gleichgeschlechtlichen Liebe—nein, Liebe geht da nicht—, na, wie hab' ich's denn das letzte Mal genannt? *(Die Papiere rascheln wieder.* Paula, Jenny, Annie *und* Hantke *gehen leise ins Botenzimmer.)*

Stechbein: (zu Widerborst*)* Hat der Saaldiener auch Ihnen mitgeteilt, daß der Herr Pfarrer memoriert?

Widerborst: War unnötig. Das riecht unsereiner.

Krachhahn: Locus a non locendi.

Biederhold: —Das war also die Päderastie,—dem rächenden Arm der Gerechtigkeit entziehen wollen. Entmenschte Weiber, die sich ruchlos der gottgewollten Frucht ihres Leibes entledigen, will man gar ihres

Stechbein: Well, all right, the others, except for the Intransigents. Also Fräulein Trankhafen. *(Hantke exits.)*

Biederhold: The family is decaying. Lewdness and intemperance are shamelessly raising their ugly heads. Non-belief is taking over the gullible masses.

Paula: *(listening from women's room)* Watch out, now he'll get to the girls.

Biederhold: Women and girls, bereft of any pious modesty,—

Jenny: It's the same thing every time.

Biederhold: —without blushing, wear their hair and their dresses so short that they actually provoke lasciviousness and sin. Their disgraceful ways of hiding from—

Wolff: That's easy for him to say.

To the left and right listeners fill up the restrooms. In the men's room are Barde, Widerborst, Krachhahn, Speicherer, Selters, *and on the women's side* Trankhafen, Wachtel, Möhre.

Biederhold: —of hiding from the true and deserved consequences of wicked desires—or, wait a minute—of sinful actions, which unfortunately are necessary to the procreation of humankind—these disgraceful conceits have become enormously popular. Even in this high house there are more and more voices that would withhold the strong arm of justice from the vice of same-sex love—no, love doesn't work there—hmm, what did I call it last time? *(Rattling of papers once again.* Paula, Jenny, Annie *and* Hantke *go quietly into the staff room.)*

Stechbein: *(to* Widerborst*)* Did the page tell you that the reverend was memorizing his speech?

Widerborst: Didn't have to, we can smell that kind of thing.

Krachhahn: *Locus a non locendi.*

Biederhold: —ah, yes it was pederasty—would withhold the vengeful arm of justice from the scandalous vice of pederasty. Barbaric women who wickedly rid themselves of the divinely blessed fruit of their

Frevels froh werden lassen. Sie rufen mir zu, Herr Kollege, ein geborenes Kind müsse auch zu essen haben.

Jenny: *(im Botenzimmer)* Jetzt bestellt er sich den Zwischenruf.

Biederhold: O, verschmähte das Volk die himmlische Speise nicht, es sollte auch der irdischen Nahrung nicht zu entraten brauchen. Aber wohin ist die Ehrfurcht geflüchtet? In den Zeitungen und auf öffentlichen Märkten wird des Erhabenen gespottet. Das Theater selbst, gedacht als Stätte der Erbauung und sittlichen Stärkung, ist zum Tummelplatz radikaler Lästerer geworden. Lachen Sie nicht, meine Herren auf der äußersten Linken! Schon wendet sich der Ungeist der Verhetzung gegen dieses hohe Haus selbst. Eines dieser Machwerke, das man sich nicht scheut, allabendlich dem Publikum vorzuspielen, verhöhnt, wie mir berichtet wird, unbekümmert sogar die demokratischen Einrichtungen des Staates selber und liefert uns alle, auch Sie, meine Verehrten ganz rechts und ganz links, der Skandalsucht der Menge aus.

Widerborst: Man kann doch uns nicht anhängen, was sich da irgendein Anarchist zusammen geschmiert hat.

Biederhold: Wenn es soweit gekommen ist, liegt da nicht der Gedanke nahe, die ewige Gerechtigkeit werde in diesen Pfuhl des Lasters und der Verwahrlosung mit allen Wettern, vielleicht gar mit einer neuen Sintflut hineinfahren wollen? Dürfen wir armen Sterblichen, frage ich, mit unserem Aberwitz der göttlichen Allmacht in den Arm fallen?

Möhre: *(in der Damenabteilung)* Das ist nur allzu wahr.

Trankhafen: Er will doch nicht gegen die Vorlage sprechen?

Biederhold: Nichts liegt uns ferner, als uns dem gesunden Fortschritt der Zivilisation entgegenstemmen zu wollen.

Selters: Die Ablehnung ist also nicht mehr zu fürchten.

Biderhold: Immerhin müssen wir unsere Zustimmung zur Regierungs-vorlage von gewissen Sicherungen abhängig machen; durch welche jedem Mißbrauch der Witterungsanlagen im Hinblick auf die göttliche Weltordnung vorgebeugt wird. Als Gewähr dafür verlangen wir

wombs—some in this house want to excuse this outrage. You shout to me, Herr Colleague, that a child that is born must also have food to eat—

Jenny: *(in staff room)* Now he's answering the interruptions from the floor.

Biederhold: Oh, if the people did not disdain the food of Heaven, then they would not also have to do without earthly nourishment. But what has happened to respect toward the divine? In any newspaper you can find on any street you will find a mockery made of the sublime. Even the theater, once considered a place of edification and moral teaching, has become an arena of radicals. Do not laugh, gentlemen of the far left! These theaters are already making pronouncements against even this high house of government! I am told that one of these conniving performances, one which is being presented every evening in front of an audience, even mocks the democratic institutions of the state and subjects us all, my colleagues on the right and the left, to the masses' thirst for scandal.

Widerborst: Well, you can't pin on us what some crazy anarchist somewhere has thrown together.

Biederhold: If it has come this far, then is it not easy to imagine that eternal justice itself might be swept away in a new deluge rushing from this cesspool of vice and degeneracy? I ask you, should not we poor foolish mortals allow ourselves to fall into the protective arms of the divine almighty?

Möhre: *(in women's room)* Yes, how true, how true.

Trankhafen: Surely he's not going to speak against the motion?

Biederhold: Nothing is farther from our desires than to try to impede the progress of civilization.

Selters: All right, we don't have to worry about a rejection.

Biderhold: Still, we must make our approval of the government's proposal dependent on certain assurances. Any abuse of the weather station with respect to the divine order of the world must be prevented. To guarantee this, we demand that the leadership of the Weather

weitgehenden Einfluß der Kirche, beziehungsweise der Wortführer christlicher Staatsgesinnung auf die Leitung des Wetteramtes.

Otti: *(in der Damenabteilung)* Was soll daraus werden?

Biederhold: Die bis jetzt in Wetterborn maßgebenden Persönlichkeiten haben, wie wir aus den Darlegungen der Bevollmächtigten in der Kommission erfuhren, die göttlichen Belange völlig vernachläßigt. Sie haben ihrem Wetterkalender die Berichte und Gutachten jeder staatlichen Aufsicht entzogen, lediglich Arbeitnehmerwünschen willfähriger Stellen zugrunde gelegt. Die strengste Beaufsichtigung dieser Leute von staatlicher und kirchlicher Seite ist umsomehr eine unabweisbare Pflicht der Gesetzgebung, als ihr völlig verantwortungsloses Schalten mit dem in ihre Hand gelegten Gut ja schon bei der regierungsseitig angeordneten Gedenkfeier zutage trat, die der Herr Wetterrat Niedermaier selbstherrlich verregnen ließ. Wir fordern eine Regelung der Dinge, durch die die Wetterbestimmung ein für alle Male der Unfähigkeit, der Weltfremdheit und der sittlichen Unreife aus der Hand genommen wird. *(Stille, Papierknistern)*

Speicherer: Das ist ja sehr schön, aber was für Anträge will denn nun die Kirchenpartei stellen?

Stechbein: Der Regierung sind die Anträge bekannt. Sie sind durchaus annehmbar.

(Damenabteilung)

Möhre: Nun, wertes Fräulein, so denken verantwortungsbewußte Menschen über Ihr Gebaren. Was sagen Sie jetzt?

Otti: Ich sehe nicht ab, was nach der Ansicht des Herrn aus unserer Genossenschaft werden soll.

Trankhafen: Eine Genossenschaft, die der Zentralmacht des Staates selber Platz machen darf, hat damit ihren Wert erwiesen und ihren Zweck erfüllt, Fräulein Jungleib. Lassen Sie sich das von einer überzeugten Sozialistin gesagt sein.

Bureau contain the strong influence of the church embodied by appropriate representatives of the Christian ideology.

Otti: *(in women's room)* What's he trying to do?

Biederhold: The leaders at Weatherspring up to now have, as we learn from the statements of their representatives in the commision, completely ignored divine interests. They have taken as the basis of their weather calendar the reports and evaluations of persons who are under no supervision of the state and who represent only the desires of the workers. It is therefore clearly the bounden duty of this legislature to establish the strict supervision of these people by the state and the church. We have already the need for this in the irresponsible way these people used this treasure that was entrusted to them: when Weather Councillor Niedermaier allowed the government-arranged dedication ceremony to be rained out. We demand the regulation of this institution, so that once and for all it is kept out of the hands of the incompetent, the worldly innocent, the morally immature. *(Silence. Rustling of papers.)*

Speicherer: That's all very nice, but what kind of motions does the Church Party intend to make?

Stechbein: The government is familiar with the motions. They are quite acceptable.

(women's room)

Möhre: Now, my dear young lady, you hear what responsible people think of your conduct. What do you have to say now?

Otti: I can't imagine what this gentleman wants to turn our collective into.

Trankhafen: Into a collective that gives way to the central power of the state. That kind of a collective would prove its value and achieve its purpose, Fräulein Jungleib. And I tell you that as a committed socialist.

(Botenzimmer)

Jenny: Der läßt sie lange zappeln. Dabei müssen sie alle bei der Kirchenpartei um gut Wetter bitten.

Brunner: Da werden sie es wieder mit den Schirmhändlern verderben.

Annie: Die rote Otti tut mir leid. Die meint, sie ist unter die Räuber geraten.

Hantke: In der Kommission war sie die einzige, der es um die Sache ging. Allen andern ging's um Parteireklame und Geschäftsaufträge.

Paula: Die werden eine nette Wetterpolitik treiben.

Wolff: Sie werden mit Wolken schieben wie mit Grundstücken und Theaterkonzessionen.

Jenny: Was sich die rote Otti von dem ganzen Umtrieb nur denken mag?

Hantke: Wieso nennt ihr sie eigentlich die rote Otti?

Paula: Beim Wetterturm heißt sie so, sie hat es uns erzählt.

Annie: O, die ist lieb. Die hält es mit den Armen.

Hantke: Still jetzt. Hochwürden räuspert sich wieder.

(Herrenabteilung)

Biederhold: *(Hüstelt sonor und spuckt mit Getöse aus. Links und rechts werden die Notizbücher wieder bereit gehalten.)* Ich eile zum Schluß. Mit den in den vorgetragenen Anträgen enthaltenen Einschränkungen und Ergänzungen ist meine Partei also bereit, der Vorlage zuzustimmen.

Krachhahn: Jetzt sind wir so gescheit wie vorher. *(Stiefengrat tritt auf, geht in eine Nische)*

Biederhold: Die Summe von rund 14 Millionen Mark an laufenden Verwaltungskosten werden wir bewilligen, ebenso die verlangten 4,8 Millionen für den Bau des Wetteramtshauptgebäudes und der erforderlichen Beamtenwohnungen in Wetterborn. Dem einmaligen Zuschuß für Instrumentenanschaffungen und die Vervollständigung der

(staff room)

Jenny: He'll let them fidget for awhile. They're going to have to go to the Church Party to ask for good weather.

Brunner: They're going to mess things up for the umbrella salesmen again.

Annie: I feel sorry for Red Otti. She must think she's fallen into a den of thieves.

Hantke: She was the only one in the commision who cared about the matter at hand. Everybody else was talking about campaign slogans and business contracts.

Paula: Don't you love how they're playing politics with the weather?

Wolff: They're going to wheel and deal with clouds on the black market, like they do with real estate or theater concessions.

Jenny: I wonder what Red Otti thinks of all these intrigues.

Hantke: Why do you call her Red Otti?

Paula: She told us that's what they call her at the weather tower.

Annie: She's so nice. She's on the side of the poor people.

Hantke: Quiet, now. The reverend is clearing his throat.

(men's room)

Biederhold: *(Coughs loudly and spits with a loud noise. To the left and right notebooks are readied once again.)* I now conclude. With the restrictions and amendments included in our motion my party is prepared to vote in favor of the government proposal.

Krachhahn: Now we know as much as we did before. *(Stiefengrat enters, goes into a urinal niche.)*

Biederhold: We will approve the sum of 14 million marks for operating and administrative costs, as well as the requested 4.8 million for the construction of the headquarters building of the Weather Bureau and for the necessary employee housing in Weatherspring. We can only

technischen Hilfsmittel des Institutes vermögen wir nur zuzustimmen, wenn die Kosten dafür die Summe von 1.800 Mark nicht überschreiten.

Hustenreiz: Dann wird eine Einigung möglich sein.

Biederhold: Unser letztes Wort hängt jedoch davon ab, daß die Loslösung des Ortes Wetterborn von der Nachbargemeinde ihren sichtbaren Ausdruck durch die Errichtung eines dem Institut unmittelbar angegliederten würdigen Gotteshauses findet.

Möhre: (in der Damenabteilung) Sehr vernünftig.

Otti: Wer soll denn da hineingehen?

Möhre: Es wird dafür gesorgt werden, daß das Wetterwerk von einer gläubigen Beamtenschaft betreut wird.

Biederhold: (in der Herrenabteilung) Dieses Gotteshaus soll eine Mahnung sein, daß die Herrschaft über Wind und Wetter im Beistand des Höchsten geübt werden muß. Das Bewußtsein, den Schlüssel zu Donner und Blitz zu verwalten, darf der Hoffart und der Begehrlichkeit des niederen Volkes keinen Raum geben. Wer Knecht ist, soll Knecht bleiben.

Barde: Ausgezeichnet.

Biederhold: Einverstanden sind wir mit der Forderung der Rechten, daß die vaterländischen Gedenktage von heiterem Sonnenschein verschönt werden sollen.

Stiefengrat: Bravo.

Biederhold: Wir fordern dasselbe auch für die christlichen Feiertage.

Widerborst: Auch der erste Mai muß gesetzlicher Schönwettertag werden.

Biederhold: Gegen Regen, Hagel oder Nebel an den schmerzlichen Erinnerungstagen bestehen keine Bedenken. Für diese und andre religiös-sittliche Festsetzungen wird beim Wetteramt eine besondere, der Rundfunk- und Filmprüfungsstelle ähnliche Abteilung geschaffen werden müssen, auf deren unumschränkte Leitung die Kirchenpartei Anspruch erhebt.

vote for the one-time expenditure for acquisition of instruments and completion of the technical appurtenances if these expenses do not exceed the sum of 1,800 marks.

Hustenreiz: We'll probably be able to come to agreement on that.

Biederhold: Our last request is this: the separation of the Weatherspring installation from the neighboring village must have as its visual expression the construction of a house of worship immediately attached to the institute.

Möhre: (in women's room) Quite reasonable.

Otti: But who will ever go into it?

Möhre: We will make sure that the weather works are operated by churchgoing employees.

Biederhold: (in men's room) This house of God shall serve as an admonition that any control over the weather must be carried out with the assistance of the Almighty. In the management of this new means of dominion over thunder and lightning there is no place for the arrogance and covetousness of the lower classes. Whoever is a servant now shall remain a servant.

Barde: Excellent.

Biederhold: We also concur with the demand of our colleagues on the right that days of commemoration for the fatherland shall always be blessed with beautiful sunshine.

Stiefengrat: Bravo.

Biederhold: We demand the same for all Christian holidays.

Widerborst: The first of May has to be a legal nice-weather day, too.

Biederhold: We have no objection to hail or fog on the sadder commemoration days. For the purpose of making these religious and moral determinations there will need to be a new department in the weather bureau, similar to the Radio and Film Review Board, and the Church Party will lay claim to the absolute leadership of this department.

Hustenreiz: Das wird zu Schwierigkeiten führen.

Biederhold: Dies ist nur selbstverständlich. Gottesleugnung und Freidenkertum dürfen bei der Mitwirkung menschlicher Werke an den himmlischen Entschließungen weder Sitz noch Stimme haben.

Trankhafen: (in der Damenabteilung) Die Kirchenpartei will die Krise!

Hustenreiz: (in der Herrenabteilung) Das bedeutet das Ende der Koalition!

Selters: Aber nicht doch. Sie werden mit sich reden lassen.

Krachhahn: Zum Kuhhandel muß man Kühe haben.

Biederhold: So möge denn—

Paula: (im Botenzimmer) Aha, er ist schon beim Möge.

Biederhold: —reicher Segen *(heftiges Papierknistern)*—im Geiste der Demut— *(Rauschen der Wasserspülung, das die weiteren Worte übertönt. Die Aborte werden fluchtartig verlassen. Links bleiben zurück* Berta, Trankhafen, Möhre *und* Otti, *rechts* Steinbott *und* Stiefengrat.)

Stiefengrat: *(bei der Waschgelegenheit)* Amen.

(Botenzimmer)

Jenny: Ob sie die Sozialisten wirklich kaltstellen wollen?

Hantke: Er hat bloß von Freidenkern gesprochen.

Wolff: Regieren lehrt beten.

Paula: Sie reden von Freiheit, und wenn du mit ihnen gehst, machen sie bei der Kirche Halt.

Brunner: Wer weitergeht, wird erschossen.

(Herrenabteilung)

Biederhold: (kommt aus der Kabine) Ah, der Herr General.

Hustenreiz: That's going to cause problems.

Biederhold: This goes without saying. There is absolutely no place for agnosticism or free thinking in the operation of a station that controls the heavens.

Trankhafen: *(in women's room)* The Church Party is going to cause a government crisis!

Hustenreiz: *(in men's room)* This means the end of the coalition!

Selters: No it doesn't. They'll be open to further discussions.

Krachhahn: If you're going to be a horse trader, you have to have horses.

Biederhold: Therefore let us—

Paula: *(in staff room)* Okay, he's at the "let us."

Biederhold: —let us with the blessings of God *(loud rustling of papers)*—in the spirit of humility— *(Sound of flushing, which drowns out the rest of his speech. Everyone leaves the restrooms hurriedly. To the left* Berta, Trankhafen, Möhre *and* Otti *remain onstage. To the right* Steinbott *and* Stiefengrat *remain.)*

Stiefengrat: *(while washing hands)* Amen.

(staff room)

Jenny: Do you think they really want to shut out the Socialists?

Hantke: He was only talking about free thinkers.

Wolff: This government really teaches you to pray.

Paula: They talk about freedom, and whenever you go somewhere with them they stop into a church.

Brunner: If you keep walking you will be shot.

(men's room)

Biederhold: *(Comes out of the stall.)* Ah, General.

Stiefengrat: Höre, Hochwürden, Sie werden die Stellung Ihrer Partei begründen?

Biederhold: Gewissen Koalitionspartnern ein bißchen einheizen.

Stiefengrat: Kann nur ersprießlich sein.

(Damenabteilung)

Otti: *(zu* Berta*)* Wird die hohe Politik immer hier hinten gemacht?

Berta: Es ist der einzige Platz im Haus, wo sie manchmal ehrlich sind.

Trankhafen: Still doch! Man muß doch hören, wie das Militär sich einstellt.

Berta: Gehn Sie da hinein, Fräulein Otti. *(öffnet ihr die Tür zum Botenzimmer)*

(Herrenabteilung)

Stiefengrat: Die Regierung will es wohl mal ohne die Rosaroten versuchen?

Biederhold: Sie müssen Bescheidenheit lernen.

Stiefengrat: Sollen sie nicht abgehalftert werden?

Biederhold: Daran können wir im Augenblick nicht denken.

Stiefengrat: Nicht? Mir schiene grade—

Biederhold: In der Opposition würden sie sofort alles madig machen, was wir unternehmen.

Stiefengrat: Wäre das so arg?

Biederhold: Exzellenz, es ist ein unschätzbarer Vorteil, wenn man jemanden hat, der die Massen bei dem Glauben erhält, es geschehe alles zu ihrem Nutzen. Sehn Sie, unsere Tätigkeit ist ja nicht überall dem Geschmack des Pöbels auf den Leib zugeschnitten.

Stiefengrat: Da haben Sie recht, Hochwürden.

Stiefengrat: So, Reverend, you are going to establish your party's position?

Biederhold: Just light a fire under certain coalition partners.

Stiefengrat: That can only help.

(women's room)

Otti: *(to* Berta*)* Do they always make big political deals back here?

Berta: This is the only place in the building where they are sometimes honest.

Trankhafen: Quiet! We need to hear where the military stands.

Berta: You go in there, Fräulein Otti. *(Opens the door to the staff room for her.)*

(men's room)

Stiefengrat: So is the government going to try to go ahead without the pinkos?

Biederhold: They need to learn modesty.

Stiefengrat: Shouldn't they be kicked out?

Biederhold: We can't think about that at the moment.

Stiefengrat: No? It seems to me—

Biederhold: In the opposition they would foul up everything we undertake.

Stiefengrat: Would that be so bad?

Biederhold: Your Excellency, it is an enormous advantage to us if we have someone whom the masses would trust, and who could convince them that everything was happening to their benefit. You know, our activities aren't exactly tailored to acommodate to the tastes of the rabble.

Stiefengrat: You are quite right there, Reverend.

Biederhold: Lassen wir die Sozialisten unter gehöriger Beaufsichtigung mittun, dann sind sie die besten Zuggäule vor unserm Wagen.

Stiefengrat: Na ja, da haben sie Stellungen zu verlieren.

Biederhold: Richtig. In ruhigeren Zeiten mögen sie berufeneren Persönlichkeiten Platz machen, da können sie getrost gegen uns stänkern. Aber wenn etwas brenzlich ist,—ins Geschirr! Ohne sie wären wir der Revolution niemals Herr geworden.

Stiefengrat: Freilich, hätten auch die Freikorps und nationalen Formationen nicht auf die Beine stellen können. Ich verstehe jetzt: Damals haben wir uns auf den Boden der Tatsachen gestellt. Jetzt müssen sie es tun.

Biederhold: So ist es. Sehn Sie, der Aufbau des Wetteramtes ist wieder eine heikle Geschichte. Der Erfinder der Sache, der ehrenwerte Herr Niedermaier, muß stelbstredend unschädlich gemacht werden.

Stiefengrat: Rücksichtslos rausschmeißen.

Biederhold: Das geht eben nicht. Es ist schwer genug, ihn von der Leitung zu entfernen. In den unteren Volksschichten wird er vergöttert.

Stiefengrat: Allerdings, seine Tätigkeit hat bereits eine höchst bedenkliche Zufriedenheit im Volke hervorgerufen.

Biederhold: Darum brauchen wir die Sozialisten. Wir geben darin nach, daß Niedermaier die Bedienung des technischen Apparates unter sich behält, und die Herren Hustenreiz und Genossen beruhigen die brodelnde Volksseele, indem sie ihr bedeuten, damit bliebe er im Grunde, was er ist und ihre eigene Beteiligung an der Regierungskoalition als Sicherung für die Wahrung der demokratischen Freiheiten und was weiß ich austrompeten.

Krampf: *(tritt auf)* Die Sitzung wird gleich eröffnet, Hochwürden. Sie erhalten als erster Redner das Wort. *(geht in eine Nische)*

Biederhold: Immerzu, Herr Präsident. Steht außer dem Wetteramt noch etwas auf der Tagesordnung?

Biederhold: Let's allow the Socialists to play along. Under our supervision, they could be the best possible horses to pull our wagon.

Stiefengrat: Well, of course, then they'll have positions that they could lose.

Biederhold: Exactly. In more peaceful times they might have to clear out in favor of more qualified personnel, and then they can go ahead and raise a ruckus against us. But if the situation is precarious, then put the harness on them! Without them we would never have gotten control of the revolution.

Stiefengrat: Indeed, we would never have been able to get the paramilitaries and the national militias on their feet. I understand now: back then we worked with the facts as they were presented to us. Now they have to do that.

Biederhold: That's the way it is. You see, the establishment of the Weather Bureau is a delicate matter. By all means we have to make the inventor of the thing, the right honorable Herr Niedermaier, completely harmless.

Stiefengrat: Toss him out on his ear.

Biederhold: That won't work. It's difficult enough to remove him from the management. The lower classes idolize him.

Stiefengrat: To be sure, his activities have evoked a dangerous sense of contentment in the people.

Biederhold: That's why we need the Socialists. We can yield the point that Niedermaier retains the operation of the technical apparatus. Herr Hustenreiz and his comrades will calm the simmering masses by making clear to them that Niedermaier basically remains what he was before, and they can shout about how their participation in the governing coalition is insurance for the protection of democracy or whatever.

Krampf: *(Enters men's room.)* The session is beginning now, Reverend. You are the first speaker on the list. *(Goes into a urinal niche.)*

Biederhold: As always, Herr President. Is there anything on the agenda besides the Weather Bureau?

Krampf: Wenn noch Zeit bleibt, erledigen wir noch die dritte Lesung des Gesetzes zum Schutz der Zufriedenheit. *(langgezogenes, wiederholtes Klingelzeichen)*

Stiefengrat: Der Herr Abgeordnete Biederhold hat mir eben klargemacht, warum die Regierung die geschätzte Mitwirkung der Rötlichen nicht entbehren möchte.

Krampf: Allerdings—solange das Wetteramt nicht eingearbeitet ist, sind sie ohne Zweifel unersetzlich. Ich habe in meiner Eigenschaft als Landtagspräsident gestern auch mit dem Herrn Staatspräsidenten Wimmerzahn gesprochen, dem besonders die Ernennung des Geheimrats Stechbein am Herzen liegt, da er die Berufung der Ministerialrätin Trankhafen als Leiterin der Personalabteilung wünscht—

Stiefengrat: Sie wird als seine Gouvernante mit wollen.

Biederhold: Als Vogelscheuche für die Tippfräuleins. *(Die drei lachen.)*

(Damenabteilung)

Trankhafen: Erbärmliche Schwätzer!

Möhre: Machen Sie sich nichts daraus, Fräulein Doktor. Wir schutzlosen Frauen müssen uns sehr in Acht nehmen, um nicht ins Gerede zu kommen.

Trankhafen: Ich wollte Ihnen längst nahelegen, dem Gerede über Sie und Herrn Regierungsassessor Hornbriller aus dem Wege zu gehen.

Möhre: Auf diese empörende Insinuation antworte ich nicht.

Trankhafen: Schweigen wird für Sie auch ratsam sein.

Möhre: Sie haben ja gehört, wie christliche Politiker von Ihrer Partei sprechen.

Trankhafen: Jesuiten sind wir noch lange nicht. *(beide keifend ab)*

Krampf: If there's enough time, we'll have the third reading on the law for the protection of domestic tranquility and happiness. *(long, repeated bell signals)*

Stiefengrat: Delegate Biederhold just now explained to me why the government would rather not do without the the participation of the reds.

Krampf: Indeed—as long as the Weather Bureau is not yet well established, they are absolutely indispensable. In my capacity as president of the provincial parliament I spoke yesterday with State President Wimmerzahn. He is very concerned about naming Privy Councillor Stechbein to a position, since he wants to appoint Ministerial Advisor Trankhafen as the director of the personnel division—

Stiefengrat: She'll want to go along as his nanny.

Biederhold: As a scarecrow against all the pretty secretaries. *(All three laugh.)*

(women's room)

Trankhafen: Miserable rumormongers!

Möhre: Don't worry about it, Fräulein Doctor. We defenseless women have to be very careful if we don't wish to be gossiped about.

Trankhafen: By the way, I've wanted to suggest to you that you might want to watch out for the gossip about you and Herr Government Assessor Hornbriller.

Möhre: I won't even dignify that insinuation with a response.

Trankhafen: It might also be a good idea for you to keep quiet.

Möhre: You just heard what Christian politicians are saying about your party.

Trankhafen: Well, we certainly aren't Jesuits! *(The two exit women's room arguing.)*

(Herrenabteilung)

Hornbriller: *(tritt ein)* Herr Präsident? Immer noch die Devise: festina lente? Es pressiert. Die Minister plazieren sich schon auf der Estrade.

Stiefengrat: Alles kampffertig zum Sturm auf die Festung Niedermaier.

Biederhold: Ein Teil der Streitkräfte ist allerdings schon vor dem hübschen Außenfort schwach geworden.

Hornbriller: Exquisites Bonmot. Hat mir übrigens imponiert, die grazile Kanaille. Eine Apologetin ihres Chefs par excellence. Das parlamentarische Debut in der Kommission war brillant.

Krampf: Es hat aber geschäftsordnungswidrige Auftritte gesetzt, sagt man.

Hornbriller: *(im Abgehen)* Ein mehr burleskes Intermezzo. Eine Sottise des Herrn Hustenreiz an die Adresse des Diktaturaspiranten Teutsch gab das Signal zu einem Recontre—*(alle vier ab)*

(Botenzimmer)

Steinbott: *(geht ins Botenzimmer)* So, jetzt gehn sie erst richtig auf den Dreckkübel. *(Sieht* Otti*; es wird unmerklich heller im vorderen Teil der Bühne.)* Entschuldigen Sie man, Fräulein.

Otti: Bitte. Ich glaube, Sie haben ganz recht.

Steinbott: Berta, komm doch! Oder wird bei dir noch regiert?

Berta: *(kommt vor)* Nein, wenn die Tribünen im Sitzungssaal voll sind, ist bei uns stille Zeit. Na, Fräulein Otti, so haben Sie sich den Landtag hinter den Kulissen wohl auch nicht vorgestellt?

Otti: Wahrhaftig nicht. Was wird aus unserm Turm werden? Der arme Niedermaier! Solange die Menschen den Sternenlauf verfolgen, denken sie darüber nach, wie man es regnen lassen kann. Jetzt können wir es, da möchten sie auch damit an der Börse schachern.

(men's room)

Hornbriller: (Enters.) Herr President? Are we still going by the motto: *festina lente*? It's time. The ministers are already taking their positions on the podium.

Stiefengrat: Everything's ready for the storming of Fort Niedermaier.

Biederhold: Of course, part of the forces have already been weakened by the pretty forward fortifications.

Hornbriller: Exquisite *bon mot*. By the way, I found her very impressive, the fair proletarian. An apologist *par excellence* for her boss. Her parliamentary debut in the commission hearing was brilliant.

Krampf: But I heard it caused some scenes that interfered with business.

Hornbriller: (while leaving) Only a burlesque intermezzo. A foolish remark by Herr Hustenreiz in response to the speech by the aspiring dictator Teutsch gave the signal for a set-to. *(All four exit.)*

(staff room)

Steinbott: (Enters staff room.) So now they're finally going to start slinging the crap. *(Sees* Otti. *The forward part of the stage gets imperceptibly brighter.)* Excuse me, Fräulein.

Otti: Please, not at all. I think you're right.

Steinbott: Berta, come here! Or is the government still doing business in there with you?

Berta: (Comes out.) No, whenever the platform is full in the meeting hall then it's quiet time for us. So, Fräulein Otti, I bet you never imagined that a view behind the scenes of the parliament would look like this.

Otti: I certainly didn't. What's going to happen with our tower? Poor Niedermaier! As long as people have been watching the stars they've been wondering how to make it rain. Now that we can finally do it, they want to haggle over it in the stock exchange.

Wolff: Wundert Sie das noch? Das Fliegen ist doch auch bloß erfunden worden, um von oben runter morden zu können, wenn es Krieg gibt.

Brunner: Oder die Arbeiter ihre Bonzen zum Teufel jagen wollen.

Otti: Wenn man vorher noch keine Bonzen gekannt hat, in diesem Haus ist Gelegenheit, sie zu studieren.

Hantke: Wißt ihr was? Wollen wir mal dem Fräulein unser Hauslied vorsingen?

Annie: Fein, wollen Sie es hören?

Otti: Natürlich, gern.

Paula: Also los. Aber Sie müssen nachher auch noch was singen. *(Alle außer* Otti *fassen einander unter und singen im Schaukeltanz.)*

> Sei dankbar, Volk, den Edeln, die dich leiten,
> Der Obrigkeit, die stets dein Heil bedenkt.
> Willst du dir selber den Geschick bereiten,
> Bald wär die Karre in den Sumpf gelenkt.
> Was weißt denn du, was für dein Wohlsein nötig ist?
> Das Volk gehorche, weil es brägenklötig ist.
> Den höhern Einsicht füge dich beizeiten,
> Und frag' nicht lang, warum der Staat dich henkt.
>
> Vertraue, Volk, den Bonzen der Parteien,
> Geborgen ist dein Glück in ihrem Schoß.
> Wenn du sie wählst, wolln alle dich befreien;
> Wenn sie gewählt sind, melken sie dich bloß.
> Stell' dir doch vor, wenn niemand dich regieren soll,
> Wovon dein Bonze dann noch existieren soll.
> Der ganze Landtag müßt' vor Hunger schreien.
> Selbst die Abortfrau wäre arbeitslos.

Steinbott: Das ist Berta ihre Extrawurst.

Wolff: Hat sie sich auch verdient.

Otti: Ist denn das Lied von Ihnen selber?

Wolff: Does that surprise you? After all, flying was just invented so they could murder people from high above whenever they have a war.

Brunner: Or whenever the workers want to run the politicans out on a rail.

Otti: Well, if someone didn't know anything about politicians, this building is the place to study them.

Hantke: You know what? Why don't we sing our house song for Fräulein Otti?

Annie: Sure, do you want to hear it?

Otti: Of course, please.

Paula: Well let's go. But later you have to sing us something too. *(All except* Otti *join hands and sing while they sway to and fro.)*

> Be grateful, people, to the ones who lead you,
> The ones who always look out for your good.
> If you should go the way you think you need to,
> Your cart won't take you where you hoped it would.
> What do you know about the dreams you seek?
> You should obey, because your minds are weak.
> And don't ask questions; no, you do not need to.
> The state will hang you when it thinks it should.
>
> People, trust the parties' delegations.
> Your happiness is all they care about.
> Vote for them, they promise liberation,
> But once they're in, your interests get tossed out.
> Imagine, if the government went away,
> Just where would all the big-shots get their pay?
> The parliament would suffer from starvation.
> The restroom lady would be down-and-out.

Steinbott: That's an extra little goody for Berta.

Wolff: She earned it, too.

Otti: Did you all write this song?

Brunner: Alles hausgemacht.

Paula: Das war, als sie die Diäten für sich selber erhöhten und für das Personal keinen Pfennig Lohnzulage bewilligten. Da mußte Berta hin und für den Betriebsrat verhandeln. Nur die Unversöhnlichen standen auf unsrer Seite.

Hantke: Die hätten aber auch nichts ausrichten können, wenn wir nicht allesamt mit Streik gedroht hätten.

Steinbott: Berta wollten sie am liebsten abbauen—

Berta: Ist ja schon gut. Jetzt den dritten Vers.

> *Gesang:*
>
> Sie haben nichts im Kopf als Paragraphen.
> Die Bonzen sind, o Volk, die Jungs im Skat,
> Verhängen Steuern über dich und Strafen,
> Und wenn due aufmuckst, dann ist's Hochverrat.
> Sie merken nie, wenn alles auf der Kippe steht,
> Sie merken immer, wo noch eine Krippe steht,
> Doch du, o Volk, du kannst geruhsam schlafen.
> Die Bonzen wachen ja, es wacht der Staat.

Otti: Das ist famos. Euch möchte ich alle mitnehmen für meinen Chor.

Annie: Wenn das ginge!

Otti: Vielleicht stellt die Trankhafen euch beim Wetteramt an.

Steinbott: Beschäftigung gäb's sicher für uns.

Brunner: Wo die Windfabrik ist, findst du und Berta genug zu tun.

Paula: Und eine Wirtschaft wird doch gewiß hinkommen.

Wolff: Mit der und der Kirche fängt es überhaupt an.

Jenny: Und ich nehm' beim Stechbein an.

Hantke: Lassen Sie uns aber erst hören, war wir bei Ihnen für Lieder lernen sollen.

Annie: Ja, jetzt müssen Sie singen. Sie haben es uns versprochen.

Brunner: All by ourselves.

Paula: That was when they raised their own per diem pay and didn't approve a single extra penny for the staff. Berta had to go and negotiate for the workers' council. Only the Intransigents were on our side.

Hantke: But they wouldn't have been able to do anything either, if we hadn't threatened to go on strike.

Steinbott: They wanted to fire Berta.

Berta: Well, all right. Let's do the third verse.

> *Song:*
>
> They study laws until their vision's blurry.
> The big-shots write the laws to earn their keep.
> They'll punish you or tax you in a hurry
> And call it treason if you make a peep.
> They never notice when you're having troubles;
> They always notice when your free time doubles.
> So people, there's no need for you to worry,
> The state is watching o'er you while you sleep.

Otti: That's terrific. I'd like to take you all home with me for my choir!

Annie: If only we could!

Otti: Maybe Trankhafen will hire you all for the Weather Bureau.

Steinbott: There'd surely be jobs for us there.

Brunner: Wherever there's hot air, there's work for you and Berta .

Paula: And there'll probably be a restaurant there.

Wolff: The whole thing is starting out with a restaurant and a church.

Jenny: And I'll keep taking Stechbein's dictation.

Hantke: But first let's hear what kind of songs we'd be learning with your choir.

Annie: Yes, now you have to sing. You promised us.

Otti: Also gut. Unser Bauernlied.

(Otti singt, Tanz andeutend.)

Wenn zur Ernte reift das Korn,
Kommt der Bauer mit der Sense,
Und am Wegrand schnattern die Gänse,
Wackeln und schnackeln voll Zorn.
Schreit nicht so, ihr Gansgevattern!
Wer nur lärmt und keift, ist dumm.
Euer Zetermordio-Schnattern
Stürzt die Macht der Welt nicht um.

Wenn der Bauer fleißig mäht,
Kommt der Gutsherr angeritten,
Prüft, ob alles gut geschnitten,
Erntet, was andre gesät.
Jag' vom Acker den Besitzer,
Bauer, duck' dich nicht vorm Geld.
Peitschenknall und Goldgeglitzer
Macht kein Saatkorn reif im Feld.

Wenn zum Strome schwillt der Bach
Und der Funke wächst zum Feuer,
Laß' ihn betteln: Rette die Scheuer!
Rett' dir dein eigenes Dach!
Parlamenteln laß' die Gänse.
Willst du frei sein, reg' die hand.
Der den Pflug führt und die Sense,
Bauer, dir gehört das Land!

Während der letzten Sätze ist Minister Blödel *im Abort zur Rechten eingetreten. Sieht sich suchend um. Horcht und tritt zögernd ein. Bleibt betroffen stehn. Nachdem das Händeklatschen sich gelegt hat, hüstelt er.*

Jenny: *(umarmt* Otti.*)* Otti!

Annie: Liebe, liebe Otti!

Otti: All right, our farmers' song.

(Otti sings, demonstrating a dance at the same time.)

When the grain has reached ripe age
The farmer comes to bring it in,
And the geese all raise a din,
Shouting, honking full of rage.
Easy does it, brother goose!
Nothing comes from shouting so!
When you let your rage fly loose
You cannot change the status quo.

When the farmer's hard at mowing,
Comes the landlord riding by,
Sees the grain's not cut too high,
Takes what others have been growing.
Drive that landlord from the land!
Farmer, don't you be afraid.
Not money, nor his cruel hand
Makes the grain ready for the blade.

When a flood flows from the stream
And the spark roars to a fire,
Let the landlord's barn expire
And you save your rafter-beams!
The geese rail at the parliament
But you can free yourself—it's true!
The land you've plowed as punishment,
O farmer, that land belongs to you!

During the last few lines Minister Blödel *appears by the men's room. He looks around as if searching for something. He hears the song and steps into the staff room hesitantly. He stands there somewhat nonplussed. After the applause has died down, he coughs.*

Jenny: *(Embraces* Otti.*)* Otti!

Annie: Dear, dear Otti!

Otti: Da steht ein Herr. Er hat sich vielleicht verlaufen.

Blödel: Ich bin der Minister für Ruhe, Ordnung und Sicherheit. Das ist doch sehr sonderbar. Sind Sie nicht die Sachverständige aus Wetterborn?

Otti: Die bin ich. Haben Sie mich gesucht, Herr Minister?

Blödel: Keineswegs. Ich finde es nur recht unpassend, daß Sie sich in Ihrer Stellung und noch dazu in solcher Stellung in der Lakaienstube antreffen lassen.

Hantke: Hier ist Freistatt für das Personal, Herr Minister. Hier hat niemand anders Hausrecht als wir.

Blödel: Ich fand nebenan niemanden. Aber der Anblick hier hat mich allerdings erschüttert.

Brunner: Ach so, der Herr Minister hat sich den Magen verdorben.

Steinbott: Na, was das Volk denkt und tut, ist ja auch nicht für jedermann. Kommen Sie man, Herr Minister, Ihr Platz ist dahinten. *(Mit* Blödel *zum Abort.)*

VORHANG

Otti: There's a gentleman standing over there. Perhaps he's lost his way.

Blödel: I am the minister for law, order, and security. This is very strange. Are you not the expert witness from Weatherspring?

Otti: That I am. Were you looking for me, Herr Minister?

Blödel: Not at all. I simply find it quite inappropriate that you, in your position, should be here in these circumstances, here in the lackey's room.

Hantke: This is the staff lounge, Herr Minister. Nobody is in charge of this room except for us.

Blödel: I didn't find anyone next door. But I was certainly shocked at what I found here.

Brunner: Oh, I see, the minister has an upset stomach.

Steinbott: Well, not everyone can stand to hear what the common people are doing and thinking. Come with me, Herr Minister, you belong back here. *(Goes with* Blödel *to the men's room.)*

CURTAIN

Drittes Bild

Der Platz vor dem Wetterturm. Vom Dorf und von den Feldern ist nichts mehr zu sehen. Stattdessen überall nüchterne Beamtenhäuser. Rechts neben dem Windrad eine kleine geschmacklose Kirche. Schräg dahinter ist die Fassade des riesigen Verwaltungsgebäudes zu sehen. Links ragt die Terrasse des im Schweizerstil gehaltenen Restaurants in die Bühne hinein. Der Platz ist planiert, vorn rechts ist ein Teil eingezäunt. Sämtliche Gebäude sind mit Girlanden geschmückt. Aus dem Turm ragen zwei Fahnenstangen auf, die mit verschiedenen, übereinander befestigten Flaggen versehen sind, darunter die schwarzweißrote, die schwarzrotgoldene, die Hakenkreuzfahne und mehrfach die landesfarben, grün und violett.

Geburtstag des Staatspräsidenten. Strahlendes warmes Wetter. Im Vordergrund der Terrasse in bekränztem Lehnstuhl Präsident Wimmerzahn, *auf Stühlen im Halbkreis um ihn herum die Ehrengäste. Links und rechts vom Präsidenten Minister* Blödel *und General* Stiefengrat, *unter den übrigen* Krampf, Krachhahn, Barde, Speicherer, Selters, Hustenreiz, F r a u Möhre, *Frau* Wachtel. *Hinter den Parlamentariern gedeckte Tische mit Festteilnehmern. Alle in Frack, Gesellschaftstoilette, Galauniform. Zwischen ihnen tänzelt* Stechbein *herum, jetzt Staatssekretär und höchster Beamter des Wetteramtes.* Paula, *in herrschaftlicher Kellnerintracht, bedient. Vor dem Turm Beamte und Angestellte des Werks, teilweise uniformiert, teilweise in Sonntagsanzügen, einige Arbeiter in Arbeitskittel.* Otti, Peters, Fischer, Annie, Niedermaier *sind gekleidet wie im ersten Bild. Die* Beamten *des Verwaltungsgebäudes stehen teils in Festtagsuniform, teils in Zylinder und Gehrock, die* Damen *in sonntäglicher Bürgerlichkeit eng gedrängt in dem Raum zwischen Turm und Restaurant.*

Act III

The square in front of the weather tower. The village and the fields can no longer be seen. Instead there is prosaic, bland housing for civil servants everywhere. On the right, next to the weathervane, is a small, tasteless church. Diagonally behind that we see the facade of a huge administrative building. To the left the terrace of a Swiss-looking restaurant looms onto the scene. The square has been leveled, and on the right in front a portion has been fenced in. All the buildings are decorated with garlands. Two flagpoles extend from the tower, and these display a variety of flags, including the black-white-red, the black-red-gold, the swastika flag, and several flags of provinces, mostly green and violet.

It is the birthday of the state president. The weather is sunny and warm. In the foreground of the terrace sits President Wimmerzahn *in a decorated reclining chair. The honored guests sit on chairs in a semicircle around him. To the left and right of the president are Minister* Blödel *and General* Stiefengrat, *and in the group are* Krampf, Krachhahn, Barde, Speicherer, Selters, Hustenreiz, *Frau* Möhre, *Frau* Wachtel. *Behind the parliament deputies are a number of tables with tablecloths, at which sit the participants in the celebration. Everyone is in formal clothes and party attire.* Stechbein *prances around them; he is now state secretary and the administrator of the Weather Bureau.* Paula *is serving them all, dressed in elegant traditional costume. In front of the tower are employees of the weather works, part of them in uniform, part in Sunday suits, some workers in overalls.* Otti, Peters, Fischer, Annie, Niedermaier *are dressed as in the first act. The* bureaucrats *from the administration building, some of them in holiday uniforms, some in top hats and morning coats, the* ladies *dressed in middle-class Sunday best, stand tightly together in the area between the tower and the restaurant.*

Hinter der Abzäunung Dorfbewohner, *darunter* Jenny, *Arbeiterin*, Berta, *Bauersfrau*, Steinbott, *Bauer*, Brunner, *Arbeiter*, Hantke, *Landarbeiter*. *Vor dem Zaun hält ein* Schutzmann *Wache. Vor der Kirche stehen weitere* Schutzleute *und ein* Polizeileutnant.

Eine Maskenzug bewegt sich vom Hintergrunde aus im Bogen am Staatspräsidenten vorbei. Man sieht Papierhelme, Allegorien der Jahreszeiten, der Gestirne und dergleichen, durch Kopfschmuck oder auf die Kleidung aufgenähte Hindeutungen bezeichnet. Die Feen, Elfen, Engel *und die im Märchenspiel auftretenden* Figuren *bilden die Prunkgruppe des Zuges. An der Spitze bewegen sich, rückwärts trippelnd und unentwegt mit den Händen taktangebend* Hornbriller *und* Trankhafen, *beide festlich angetan*.

Trankhafen: Eins, zwei—links, rechts.

Hornbriller: Tempo, Takt—Tempo, Takt. Korrekte Pas, speziell die Tête.

Trankhafen: Links, rechts—eins, zwei. Aufpassen! Genau zehn Schritte vor dem Herrn Präsidenten.

Hornbriller: Präzise aufs Signal das Chanson intonieren!

Trankhafen: Achtung links, rechts, links—eins—zwei—*(große Gebärde)*—drei!

Gesang. Ungepflegte Stimmen, unreine Töne, falsche Akkorde, ungleiches Einsetzten, gänzlich ausdrucksloser, schleppender und plärrender Vortrag.

> In den Tälern, auf den Höhn,
> Ei, wie ist die Luft so schön!
> Welches Licht und welche Pracht!
> Ei, wer hat denn das gemacht?
> War's der liebe Gott allein?
> Alles liegt in seiner Hand.
> Doch den menschlichen Verstand
> Läßt er sich behilflich sein.
> Darum ist heut Sonnenschein.

Behind the fence are residents of the village, *among them* Jenny *as a worker,* Berta *as a farmer's wife,* Steinbott *as a farmer,* Brunner *as a worker,* Hantke *as a farm worker. In front of the fence a* policeman *stands guard. In front of the church are more* police officers *and a* police lieutenant.

A costumed parade moves from the background in a curve around the state president. We see paper helmets, allegorical figures for the seasons, the stars, and so on, all indicated by headdresses or attachments sewn onto the costumes. The Fairies, Elves, *and* Angels *and the* characters *in the play are the showiest part of the parade. At the head of the parade are* Hornbriller *and* Trankhafen, *tripping backward and tirelessly keeping a beat with their hands. Both are dressed festively.*

Trankhafen: One, two—left, right.

Hornbriller: Tempo, beat—tempo, beat. Correct steps, there, hold the *tête* in place!

Trankhafen: Left, right—one, two. Watch out! Exactly ten paces in front of the president.

Hornbriller: Everyone begin the *chanson* precisely on the signal!

Trankhafen: Careful, left, right, left—one—two *(large gesture)*—three!

Song. Untrained voices, rough tone, wrong chords, uneven entrances, the whole performance is an unexpressive, dragging, howling mess.

> On the hill and in the vale
> The lovely sky is blue and pale!
> O, what splendor! O, what light!
> Say, who made this lovely sight?
> Was it the Lord God alone?
> Everything is in His hands.
> And each human understands
> For the Lord has made it known,
> And the sun shines from His throne.

Jedes Ding hat seine Zeit:
Trockne Luft wie Feuchtigkeit.
Strahlt's von oben oder gießt's,
Die Regierung—hei!—beschließt's,
Die des Volkes Bestes kennt.
Also dankt nun insgesamt
Gott und auch dem Wetteramt.
Heiter bleib das Firmament,
Heiter auch der Präsident!

Wimmerzahn: (macht täppisch Winkewinke) Danke, danke! Sehr schön—ja. Danke.

Möhre: Nein, wie reizend!

Selters: Da wird man neugierig, wer der gegnadete Dichter ist.

Hustenreiz: Verrate ich ein Geheimnis, Herr Staatssekretär—?

Stechbein: Ich bitte Sie—

Blödel: Unser Herr Staatssekretär! In der Tat sehr hübsch.

Stechbein: Nicht doch, ist ja nicht der Rede wert.

Krachhahn: Wieso denn? Ausgezeichnete Dichtung. Höchst gemütvoll. Hätt' ich Ihnen gar nicht zugetraut.

Der Zug geht noch einmal um den Platz. Hornbriller *und* Trankhafen *regeln mit erhobenen Fingern den gleichen Schritt und Tritt.*

Hankte: Affenparade.

Berta: Und das dumme Geplärr.

Steinbott: Ewige Feiertage und nie ein Tropfen Regen.

Berta: Dafür schüttet es in der Erntezeit, daß alles verfault. Ich an Niedermaiers Stelle hätt' ihnen den Dreck längst vor die Beine geschmissen.

Hantke: Das ist leicht gesagt. Schließlich hat er und Peters und die rote Otti doch das Ganze hingestellt.

There's a time for everything:
For sunshine and the rains of spring.
If it pours or if it shines,
The government makes all designs,
Because it's so benevolent.
So let's thank them, then, also,
Thank God and the weather bureau.
Fair remains the firmament,
And fair remains our president!

Wimmerzahn: *(Makes awkward waving motions.)* Thank you, thank you. Very nice—yes. Thank you.

Möhre: Well, wasn't that charming!

Selters: I'm curious to know who the author is.

Hustenreiz: Can I tell the secret, Herr State Secretary?

Stechbein: Oh, please—

Blödel: Our state secretary! Really, it's quite cute.

Stechbein: Oh, really, it's not worth talking about.

Krachhahn: Why not? It's an excellent song. Full of feeling. I wouldn't have suspected that you wrote it.

The parade goes around the square once more. Hornbriller *and* Trankhafen *maintain the pace with raised hands.*

Hankte: What a parade of trained monkeys.

Berta: And that stupid yowling.

Steinbott: We're forever having holiday celebrations and never a drop of rain.

Berta: Instead it'll be pouring at harvest time and everything will rot in the field. If I were Niedermaier I would have told them a long time ago where to stick their nice weather.

Hantke: That's easy to say. After all, he and Peters and Red Otti set up the whole thing.

Jenny: Otti hat gestern wieder so geweint.

Steinbott: Wir auf dem Feld können das garnicht begreifen, wo die Beamten eigentlich mit ihrem Wetter hinwollen.

Brunner: Paß auf: Was die Bürokraten im Hirn haben, das nennt man Staatskunst. Wenn ihr damit misten könntet, brauchtet ihr keine Kunstdünger.

Der Zug bleibt in der Mitte des Platzes stehen.

Trankhafen: Halt. So, jetzt muß der Zug sich auflösen. Wer im Stück nicht mitspielt, stellt sich vor dem Turm auf, die andern bleiben hier. *(Läuft überall ordnend herum und verwirrt alles. Vor dem Turm.)* Hier muß aber Platz gemacht werden. Das ist für unseren Festzug. Die Arbeiter und Angestellten müssen weiter zurück. Bis ganz an die Kirche bitte. *(Murren)* Da können Sie immer noch sehen.

Fischer: Wär auch schade, wenn uns was entginge. *(langsame Umgruppierung)*

Hornbriller: *(kommt hinzu)* Dalli, dalli! *(stößt auf* Niedermaier *und* Otti*)* Parbleu! Die technische Direktion auf dem Galerieplatz! Aber der Herr Diplomingenieur sollte doch bei den Experten plaziert werden. Für Herrn Wetterrat und sein Fräulein Assistentin müssen a tempo auf der Terrasse separierte Plätze reserviert werden.

Niedermaier: Lassen Sie mich nur da bleiben, wo meine Windjacke keinen Anstoß erregt.

Hornbriller: Kommen Sie ungeniert zu den Honoratioren. Ihre Meriten dispensieren Sie von der Konvention. Das Genie hat das Prae, originell sein zu dürfen.

Niedermaier: Danke wirklich. Ich gehe hinter die Absperrung. Otti, kommst du mit? *(Setzt sich mit* Otti *in Bewegung, gefolgt von* Peters, Fischer, Annie *und anderen. Nur die uniformierten und aufgeputzten* Angestellten *gehen an den Platz zwischen Windrad und Kirche, den die* Trankhafen *ihnen anweist.)*

Hornbriller: *(begleitet* Niedermaier, *auf ihn einredend)* Nicht so desolat. Die prominenzen reflektieren auf ihre Teilnahme am Cercle.

Jenny: Yesterday Otti was crying her eyes out again.

Steinbott: We field workers don't have a clue what the government wants to do with the weather.

Brunner: You know something? They call that stuff the bureaucrats have in their heads "statesmanship." If you all could spread that manure on your fields, you wouldn't need any other fertilizer.

The parade stops in the middle of the square.

Trankhafen: Halt. All right, now the parade can break up. Whoever is not part of the play should stand in front of the tower, the others should stay here. *(Runs around everywhere organizing things, and makes everything more and more confused. In front of the tower.)* But we need to clear some space here. This is for our procession. The workers need to move back. All the way back to the church, please! *(Grumbling from the crowd.)* You can still see from there.

Fischer: Yes, it would be a shame if we missed something. *(They move back slowly.)*

Hornbriller: *(Steps forward.)* Dum diddley um! *(Comes over to* Niedermaier *and* Otti.*) Parbleu!* The technical managers are in the gallery! But Herr Engineer Niedermaier should be placed with the experts. We need to reserve separate places on the terrace for the Weather Councillor and his assistant *à tempo.*

Niedermaier: Let me stay over here where my windbreaker won't bother anyone.

Hornbriller: Oh, please come over with the honorees. Your achievements excuse you from certain conventions. Genius has the prerogative of being a bit peculiar.

Niedermaier: Thanks, really. I'll go over here behind the barrier. Otti, will you come along? *(Starts moving with* Otti, *followed by* Peters, Fischer, Annie, *and others. Only the uniformed and dressed-up* employees *go to the place indicated by* Trankhafen, *between the wind wheel and the church.)*

Hornbriller: *(Walks with* Niedermaier, *talking insistently with him.)* Please don't be so melancholy. The prominent guests will appreciate

Ihre Zelebrität ist eine Attraktion. Das Exterieur ist dabei relativ irrelevant. Ohne Komplimente—

Niedermaier: Sie bemühen sich unnötig, Herr Regierungsassessor.

Hornbriller: Sie sind intolerant. Weil Ihnen in der Administration dès Institutes kein plein pouvoir mehr konzediert werden konnte, fühlen Sie sich degradiert. Der casus muß sine ira et studio ventiliert werden—

Otti: Dann hören Sie nur mal bei den Bauern und Arbeitern herum.

Hornbriller: Auch Sie sind präokkupiert, Mademoiselle. Man kann doch den populären Sentiments nicht ad libitum Konzessionen machen. Das Primat hat das Staatsinteresse. Das ist eine generelle Maxime. *(Sie sind bei der Absperrung angelangt. Verschwinden in der Menge.)*

Wolff: *(drängt sich mit einer bunt beklebten Leiter von links her durch)* Wo soll das Dings zu stehn kommen?

Trankhafen: Aha, die Bühne. Hierher. *(weist einen Platz von der Terrasse an)*

Wolff: Platz da!

Wachtel: *(kommt suchend von der Terrasse herunter)* Au! Sie stoßen mich ja mit der Leiter vor den Leib.

Wolff: Halten Sie doch Ihren Bauch woanders hin.

Wachtel: *(ruft zu* Paula *hinauf)* Um Gotteswillen, Fräulein, wo ist denn das hier?

Paula: Durchs Lokal. Ich gebe Ihnen den Schlüssel.

Wachtel: Schrecklich, das kann ja ein Unglück geben.

Wolff: Laufen Sie man, eh das Unglück geschen ist.

Trankhafen: Herr Regierungsassessor, da sind Sie ja. Hier rennt alles durcheinander. Auf mich hört kein Mensch.

your participation in the group. Your celebrity is something of an attraction. So your exterior is relatively irrelevant. Not to flatter you, but—

Niedermaier: You are wasting your breath, Herr Government Assessor.

Hornbriller: You are being intolerant. Just because the administration of the institute can't concede to you full power over its operation, you feel debased. The whole matter has to be considered and discussed without emotion, *sine ira et studio*—

Otti: Then you should listen to the farmers and workers sometime.

Hornbriller: You too seem preoccupied, mademoiselle. But one simply cannot make concessions to the popular sentiment *ad libitum*. The interest of the state comes before anything else. That is a general principle. *(They have come to the barrier. They disappear into the crowd.)*

Wolff: *(Pushes his way through from the left with a brightly decorated ladder.)* Where should I put this thing?

Trankhafen: Aha, the stage. Over here. *(Points to a spot in front of the terrace.)*

Wolff: Watch out, coming through!

Wachtel: *(Comes down from the terrace as if looking for something.)* Ouch! You ran that ladder right into me!

Wolff: Well, you should move your belly somewhere else.

Wachtel: *(Calls up to* Paula.*)* For God's sake, waitress, where is one around here?

Paula: Through the restaurant. I'll give you the key.

Wachtel: This is awful, you could cause an accident with that thing.

Wolff: Well, you'd better run before an accident happens.

Trankhafen: Herr Government Assessor, there you are. Everything is chaos, no one is listening to me.

Hornbriller: Die Inszenierung darf nicht inkommodiert werden. Das Terrain im Zentrum nur für die Akteure. Das Requisit direkt dem Parkett vis-à-vis. Monteur, evakuieren Sie die Arena.

Wolff: Platz! Weg da! *(Gedränge)*

Stiefengrat: Das dauert ja unheimlich. Da fehlt der soldatische Schmiß.

Barde: Unsre ganze Kunst ist jüdisch verseucht.

Möhre: Gott, es sind ja nur Liebhaber.

Hustenreiz: Wie ich höre, wirken nur die Damen von hiesigen Beamten mit.

Krachhahn: Ist das Stück, das sie da steigen lassen wollen, auch von Ihnen, Herr Staatssekretär?

Stechbein: Im Vertrauen, Herr von Krachhahn, das Stück ist von Fräulein Ministerialrätin selbst. Ich habe nur bei den Reimen nachgeholfen.

Blödel: Muß sehr schwierig sein. Etwas Ungereimtes bringt unsereiner ja eher fertig.

Hornbriller: *(tritt dazu.)* Ein Moment noch, dann ist alles perfekt.

Selters: Viel Arbeit für Sie heute, Herr Regierungsassessor.

Hornbriller: Inspizieren, die Defekte der Regie korrigieren. Sind ja alles Amateure.

Speicherer: Gingen Sie nicht mit dem Wetterrat da herunter? Wollen er und das schöne Fräulein nicht beehren?

Hornbriller: Total obstinat. Fraternisieren mit der Galerie.

Krachhahn: Da gehören sie auch zwischen.

Hornbriller: Dieser pathologische Ingenieur kokettiert aus Ressentiment mit seinem ramponierten Prestige. Ein infantiler Querulant. Und die Personnage mit der roten Coiffure akkompagniert ihn mit effektvollen Vulgärargumenten.

Blödel: Sie haben also die Form gewahrt und sie hergebeten?

Hornbriller: The performance must not be incommoded. The space in the center is only for the actors. The stage properties must be *vis-à-vis* from the orchestra. Mechanic, please clear the arena.

Wolff: Make way there! Coming through! *(pushing through the crowd)*

Stiefengrat: This is taking forever! They need a little military discipline.

Barde: All our artworks are contaminated by Jews nowadays.

Möhre: My God, they're all just amateurs.

Hustenreiz: I heard that only the wives of the local bureaucrats are participating.

Krachhahn: Is this play that they're putting on written by you as well, Herr State Secretary?

Stechbein: To tell the truth, Herr von Krachhahn, the play is by Fräulein Trankhafen herself. I only helped with the sense of some of the lines.

Blödel: That must have been difficult. We're usually more used to producing nonsense.

Hornbriller: *(Comes over to the group.)* Just one more moment, then everything will be perfect.

Selters: This is a lot of work for you today, Herr Assessor.

Hornbriller: Yes, I must scrutinize everything, correct mistakes in the staging. They're all just amateurs.

Speicherer: Weren't you speaking with the weather councillor a minute ago down there? Won't he and the lovely young lady join in the honors?

Hornbriller: Completely obstinate. They're fraternizing with the gallery.

Krachhahn: That's where they belong, after all.

Hornbriller: This pathetic engineer is playing coy with his enormous prestige, just because of his own prejudices. He's being childishly peevish. And the person with the red coiffure follows him around with her vulgar arguments.

Blödel: I trust you maintained good form and invited them over?

Hornbriller: Ohne succès. Meine superlativischen Elogen reussierten nicht. Die simple Gratulationen mit Nonchalance ignoriert. Man will sich à tout prix mit der misera plebs solidarisieren.

Stiefengrat: Diese Leute hätten längst von hier entfernt werden müssen.

Barde: Sehr richtig.

Stechbein: Das hätte böses Blut gemacht. Niedermaiers Absetzung von der Leitung wird uns schon als Undank ausgelegt.

Biederhold: Dann könnte man ihm in Gottes Namen einen Ruhesold aussetzen und eine Straße nach ihm benennen.

Hornbriller: Ein fait accompli, ohne das Dekorum zu lädieren.

Hustenreiz: Die Unversöhnlichen hätten die Massen doch verhetzt.

Speicherer: Die breite Masse findet sich mit Tatsachen immer ab. Der Lärm der Gasse schreit sich vor tauben Ohren müde.

Selters: Die Hauptsache ist, daß dem Manne die Bestimmung der Witterung entzogen ist.

Wachtel: Wenn ich nur an das Grundsteinjubiläum denke. Es zog so, daß mir wochenlang elend zu Mut war.

Möhre: Dafür haben wir heute umso schöneren blauen Himmel.

Wimmerzahn: Prächtig, jawohl, ganz prächtig.

Stiefengrat: Das wahre Hohenzollernwetter!

Trankhafen: Die Engel, Feen und Elfen jetzt im Halbkreis um die Leiter. Sonnenscheinchen und Schönwetterchen verbergen sich hinter den Kleidern der etwas beleibteren Damen, ebenso die Tierstimmen.

Sausewind: Und wir? *(Sausewind, Schnee und Regen gehen bis zur Schutzmannskette zurück.)*

Trankhafen: Richtig, bleiben Sie aber beim Herrn Polizeileutnant stehen, damit Sie nicht den Leuten da hinter der Absperrung zu nahe

Hornbriller: Without success. My extravagant words of praise had no effect. He ignored it all quite nonchalantly. They seem to want to show solidarity with the rabble *à tout prix.*

Stiefengrat: These people should have been removed from here long ago.

Barde: Quite right.

Stechbein: That would have created bad blood. Niedermaier's removal from the management is already being interpreted as ingratitude on our part.

Biederhold: Then we could buy his silence by naming a street after him.

Hornbriller: That would be a *fait accompli,* without violating decorum.

Hustenreiz: The Intransigents would have gotten the masses all worked up.

Speicherer: The great masses always resign themselves to the facts. The noisemakers in the streets always shout until they're hoarse, and all their noise falls on deaf ears.

Selters: The main thing is to take the planning of the weather out of that man's hands.

Wachtel: When I think about that day we celebrated the building of the tower! It was so windy that I was miserable for weeks!

Möhre: Well, today the skies are all the more beautiful.

Wimmerzahn: Splendid, yes, quite splendid.

Stiefengrat: Truly imperial weather!

Trankhafen: The Angels, Fairies, and Elves should all make a semicircle around the ladder. Little Sunshine and Little Blue-Skies, you hide behind the skirts of the larger ladies there, and the animal voices, you hide as well.

Gusty-Wind: And us? (Gusty-Wind, Snow, *and* Rain *go back to the line of* police officers.)

Trankhafen: Right, but you stay there by the lieutenant, so you don't get too close to the people behind the barricade. And where is Gnome?—

kommen. Und wo ist der Gnom?—Sie stellen sich nur einfach vor den Masken auf, Fräulein. Sitzt Ihr Bart auch gut? Schön. Jetzt noch der Laubfrosch. Sie setzen sich also auf die Erde neben der Leiter und blicken sinnend hinauf. *(läuft anordnend von einem zum anderen)*

Jenny: Sie, Herr Schutzmann, wir wollen doch noch was andres sehn, als Ihre Hinteransicht.

Schutzmann: Ich muß aufpassen, daß die Sperre nicht durchbrochen wird.

Peters: Die Engel da vorn kriegen wir doch auch bloß von hinten zu sehn.

Berta: Laßt doch Herrn Niedermaier und Otti mal durch.

Niedermaier: Ist nicht wichtig für mich. Aber Otti kann vielleicht von der Trankhafen was für ihren Chor lernen.

Otti: Soviel wie du vom Stechbein fürs Wetter.

Annie: Wir müssten denen mal mit dem Jugendchor einfach dazwischen tanzen. Kuck dich mal um, Otti, hier hinten fehlt fast keiner von uns.

Otti: Wir wollen uns lieber vorläufig mit dem Dorfplatz unten begnügen. Hier oben tanzen wir erst wieder, wenn wir hier oben wieder mitzureden haben.

Hantke: Die Zeit kommt auch.

Wolff: *(kommt und stellt sich außerhalb der Sperre)* So. Jetzt kann der Zauber losgehn.

Hornbriller: *(steigt mit einem Gong auf die Leiter)* Ist die Szenerie parat? Silentium! Absolute Ruhe für das Ensemble! *(schlägt den Gong)*

Wolff: Ein Dutzend Mal hab' ich es schon bei den Proben gesehn.

Otti: Ein hartes Los.

Laubfrosch: Ein hartes Los, fürwahr, ward mir zuteil.
Am frühen Morgen, wenn die Hähne krähn,

Tierstimme: Kikeriki!

Laubfrosch: Muß ich schon wissen, was der Himmel plant.
Denn Mensch und Tiere wolln es von mir wissen.

You just stand in front of the masks, miss. Does your beard fit you? Good. Now Treefrog. You sit on the ground next to the ladder and look around thoughtfully. *(She runs from one to the other as she arranges them.)*

Jenny: Say, officer, we want to see something besides your back.

Policeman: I have to make sure the barricade isn't penetrated.

Peters: We can only see those angels up there from the back anyhow.

Berta: Let Herr Niedermaier and Otti through there.

Niedermaier: It doesn't matter to me. But maybe Otti can learn something from Trankhafen for her choir.

Otti: Yeah, just as much as you can pick up from Stechbein about the weather.

Annie: We ought to just dance through them with our youth choir. Look around, Otti, almost all of us are here.

Otti: Oh, I think we ought to just settle for dancing on the village square for the time being. We ought not to dance up here again until we have a say in what happens here.

Hantke: That time will come.

Wolff: *(Comes and stands outside the barricade.)* All right. Now the magic can begin.

Hornbriller: *(Climbs onto the ladder with a gong.)* Is the scenery ready? Silence! Absolute silence for the ensemble! *(Strikes the gong.)*

Wolff: I've seen the rehearsals for this a dozen times.
Otti: What a hard fate.

Treefrog: What a hard fate, indeed, does fall my way
Each early morning, when the roosters crow,

Animal: Cockledoodledoo!

Treefrog: For I should know just what the skies have planned.
Both man and beast await to hear from me.

Kulturbeleckt die Großstadtpflanzen nur
Befragen lieber ihre Barometer.
Der Bauersmann dagegen und die Rinder,
Wenn freudig blökend sie zur Weide ziehn,

Tierstimme: Muh!

Laubfrosch: Die kommen nur zu mir. Ei, lieber Laubfrosch,
Verrate uns, was für ein Wetter wird.
Soll lichter Glanz die Felder überfluten,
Bezieungsweise soll, ob Flur und Rain,
Des Regens Naß die liebe Erde tränken?
Ich Ärmster bin die reinste Auskunftei.
Quecksilbrig muß ich auf- und abwärts turnen.
Denn die Insekten, die mir Mahlzeit sind,
Bei trüber Wittrung sumsen sie am Boden,

Tierstimme: Summsummsumm!

Laubfrosch: Bei klarer Luft hingegen steigen sie
Beseligt auf in das azurne Blau.
Grasmückchen zirpt,

Tierstimme: Zizizizizi!

Laubfrosch: Der Vögel muntre Schar
Sie hüpft von Zwieg zu Zweig und zwitschert,

Tierstimme: Ztschztschzi!

Laubfrosch: pfeift,

Tierstimme: Fftiffitff!

Laubfrosch: Und trilleriert,

Tierstimme: Trillerillerie!

Laubfrosch: Und treibt der Kurzweil viel.
Indeß, ich grüner Tor, da schwätz ich nun,
Verträume meine Zeit und weiß noch nicht,
Soll ich mich hurtig auf die Leiter schwingen,
Und also sonnig Wetter prophezein?
Soll ich inmitten ihrer Sproßen sitzen,
Daß jeder wähnt: aha, veränderlich!?

The cultured creatures of the giant city
Ask their barometers what clouds will come.
The farmer, though, and all the cows and calves,
When they come to the meadow peacefully,

Animal:　　　　　　　　　　　　　　　　Moo!

Treefrog:　They only come to me. "Say, good Treefrog,
　Please tell us what the weather's going to be.
　Will shining sun flood over all the fields,
　Or will we rather see in hill and meadow
　The lovely earth become all soaked with rain?"
　I, poor Treefrog, give everyone the news.
　I must leap up and down as in a flash.
　The insects, who are my own daily food,
　Hum on the ground when thunderstorms arrive.

Animal:　　　　　　　　　　　　　　　　Hmmmmm!

Treefrog:　And when the air is clear they fly on up
　And up and up into the heavenly blue.
　Grasshoppers chirp,

Animal:　　　　　　　　　　　　　　　　Chirp chirp chirp!

Treefrog:　　　　　　　　and hosts of noble birds
　They hop from branch to branch and tweet

Animal:　　　　　　　　　　　　　　　　Tweet tweet tweet!

Treefrog:　　　　　　　　　　　　　　　and sing

Animal:　　　　　　　　　　　　　　　　Wheet wheet wheet!

Treefrog:　And trill

Animal:　　　　　　　　　　　　　　　　Tweedledeedledee!

Treefrog:　　　　　and gaily, merrily pass the day.
　Meanwhile, I watch and prattle, all in green,
　And dream away the day, and ask myself,
　Should I now nimbly hop high on the ladder
　And thus foretell another sunny day?
　Should I sit among its buds so small
　So everyone will know the weather changes?

Hinwiederum, weil ich am Fuß derselben,
Und künde klagend Hagel und Gewitter?
Der Laubfrosch darf nicht nach Belieben amten.
Verantwortsvolle Zuverläßigkeit
Sei immerdar die Richtschnur seines Waltens.
(schaut sinnend in die Ferne)

Speicherer: Das ist wirklich mal etwas außerordentlich liebens-
würdiges.

Barde: Muß selber zugeben—ulkig!

Fischer: Das ist ja um Junge zu kriegen.

Laubfrosch: Sieh da, herr Gnom, der gute Geist der Menschen
Und auch der himmlichschen Gewalten Freund.
Der wird gewiß mich nicht zum Besten halten.

(Der Gnom *kommt heran.)*

Heda, kommt doch mal näher, guter Gnom.
Was steht geschrieben denn am Himmelsdom?
Der heut'ge Tag, wird trüb er oder heiter?
Wo nehm' ich Platz auf meiner Wetterleiter?

Gnom: Grüß euch, Gevatter Laubfrosch, schmeckt die Fliege?

Laubfrosch: Wo kommt ihr her?

Gnom: Von Esel, Schaf und Ziege.

Tierstimmen: Y-ah! Bäh! Meckmeck!

Brunner: Er scheint vom Landtag zum kommen.

Laubfrosch: Und wußten die, wie's Wetter wird, Bescheid?
O, sagt es mir, Gevatter.

Gnom: Tut mir leid.
Wißt ihr denn noch nicht, daß die Menschen jetzt
Ihr Wetter trefflich selber machen können?
Prunkvolle Bauten haben sie errichtet,
Auch einen Turm, ein Windrad steht daneben,
Ein Kirchlein gar, daß alles wohl gedeihe.

Or should I sit here at the ladder's feet
And warn of summer hail and thunderstorms?
The treefrog must not act just as he wants.
Responsible reliability
Is always the true guide of all his tasks.
(Looks pensively into the distance.)

Speicherer: This is really extraordinarily lovely.

Barde: I have to admit, it's funny.

Fischer: These folks are crazy as coots.

Treefrog: Look there, the Gnome, the human's goodly spirit,
And also friend to heaven's mighty powers.
He surely will not dare make fun of me.

(Gnome comes in.)

Hello, come close, O Gnome, come closer by.
What message is now written in the sky?
Will this day turn out gray, or rather fair?
Should I sit here, or should I sit up there?

Gnome: Good day, friend Treefrog, how are the flies today?

Treefrog: Where have you been?

Gnome: With donkey, sheep, and goat.

Animals: Hee-haw! Baaah! Maaah!

Brunner: It looks like he came from the parliament.

Treefrog: And did they know what weather's coming, pray?
Oh, tell me.

Gnome: I regret, they didn't say.
Have you not heard that human beings now
Can make whatever weather pleases them?
They've built some splendid buildings in the land,
With a great tower, and there's a windwheel, too,
And even a small church, so all might thrive.

Biederhold: Lobenswert von der Sozialistin, dessen zu gedenken.

Gnom: Hoch ragen Warten, fern in Afrika,
Auf zackigem Grat und in den fernen Cordilleren
Belauschen sie so Wind wie Meereswogen,

Peters: Die peilen den großen Ozean auf dem Chimborasso aus.

Gnom: Auf daß sie hierzuland das Wetter haben,
Wie es das Volk am besten brauchen kann.

Jenny: Um Hunger zu leiden.

Laubfrosch: Wohl hörte ich davon. Doch leider, leider
Fehlt's an Beziehung mir zum Wetteramt.
Ich muß die Nase in die Lüfte strecken,
Um zu ergründen, wie die Winde gehn.

Möhre: Sie befinden sich wieder wohler, Kollegin Wachtel, ja?

Laubfrosch: Euch aber, Vetter Gnom, bleibt nichts verborgen.
Bleibt ihr auch unsichtbar den Menschenkindern,
So dürft ihr doch dabei sein, wie sie's halten,
Beglaubigt als des Erdgeists Botschaftsrat.

Krachhahn: Famos, was?

Selters: Diese Anspielungen, ebenso geistreich wie zartsinnig.

Gnom: Das stimmt; jedoch in dieser Eigenschaft
Bin streng ich zur Verschwiegenheit verpflichtet.
Wie's Wetter wird, verfügt die Staatsregierung,
Beraten von der Weisheit der Parteien.
Das Nähere bestimmt das Wetteramt.

Otti: Die Verse geschehen ihnen ganz recht.

Niedermaier: Na, Otti, sei nicht zu grausam.

Gnom: Zu aller Heil regiert der Präsident,
Vom Volk erkoren, wie es Recht und Brauch.

Laubfrosch: Dann ist's das Volk, das sich das Wetter aussucht?

Biederhold: Very commendable that my Socialist colleague
remembered to think of that.

Gnome: Observers watch in farthest Africa,
On jagged peaks and high upon the mountains
They listen to the wind and to the waves,

Peters: Sounds like they're taking ocean soundings from on top of Mt.
Chimborazo.

Gnome: So that the weather here in our fair land
Is just the weather that the people need.

Jenny: So we can starve.

Treefrog: I think I've heard of that. But, sad to say,
I have no contacts with the Weather Bureau.
I must still stick my nose up in the air
So I can find out where the winds will blow.

Möhre: You're feeling better now, Frau Wachtel, I hope?

Treefrog: But you, friend Gnome, hear all there is to hear.
If you stay hidden there among the humans,
Then you can be present as they work,
Attesting, as a messenger from earth.

Krachhahn: Great, isn't it?

Selters: These allusions are both ingenious and lovely.

Gnome: That's true enough, but as that messenger,
I am obliged to maintain strictest silence.
The government determines all the weather,
With the advice and wisdom of the parties.
The Weather Bureau works out the details.

Otti: These foolish verses are just what they deserve.

Niedermaier: Now, Otti, don't be too cruel.

Gnome: The president governs for the common good,
Elected by the people, in their law.

Treefrog: And so the people really make the weather?

Gnom: Des Volkes Laune gleicht der Wetterfahne,
Die sich nach jeder Himmelsrichtung dreht,
Und ohn' zu fragen, wer es wohl versteht,
Wählt es heut Umsturz, morgen vaterländisch.
Doch die Regierung ist nicht wetterwendisch.
Beschließt sie Schneesturm oder Windesstille,
Wie sie es vorschreibt, ist's des Volkes Wille.
Denn sei es Sonnenglanz, sei's Sturmgebraus—
Die Staatsgewalt, sie geht vom Volke aus!

(heftiges Händeklatschen auf der Terrasse)

Blödel: Ausgezeichnet, ganz allerliebst.

Krachhahn: Trotz gewisser demokratischer Wendungen garnicht übel.

Stiefengrat: Man muß sogar zugeben, das mit der wetterwendischen
Volksmeinung ist ein durchaus nationaler Gedanke.

Möhre: Und die entzückenden Reime. Unser Herr Staatssekretär ist ein
gottbegnadeter Dichter.

Stechbein: Was einem die Muse so eingibt.

Jenny: Sieh doch mal rüber, Annie—die Paula! Die stirbt ja vor
Lachen. *(Paula steht im Hintergrunde der Terrasse und schüttet sich
aus vor Lachen.)*

Wolff: Der ist die wahre Kunst noch nicht aufgegangen.

Berta: Wenn sie es bloß nicht merken!

Brunner: Die Obrigkeit merkt nie, das man über sie lacht.

Laubfrosch: Doch weiß ich noch nicht, wird es grau, wird's heiter,
Und wohin tret' ich auf der Wetterleiter?

Gnom: Jenun, Gevatter Frosch, ihr dauert mich.
Erratet drum, was ich euch nicht darf sagen.
Ich war in Wetterborn und sah geschäftig
Beamte dort und Angestellte schalten.
Girlanden zogen sie den First entlang
Und hißten Fahnen auf des Turmes Zinnen.
Mann, Weib und Kindlein tragen Festgewand

Gnome: The people's mood is like a weather flag
   Which waves in each direction, with the wind,
   And never asking how, or why, or when,
   First revolution, next the fatherland,
   The government, though, blows not with the weather.
   If it says "snowstorm," or prescribes calm breeze,
   The people's will stands behind its decrees.
   For if the sun should shine, or storms should roar,
   State power is people's power, now evermore.

(passionate applause on the terrace)

Blödel: Excellent, quite lovely.

Krachhahn: In spite of certain democratic phrases, not bad at all.

Stiefengrat: You have to admit, that business about the changeable
mood of the people is a thoroughly nationalist idea.

Möhre: And those charming rhymes. Our Herr State Secretary is really
a gifted poet.

Stechbein: The muses must have touched him.

Jenny: Look over there, Annie! Paula's dying laughing! *(Paula is
standing in the background doubled over with laughter.)*

Wolff: She must never have experienced true art.

Berta: I only hope they don't notice her.

Brunner: The authorities don't ever notice when people are laughing
about them.

Treefrog: But still I don't know if it's cloudy or fair,
   Or where I should sit on this weather ladder.

Gnome: Well, good friend Frog, I really pity you.
   You'll never guess what I now have to tell:
   I was in Weatherspring, and there I saw
   The officers and workers switching things.
   They put some garlands all along the roof
   And raised some flags high up upon the tower.
   Men, women, children, all were dressed up fine,

Und Lust und Frohsinn lacht aus aller Augen.
Ein jeder winkt dem andern freudge Zeitung:
Geburtstag nämlich ist in Vorbereitung.

Laubfrosch: Und feiert ihn, wen Hoch und Niedrig kennt?

Gnom: Ei ja, Herr Frosch, des Staates Präsident!

Laubfrosch: Hurra! Da wird's nicht hageln und nicht blitzen.
Hoch oben kann ich auf der Leiter sitzen.
Doch wehe! Schon erfüllt mich neues Bangen.
Kommt da nicht Meister Nebel angegangen?

(Nebel *tritt suchend auf.*)

Nebel: Ach bitte, saht ihr meine drei Kollegen,
Die Brüder Schnee und Sausewind und Regen?
Sind sie heut früh noch nicht vorbeigekommen?

Laubfrosch: Hier nicht.

Nebel: Dann haben sie Reißaus genommen.
Wo sie nicht sind, da bin auch ich nichts nütze,
Muß niederlegen mich als feuchte Pfütze.
Nur wenn ein nasser Wind weht in den Zweigen,
Darf ich als Wolke in den Himmel steigen.

(legt sich nieder)

Laubfrosch: Ha, dieser stirbt. Doch seht nur, hell besonnt
Naht eine Lichtgestalt am Horizont.
Juchhe, das ist ja unser Sonnenscheinchen.
Voll Anmut hebt es seine Strahlenbeinchen.

Biederhold: Schade, einen solchen Ausdruck hätte ich gern vermieden
gesehn.

Stechbein: Er war des Reimes wegen leider unvermeidlich, Hochwürden.

Gnom: Ja, ihr habt recht. Grad kommt es auf uns zu,
Freudig begrüßt von Hühnern, Geis und Kuh.

Tierstimmen: Krähen, Glucken, Meckern, Blöken.

And all had looks of joy upon their faces.
They greeted with glad tidings and with mirth,
Because today they celebrate a birth.

Treefrog: The birth of him who's known to small and great?

Gnome: Yes, Treefrog, of our president of state!

Treefrog: Hurrah! Then no storms will be blowing by!
And I can hop up on the ladder high!
But wait! I'm a bit worried once again.
Is that not Mr. Fog there, rolling in?

(Fog *enters tentatively.*)

Fog: Excuse me, have you seen my three good friends,
My colleagues Snow and Rain and Gusty-Wind?
Did they not come through here early today?

Treefrog: Not here.

Fog: They must have gone their merry way.
If they're not here, then I should leave as well.
I'll lie down as a puddle in this dell.
Only when wet winds blow is it allowed
For me to rise up as a mighty cloud.

(*Lies down.*)

Treefrog: He's dead! And look, there on the far horizon,
I think I see a light there, slowly rising.
It is the Sun! She comes to us so bright,
And stretches out her lovely legs of light.

Biederhold: Oh, I really wish that kind of language could have been avoided.

Stechbein: I'm afraid it was necessary for the rhyme, Reverend.

Gnome: Ah yes, you're right! She's coming to us now,
And greeted by the chickens, goats, and cows.

Animals: Cluck, maah, moo.

Steinbott: Das klingt, als ob die Kühe Gänse wären.

Wolff: Sind sie auch.

(Sonnenscheinchen *tritt auf.*)

Gnom: Wie glitzert ihr der Garbe Gold im Arm!

Laubfrosch: Ich steige auf die Leiter. Mir wird warm.

Sonnensch.: Ich werfe Lichter auf das Festgewimmel
Niederkommen bin ich grad vom Himmel.

Brunner: Senkrecht aus dem Wochenbett, scheint's.

Gnom: Nun wird im ganzen Lande Freude sein.

Sonnensch.: Seht nur, schon kommt mein trautes Schwesterlein.

(Schönwetterchen *tritt auf.*)

Gnom: Schönwetterchen im blauen Florgewand,
Ein Füllhorn, bunt von Blumen, in der Hand.
Geht, Laubfrosch, gleich noch höher ein paar Stufen.

Schönwetter: Das menschliche Genie hat uns gerufen.

Laubfrosch: Dann fürcht ich heut nichts mehr von den Wettern
Und will sofort zur höchsten Stufe klettern.

Sonnensch.: Ja, seit der Staat in Obhut uns genommen,
Ist's uns vergönnt, gar oft zu euch zu kommen.

Gnom: Ihr labt uns nun schon viele frohe Wochen.
Das bös' Gewölk, es hat sich ganz verkrochen.
Nur selten war die Welt so lange Zeit,
Ohn' Unterlaß von euch, ihr Zwei, erfreut.

Niedermaier: Da hat er mal recht, der Gnom.

Schönwetter.: Doch heut hat uns das Wetteramt beschieden
Zu leuchten über Freude, Glück und Frieden.
Den Präsidententag soll garnichts stören.

Gnom: Die Glöckenblümlein kann ich läuten hören.

Steinbott: Those cows sound like geese.

Wolff: I think they are.

(Little Sunshine *enters.*)

Gnome: I say, look how she's bringing gold in sheaves.

Treefrog: I'm getting warm—I'll climb up to the leaves.

Sunshine: I cast my light down on this happy day.
   From heaven above to earth I make my way.

Brunner: Looks like she just fell out of bed.

Gnome: Now people will be happy everywhere.

Sunshine: And look, my little sister's coming there.

(Little Blue-Skies *appears.*)

Gnome: Little Blue-Skies comes dressed in flowers there,
   A wreath of lovely flowers in her hair.
   Go, Treefrog, climb up higher in the tree.

Blue-Skies: The humans' genius caused us here to be.

Treefrog: Then of the weather I have naught to fear.
   I'll hop up to the top of this tree here.

Sunshine: Yes, since the state has told us what to do
   We can come almost daily unto you.

Gnome: You've brought such joy and gladness to this place
   That the storm-cloud dares not show his face.
   The world has never known so long a time
   That we've enjoyed such Blue Skies and Sunshine.

Niedermaier: You're right about that, Gnome.

Blue-Skies: Today the Weather Bureau does command
   That we should shine on this fair, peaceful land.
   Nothing should trouble this, our president's day.

Gnome: I think I hear the blue-bells down the way.

(Helles Gebimmel)

Laubfrosch: Weh, seh ich recht?

Gnom: Das Glöcklein jäh verstummt.

Sonnensch.: Die argen Feinde schleichen her vermummt.
  Schnee, Sausewind und Regen, die Gesellen,
  Sie wollen das Geburtstagsfest uns vergällen.

Regen *mit Gießkanne,* Schnee *mit Kopfkissen,* Sausewind *mit Besen treten auf.*

Gnom: Was führt euch her, die Lust uns zu verdrießen?

Regen: Ich bin der Regen, will das Land begießen.

Schnee: Ich bin der Schnee und will mein Kissen schütteln.

Sausewind: Ich Sausewind will an den Bäumen rütteln.
  Mein Besen soll das Fest zusammenfegen.

Schnee: Hol' du den Laubfrosch mal herunter, Regen!

Laubfrosch: Ich will ja ganz allein heruntergehn.

Schönwetter.: Ein andermal könnt ihr ja schnein und wehn.

Regen: Der Boden ist schon viel zu lange trocken.

Schnee: Mein Sack ist bis zum Rande voll von Flocken.

Sausewind: Und meine Lungen werden bald asthmatisch.
  Nur lauter schöne Tage tun nicht gut.

Gnom: Klugschwätzer du, dies Land ist demokratisch,
  Nur die Regierung weiß, was nötig tut.

Blödel: Man kann sagen, was man will, es ist ein vorzügliches Stück.

Möhre: Ich bin so gespannt, wie es weitergeht.

Jenny: Man müßte denen mal ein Stück vorspielen, aus dem sie sehn
  könnten, was sie mit der Dürre wirklich anrichten.

Brunner: Wenn sie das begreifen sollen, mußt du sie beim Zusehn bis
  zum Halse in heißen Sand einbuddeln.

(a bright tinkling of bells)

Treefrog: Oh no, what's that?

Gnome: The blue-bells have gone still.

Sunshine: The evil fiends are sneaking o'er the hill.
   Snow, Gusty-Wind, and Rain, those wicked beasts,
   They aim to spoil our president's birthday feast.

Rain *enters with a watering can,* Snow *with a feather pillow,* Gusty-Wind *with a broom.*

Gnome: What brings you here to vex our day of mirth?

Rain: I am the Rain, I water all the earth.

Snow: I am the Snow, I've come to shake my pillow.

Gusty-Wind: I, Gusty-Wind, blow through the weeping willow.
   And with my broom I'll sweep this feast away.

Snow: You bring that Treefrog down, Rain, from on high.

Treefrog: Oh, I can come down on my own just fine.

Blue-Skies: You snow and blow through here some other time.

Rain: But the poor ground is dry as it can be.

Snow: My bag of snowflakes is too big for me.

Gusty-Wind: And in my lungs I feel a bit asthmatic.
   To have just sunny days is dangerous.

Gnome: Be still, you scamp, this land is democratic.
   Only the government knows what's good for us.

Blödel: You can say what you like, this is an excellent play.

Möhre: I'm really eager to see how it turns out.

Jenny: Somebody ought to do a play for these people and show them
   what really happens because of this drought they've made.

Brunner: For them to understand you'll have to bury them up to their
   necks in hot sand while they watched it.

Sonnensch.: Wolln sie von selber nicht von dannen ziehn,
Solln sie vor unserer Kraft und Schönheit fliehn.
Herbei, ihr Feen, ihr Engel und ihr Elfen,
Ihr sollt die Bösen uns verjagen helfen.

Feen, Engel *und* Elfen *laufen herbei und schlagen mit Pfauenfedern und ähnlichen Waffen auf die drei ein.*

Stiefengrat: Jetzt kommt doch Leben in die Bude.

Barde: Immer feste druff!

Sausewind: O weh, wir sind der Übermacht erlegen.
Ich führ euch fort, kommt mit mir, Schnee und Regen.

Nebel: *(steht auf)* Auch ich enteile hinter Ried und Busch.

Sie fliehen, verfolgt von den Feen, Engeln, Elfen.

Engel, Feen, Elfen: Fort mit euch Unheilstiftern, fort—husch, husch!

Gnom: Hei, siegreich sind sie in die Flucht geschlagen.

Schönwetter.: Komm, Sonnenscheinchen, jetzt soll Freude tagen.

Sonnensch.: Ja, Schwester, nun wir diesen Spuk verscheuchten,
Soll Jubelglanz dem Präsidenten leuchten.

Sie zünden bengalische Streichhölzer an. Hornbriller *und* Trankhafen, *beiderseits vor der Terrasse postiert, werden hell beleuchtet.*

Krachhahn: Alle Wetter! Hochkünstlerische Wirkung.

Otti: In der Beleuchtung kommen die Trankhafen und der Hornbriller als die Eckpfeiler des Staates erst zur rechten Geltung.

Gnom: Ihr Elfen, Engel, Feen all hervor!
Zum Ringelreihen singen wir im Chor:

Alle Mitwirkenden stellen sich vor der Terrasse auf, machen von Trankhafen *und* Hornbriller *wie zuvor mit den Händen dirigiert, hopsende Tanzschritte, worauf der Gesang beginnt, in den auch die vor dem Turm aufgestellten* Zugteilnehmer *einstimmen.*

Sunshine: If those three still refuse to leave these places,
  We'll drive them out with our bright sunny faces.
  Come, Fairies, Angels, Elves, come help us out,
  We have some enemies that we must rout.

Fairies, Angels, *and* Elves *run onstage and begin beating the three with peacock feathers and similar weapons.*

Stiefengrat: Now it's getting lively!

Barde: Hit 'em again!

Gusty-Wind: Oh, we have met our match! O pain! O woe!
  Come, I'll lead us to safety, Rain and Snow.

Fog: *(Stands.)* I too will flee behind these bushes here.

They run away, chased by the Fairies, Angels, *and* Elves.

Angels, Fairies, Elves: Away, you mischief-makers! Flee in fear!

Gnome: Ah, victory! The enemy's been destroyed!

Blue-Skies: Come, Sunshine, let us greet the dawn of joy!

Sunshine: Yes, sister, since these villains have been banned,
  Let's light a light for the president of our land.

They light sparklers. Hornbriller *and* Trankhafen, *standing on either side of the terrace, are suddenly brightly lit.*

Krachhahn: Thunderation! What an effect!

Otti: That light shows off Trankhafen and Hornbriller as the true cornerstones of the state.

Gnome: Come, Angels, Fairies, Elves, come all along,
  And let us raise our voices now in song:

All the cast members *come in front of the terrace and dance some hopping steps as* Trankhafen *and* Hornbriller *lead them with hand movements. The song begins. The* participants *in the parade, who have been standing in front of the tower, join in.*

Gesang: Lieblich ist der Erde Pracht,
Wenn die Sonne freundlich lacht,
Wenn der liebe Himmel blaut,
Treulich uns ins Auge schaut.
Heute strahlt das firmament,
Weil der erste Mann im Staat
Heißa! den Geburtstag hat.
Unsre Liebe heiß entbrennt.
Hoch des Staates Präsident!

Die Mitwirkenden *vollführen einen Ringelreihen und flattern an der Leiter vorbei rückwärts über den Platz zurück, verschwinden hinter dem Windrad. Großer Beifall auf der Terasse und bei den* Beamten. *Lautes Gelächter hinter der Absperrung.*

Stechbein: Es ist aber jetzt Zeit, den Herrn Staatspräsidenten aufzuwecken. Ich werde dann wohl am besten gleich mit der Festrede beginnen.

Hustenreiz: Fangen Sie ruhig an, Herr Staatssekretär. Ich bemühe mich inzwischen um den Präsidenten. Herr Präsident!

Polizeioffizier: *(geht vor die Sperre)* Benehmen Sie sich hier anständig. *(zu* Wolff*)* Was haben Sie außerhalb der Sperre zu suchen?

Wolff: Nicht weniger als die Ochsen und Schafe in dem Stück.

Leutnant: Unterlassen Sie derartige Bemerkungen. Zurück hinter den Zaun!

Wolff: *(kriecht durch, von drüben)* Die Laubfroschleiter tragen Sie wohl weg, Herr Leutnant. Hingestellt hab' ich sie.

Leutnant: Sie sind hier beschäftigt? Das kann ich Ihnen doch nicht ansehn.

Wolff: Das nächste Mal zieh' ich mich richtig an: Zylinder auf den Kopf, Flügel am Buckel oder Riemen um den Bauch.

Krampf: Wacht der Herr Präsident jetzt?

Wimmerzahn: Ach so, freilich. *(steht auf)* Es ist mir ein Herzensbedürfnis—

Song: The earth's glory is all around
   When the lovely Sun shines down.
   When the skies are all bright blue,
   We can see their beauties, too.
   Sunbeams from the firmament,
   For the top man in our state;
   His birthday we celebrate.
   Our best wishes we have sent.
   Hail to our state president!

The cast members *do a ring dance and flutter past the ladder backwards over the square, then disappear behind the wind wheel. Great applause on the terrace and among the* bureaucrats. *Loud laughter behind the fence.*

Stechbein: It's time to wake the president. I probably ought to get started with my speech.

Hustenreiz: Go ahead and begin, Herr State Secretary. I'll deal with the president. Herr President!

Policeman: *(Walks in front of the barricade.)* You people behave over here. *(to* Wolff*)* What are you doing outside the barricade?

Wolff: At least as much as the cows and sheep in that play.

Lieutenant: Let's dispense with those kinds of remarks. Get back behind the fence!

Wolff: *(Crawls through. From the other side:)* Then you can carry the treefrog's ladder away, Herr Lieutenant. I put it up there.

Lieutenant: You're working here? I couldn't tell by looking at you.

Wolff: Next time I'll dress properly: top hat, tails, cummerbund.

Krampf: Is the president waking up now?

Wimmerzahn: Ah yes, of course. *(Stands.)* It is an honor for me—

Hustenreiz: Noch nicht, Herr Präsident. *(zieht ihn auf den Stuhl zurück)*

Krampf: Ich bitte nunmehr, den Herrn Staatssekretär Stechbein das Wort zu nehmen.

Stechbein: Hochverehrter Herr Staatspräsident! Verehrte Festversammlung! Jahre sind vergangen, seit diese Stätte zum letzten Male der Schauplatz eines Staatsbesuches war. Unter Führung des Herrn Ministers Dr. Blödel erschienen auch damals hier die Vertreter der Regierung und des Parlamentes, um die Fünfjahresfeier der Grundsteinlegung zum Wetterturm zu begehen und zugleich namens der Staatsregierung den Beschluß anzukünden, die noch junge Kunst, das Wetter zu beherrschen, durch die Schaffung eines eigenen staatlichen Wetteramtes der Erfüllung ihrer Aufgaben für die Menschheit erst zuzuführen. An jenen ersten Besuch hier knüpfen sich peinliche Erinnerungen—

Otti: Die haben es noch nicht verschmerzt.

Stechbein: —die zu erwecken deshalb gestattet sei, weil der heutige Tag kein andres Gefühl, als das der Freude und Genugtuung aufkommen läßt, zumal heute zum ersten Mal der Herr Staatspräsident in eigener Person hier weilt, um durch die Wahl von Wetterborn zur Begehung seines Geburtsfestes unser Werk in sinniger Form zu ehren.

Selters: Bravo!

Stechbein: Welche Errungenschaften seit jener mißglückten Feier! Stolz erhebt sich das mächtige Verwaltungsgebäude vor Ihren Blicken, in welchem das damals noch ungeborene Wetteramt in emsiger Arbeit seine Pflicht erfüllt. Wahrlich, das Wetteramt darf mit Stolz auf seine Leistungen zurückblicken. An ihm hat sich das parlamentarische System unseres Staatswesens glänzend bewährt.

Trankhafen: Sehr richtig.

Stechbein: Schwierigkeiten bei der Ämterbesetzung zu Anfang, da jede Partei den berechtigten Anspruch erhob, gemäß ihrer Stärke an der Verantwortung teilzunehmen—

Jenny: Gehälter einzusacken.

Stechbein: —konnten durch die politische Einsicht aller Beteiligten behoben werden. Die Befriedigungskoalition, welche alle

Hustenreiz: Not yet, Herr President. *(Pulls him back down onto the chair.)*

Krampf: I now give State Secretary Stechbein the floor.

Stechbein: Honored Herr State President! Worthy guests! It has been several years since this site was the object of a state visit. At that time, under the leadership of Minister Blödel, representatives of the government and of the parliament gathered to celebrate the fifth anniversary of the laying of the cornerstone of the weather tower, and at the same time to announce the government resolution creating a state Weather Bureau. This Weather Bureau would place the recent invention enabling control of the weather under the control of the state, in fulfillment of its duty to humanity. Memories of that first visit are, to be sure, somewhat painful—

Otti: They still haven't gotten over it.

Stechbein: —but I mention the memory of that time because today is filled with feelings of joy and satisfaction. This is especially true since our state president is visiting this site for the first time in order to celebrate his birthday, thus bringing honor to our weather works.

Selters: Bravo!

Stechbein: Much has been achieved since that unfortunate ceremony. I am proud to present to you the mighty administration building, in which the Weather Bureau, at that time not yet constituted, carries out its duties. Indeed, the Weather Bureau can look back on its accomplishments with pride. It is an exemplary manifestation of our state's parliamentary system.

Trankhafen: Quite right.

Stechbein: Although there were some difficulties in the beginning involving the assignment of official positions, since each party wished to participate according to its strength in the parliament—

Jenny: So they could get bureacratic salaries.

Stechbein: —we were able to overcome these difficulties thanks to the good political judgment of all involved. The coalition of appeasement,

staatserhaltenden Parteien umfaßt von der Arbeiterrassenpartei, bis zu
den Sozialisten *(Beifall)* ist nicht zuletzt dem Bestreben zu danken,
grade im Wetteramt die Referate gerecht und niemand zu Leide zu
verteilen. Die Notwendigkeit, alle Richtungen mit der einzigen
Ausnahme der Umsturzpartei im Verhältnis ihrer Mandatszahl zu
berücksichtigen, ergab sich nach dem Ausfall der letzten Wahlen von
selbst. Der Umstand, das die Unversöhnlichen seither über die absolute
Mehrheit im Landtage verfügen, konnte unbeschadet unserer
demokratischen Auffassungen nicht dahin misdeutet werden, das nun
etwa ihnen der geringste Einfluß auf eine so wichtige Staatseinrichtung
einzuräumen wäre.

Hustenreiz: Sehr wahr!

Otti: Nette Demokratie!

Stechbein: Die Grundlagen seiner Wirtschaftsordnung darf ein
pflichtbewußter Staat auch von einer Wählermehrheit nie und nimmer
antasten lassen.

Speicherer: Vortrefflich!

Stechbein: Wer aber war es, der die Staatsnotwendigkeit sogleich
zielsicher erkannte und mit würdiger Festigkeit den gordischen Knoten
zerhieb?

Selters: Präsident Wimmerzahn.

Stechbein: Sie sagen es: Präsident Wimmerzahn rief zur Sammlung
aller Wohlgesinnten und zögerte nicht, die verfassungsmäßigen
Machtmittel anzuwenden, welche ihm bei Gefahr in Verzug in die
Hand gegeben sind, um gegen eine entartete Parlamentsmehrheit den
gesunden Menschenverstand zum Siege zu führen. *(Beifall)*

Steinbott: Wozu haben wir eigentlich gewählt, möcht ich wissen.

Hantke: Das hättet ihr euch vor der Wahl fragen sollen.

Stechbein: Indem so der Präsident die Stimmen nicht zählte sondern
wog, setzte er das Wetteramt und namentlich die Personalreferentin,
Fräulein Ministerialrätin Dr. Trankhafen, in die Lage, überall den
rechten Mann an den rechten Platz zu stellen und die hohen
Errungenschaften der Wissenschaft und der Technik den Erfordernissen des Vaterlandes und der Parteien anzupassen. Konnten wir

which includes all the parties in favor of preservation of the state, from the Workers' Race Party to the Socialists *(applause)*, that coalition owes its existence in no small measure to the efforts to distribute positions in the Weather Bureau fairly and without harm to any party. The necessity of recognizing all ideologies in proportion to their number of seats in parliament—except for the revolutionary party—was made clear after the losses in the last election. No one should mistakenly believe, just because the Intransigents have an absolute majority in parliament, that they have even the slightest influence over such an important institution of the state.

Hustenreiz: Very true!

Otti: This is a swell democracy!

Stechbein: A conscientious state must never allow the fundamental economic order to be violated even by a majority of the voters.

Speicherer: Excellent!

Stechbein: And who was it who recognized at once the needs of our state, and cut the Gordian knot with firm resolve?

Selters: President Wimmerzahn.

Stechbein: You have said it yourselves: President Wimmerzahn called an assembly of all right-thinking parties and did not hesitate to invoke the constitutional powers granted him in case of emergency, and thus led the healthy forces of human reason to a victory over a degenerate parliamentary majority! *(applause)*

Steinbott: Why did we vote, then, that's what I'd like to know?

Hantke: You all should have asked that before the election.

Stechbein: By carefully weighing rather than actually counting the votes, our president gave the Weather Bureau and its personnel director, Fräulein Ministerial Advisor Dr. Trankhafen, the power to place the right man in the right position in all cases, and to adapt the great scientific and technological achievements of this invention to the needs of the fatherland and of the parties. Today, on the birthday of our

heute am Geburtstage des verehrten Präsidenten, gleich den elbischen Wesen in unserem Märchenspiel die dräuenden Geister des Unwetters siegreich in die Flucht schlagen,—

Otti: Gott, wie sinnig!

Möhre: Gott, wie sinnig!

Stechbein: —so gebührt dem Geburtstagskinde selbst dafür der Dank, Glück, Segen, Gesundheit und langes Leben sei sein Lohn. Unser allverehrter Herr Staatspräsident, er lebe hoch! hoch! hoch!

Wimmerzahn: War sehr schön, vollständig zutreffend, jawohl. Danke, danke.

Otti: Für den Schöpfer des Ganzen, für die Arbeiter im Werk nicht ein Wort.

Wolff: Der eine richtet die Schüssel an, der andre frißt sie leer.

Brunner: Klar, oder haben vielleicht die Brüder da, die das Kracheisen für uns locker halten, das Schießpulver erfunden?

Krampf: Ich bitte nun um allgemeine Aufmerksamkeit für Herrn Staatspräsidenten Wimmerzahn.

Rufe: Ah! Ruhe!

Hornbriller: Silentium! *(Wimmerzahn richtet sich langsam auf.)*

Niedermaier: Meinetwegen können sie sich an unserm Kuchen sattfressen. Aber wenn es im Turm da für alle Zeit bloß noch nach Parteigunst und Kurszettel gehn soll, dann kann der Tag kommen, wo ich mein eigenes Werk in die Luft sprenge.

Schutzmann: Ruhe da! Der Staatspräsident redet.

Annie: Aber nicht für uns.

Wimmerzahn: Es ist mir ein Herzensbedürfnis, jawohl, Ihnen allen meinen wärmsten Dank auszusprechen—ja, wärmsten Dank also. Wenn ich heute meinen dreiundsiebzigsten Geburtstag—wie? ach ja, den vierundsiebzigsten Geburtstag in seltener geistiger Frische zurückzulegen vermag, ja—so verdanke ich das—verdanke ich also dem—der—dem—

honored president, as we victoriously drive the evil spirits of bad weather out of our midst, just as in our fairy-tale play we have just seen—

Otti: My God, how thoughtful!

Möhre: My God, how thoughtful!

Stechbein: —we owe the birthday boy all our thanks, good luck, happiness, blessings, good health, and a long life. Cheers for our most honorable Herr State President! Hurrah! Hurrah! Hurrah!

Wimmerzahn: That was very nice, quite appropriate, yes indeed. Thank you, thank you.

Otti: Not a single word for the creator of the whole thing, not a word for the workers in the tower.

Wolff: Some people cook and serve the food and other people eat it.

Brunner: Right. Or maybe those guys there who are holding rifles ready for us, maybe they invented gunpowder.

Krampf: Attention, please! Could I ask for your attention for our State President Wimmerzahn?

Shouts: Quiet!

Hornbriller: Silentium! (Wimmerzahn *slowly gets ready to speak.*)

Niedermaier: As far as I am concerned they can eat all of our cake they want. But if the tower is going to be run for the rest of time just the way the parties and the stock exchange want it, then the day might come when I blow up my own work.

Policeman: Quiet there! The president is speaking.

Annie: But not for us.

Wimmerzahn: It is an honor for me, indeed, to express my warmest thanks to you all—yes, my warmest thanks. If I am able to pass my seventy-third birthday today—what? ah, yes, fine, my seventy-fourth birthday today in such rare mental freshness as this, then I owe my thanks to—I must thank—I give thanks to—

Stiefengrat: Dem Vaterlande.

Hustenreiz: Der Liebe des Volkes.

Biederhold: Gottes Hilfe.

Krachhahn: Dem Roggenbrot.

Wimmerzahn: —in erster Linie dem schönen Wetter, das mir in meinem schweren Amt, jawohl, die Gelegenheit gibt, von den Staatsgeschäften gewissermaßen auszuruhn. Vielmehr wollte ich sagen im Sonnenschein spazieren zu gehn—jawohl. An dieser Stätte, wo das Wetter also sozusagen im Dienste der Gesamtheit, der Gemeinschaft, ja—

Jenny: —der Gemeinheit.

Wimmerzahn: —wie ich sagen möchte, seine Weisungen empfängt, ist es mir also vergönnt, in verhältnismäßig jugendlicher Frische, nicht wahr, und Rüstigkeit unter dem blauen Himmel des Wetteramtes gewissermaßen die Spitzen des Vaterlandes ja, um mich versammelt zu sehn. Eine Pflegstätte der Pflichttreue gewiß, und der Gewissenhaftigkeit möge denn unser herrliches Kulturwerk eben sozusagen auch fernerhin dem ganzen Volke als Vorbild einer, ich möchte sagen, moralischen Anstalt also voranleuchten. Gerührt von den vielen Beweisen, jawohl, treuer Anhänglichkeit und, nicht wahr, erhebender Staatsgesinnung erwidere ich gewissermaßen die dargebrachten Wünsche und das anmutige, ja eben, die sinnige Darbietung des schönen Märchens—jawohl, Märchenspieles und spreche den Dank und die gewissermaßen vertrauensvolle Anerkennung des Vaterlandes aus allen, denen es, nun ja, obliegt, den Wetterdienst also sozusagen den Belangen des, ich möchte sagen des Volksganzen eben einzuordnen. In diesem Sinne unser teures Vaterland also und natürlich, jawohl, unser nun denn treffliches Wetteramt—hoch! hoch! hoch! (*Setzt sich. Die Terrasse, die* Beamtenschaft *und der* Maskenzug *stimmen in das Hoch ein.* Trankhafen *und* Hornbriller *gehen auf* Wimmerzahn *zu.*)

Hornbriller: Akzeptieren Herr Präsident mit den Ovationen der enthusiasmierten Gratulanten auch unser Kompliment. Die labile Eloquenz Ihrer Rhetorik ist sans phrase exzeptionell.

Trankhafen: Es war eine wahrhaft staatsmännische Rede.

Stiefengrat: The fatherland.

Hustenreiz: The love of the people.

Biederhold: God's help.

Krachhahn: Rye bread.

Wimmerzahn: —primarily to the beautiful weather, which affords me the opportunity in my high and weighty office to take a little rest from the business of state. That is, to take a lovely walk in the sunshine—yes indeed. In this place, where the weather receives itsinstructions according to the common good, for the the community, yes—

Jenny: —for common meanness.

Wimmerzahn: —as I want to say, in this place I have the opportunity, in relatively youthful vigor and freshness, you know, to see the leaders of the fatherland gathered around me under the blue skies of the Weather Bureau. May this glorious cultural artifact of ours light the path for our entire population, yes, may this shrine to civic duty and to conscientiousness serve us all as a model moral institution. I am touched by all this evidence, indeed, of your loyal devotion and, you know, statesmanlike views, and I respond to these good wishes, to a certain extent, and to the charming and, ahh, appropriate fairy tale—I mean, fairy-tale play—as I express thanks and and, ahh, a certain acknowledgment of your patriotism, to all who are charged with holding the weather service true to the needs of all the people. In that spirit, ahh, and to our dear fatherland and, of course, ahh, to our very fine Weather Bureau—hurrah! Hurrah! Hurrah! *(Sits down. The terrace, the* bureaucrats*, and the* members *of the parade all join in the cheer.* Trankhafen *and* Hornbriller *go over to* Wimmerzahn.*)*

Hornbriller: Herr President, along with the ovation of these enthusiastic admirers please accept our compliments as well. The eloquence of your rhetoric was exceptional, *sans phrase.*

Trankhafen: It was truly a statesmanlike speech.

Wimmerzahn: Danke, sehr aufmerksam, jawohl, danke. Auch Ihr Stück, sehr schön, wirklich sehr reizend, gewiß ja.

Hornbriller: Eine pittoreske poetische Allegorie.

Wimmerzahn: Ganz richtig, ja, sehr gut. Sie gehören der Kirchenpartei an, der Kirchenpartei, Fräulein Ministerialrätin, nicht wahr?

Trankhafen: Ich bin Sozialistin, Herr Präsident.

Wimmerzahn: Soso, Sozialistin, natürlich ja. Sehr ehrenwert, jawohl, sehr ehrenwert, wie Sie Ihre Gesinnung in dem Stück eben sozusagen zu verbergen gewußt haben.

Trankhafen: Zu liebenswürdig, Herr Präsident. Aber wo dem Staatswohl gedient werden soll, dürfen Überzeugungen keine Rolle spielen.

Krampf: Der Herr Abgeordnete Biederhold macht den Vorschlag, nunmehr den Kirchgang folgen zu lassen. Wie denken Herr Präsident darüber?

Wimmerzahn: Kirchgang? Jawohl, Gottesdienst, verstehe. Gewiß doch.

Stechbein: Vielleicht will noch einer der Herren vorher ein Glas Bier trinken; ich werde inzwischen das Notwendige anordnen.

Biederhold: Zu einem Gläschen hat es freilich Zeit. Aber dann gedenken wir unverweilt des Höchsten.

(Rechts der Kirche erscheint Schönbrod *an der Spitze einer* Bauern-abordnung.*)*

Schutzmann: Halt, hier kommt keiner mehr durch.

Schönbrod: Wir gehn da durch, daß Sie das man wissen.

Schutzmann: Es ist streng verboten, den Platz zu betreten..

Schönbrod: Das ist einerlei. So kriegen wir die nie wieder zusammen. Jetzt wird damit gesprochen.

Schutzmann: Keinen Schritt weiter, sag' ich.

Wimmerzahn: Thank you, you are very attentive, yes indeed, thank you. Your play, too, very nice, quite charming, certainly, ahh.

Hornbriller: A vivid poetic allegory.

Wimmerzahn: Quite right, yes, very good. I believe you belong to the Church Party, to the Church Party, Fräulein Ministerial Advisor, don't you?

Trankhafen: I am a Socialist, Herr President.

Wimmerzahn: Ah, I see, a Socialist, of course, yes. Very admirable, indeed, very admirable the way you were able to conceal any hints at your ideology in your play, so to speak.

Trankhafen: You're too kind, Herr President. But you know, when the good of the state must be served, there is no place for convictions.

Krampf: Delegate Biederhold has suggested that we walk over to the church now. What do you think of that, Herr President?

Wimmerzahn: To the church? Ah yes, worship service, I understand. Of course.

Stechbein: Perhaps some of the gentlemen would like to have a glass of beer beforehand. I will arrange everything.

Biederhold: Well of course, there's time for a quick one. But then we we will honor the Almighty right away.

(To the right of the church Schönbrod *appears leading a delegation of* farmers.)

Policeman: Stop. No one is allowed through here.

Schönbrod: Well, we're going through, you know.

Policeman: It is strictly forbidden for anyone to enter the square.

Schönbrod: I don't care. We'll never again have these people together in one place. We're going to speak with them now.

Policeman: I said don't take another step.

Hankte: Was ist denn da bei der Kirche los?

Niedermaier: Der alte Schönbrod. *(Polizeileutnant läuft hinzu.)*

Barde: Wirtschaft! Bier!

Paula: Bitte.

Krachhahn: Mir auch und einen Korn dazu.

Biederhold: Dann will ich mich doch ebenfalls stärken, liebes Fräulein.

Wachtel: Wollen Sie mir bitte einen Magenbittern bringen?

Paula: *(schreibt die Bestellung auf)* Sofort. *(Will gehen, sieht hinaus, geht an die Brüstung, bleibt gebannt stehen.)*

Barde: Wird's bald!—Was geht denn da hinten vor?

Leutnant: Zum letzten Mal, zurück!

Schönbrod: Wir wollen durch. Ich steh' für nichts.

Jenny: Es wird ernst, glaub' ich.

Schönbrod: Weg da! Vorwärts!

Leutnant: *(faßt ihn an die Brust)* Halt! *(Gibt Pfeifensignal. Schutzleute kommen im Laufschritt dazu.)*

Berta: Sie wollen den Schulzen verhaften!

Krachhahn: Scheint Klamauk zu geben da drüben. *(Paula läuft mit rascher Kehrtwendung ins Lokal.)*

Leutnant: Nehmen Sie den Alten fest! *(Schutzleute stürzen sich auf* Schönbrod.*)*

Niedermaier: Wir müssen ihm helfen!

Otti: Die Latte runter! *(Die Sperre wird durchbrochen. Alle laufen auf die* Polizisten *zu. Getümmel.)*

Speicherer: Das sieht ja ordentlich gefährlich aus da.

Möhre: Es werden wohl wieder Betrunkene sein.

Krachhahn: Genügend Polizei ist da. Brauchen uns nicht stören zu lassen. *(Paula kommt zurück, Tablett ohne Getränke in der Hand. Blickt angestrengt hinaus.)*

Hankte: What's going on over by the church?

Niedermaier: Herr Schönbrod. *(Police lieutenant runs over.)*

Barde: Waitress! Beer!

Paula: All right.

Krachhahn: Me too, and a whisky with it.

Biederhold: Then I think I'll have a little reinforcement as well, Fräulein.

Wachtel: Would you also please bring me some bitters?

Paula: *(Writes down the order.)* Right away. *(Starts to go, then looks out, goes to the banister, stands gazing intently.)*

Barde: Make it quick! What's going on back there?

Lieutenant: For the last time, get back!

Schönbrod: We're coming through. I'm not standing here.

Jenny: I think it's getting serious.

Schönbrod: Out of the way! Forward!

Lieutenant: *(Grabs him around the chest.)* Stop! *(Blows his whistle. Police officers run onto the scene.)*

Berta: They're trying to arrest the mayor!

Krachhahn: Looks like some hullaballoo over there. *(Paula turns quickly and runs into the restaurant.)*

Lieutenant: Arrest the old man! *(Officers jump on Schönbrod.)*

Niedermaier: We have to help him!

Otti: Tear down the fence! *(The barricade is broken down. Everyone runs toward the policemen. Pandemonium.)*

Speicherer: That looks downright dangerous.

Möhre: It's probably just some more drunkards.

Krachhahn: There are enough police there. We don't need to worry about it. *(Paula comes back carrying a tray without drinks. Glances outside intently.)*

Barde: Was heißt denn das? Bekommen wir nicht endlich unser Bier?

Paula: *(schmeißt ihr Tablett zwischen die* Abgeordneten.*)* Holt euch euer Gesöff selber! *(stürzt hinunter dem* Gedränge *zu)*

Trankhafen: Das ist ja unbeschreiblich.

Hornbriller: Man scheint aggressive Tendenzen zu haben.

Blödel: Ja, die Trunksucht, die leidige Trunksucht.

Leutnant: Zurück! *(Die* Schutzleute *werden von der* Masse *bedrängt, fangen an zu weichen.)* Pistolen heraus!

Niedermaier: Begehen Sie keine Unbesonnenheiten, Mensch!

Otti: Der ganze Platz ist voll von Unbeteiligten.

Leutnant: Gehn Sie eben aus dem Wege!

Niedermaier: Herr Polizeileutnant! Ich bin der Wetterrat Niedermaier.

Leutnant: *(stutzt)* Gut. Ich werde den Staatssekretär anfragen, ob ich die Leute durchlassen soll. *(spricht leise mit einem* Schutzmann, *der zur Terrasse läuft)*

Schönbrod: Dann wollen wir den Augenblick noch zuwarten. *(Die* Masse *bleibt in drohender Haltung stehen.)*

Schutzmann: *(vor der Terrasse)* Der Herr Leutnant läßt bitten, von der Schußwaffe Gebrauch machen zu lassen.

Barde: Na, selbstredend.

Krampf: Geschossen soll werden? Dagegen werden sich immerhin Bedenken geltend machen können.

Hustenreiz: Vor übereilten Schritten möchte ich doch warnen.

Krachhahn: Keine Schwäche gegen das Gesindel!

Möhre: Daß es nur nicht grade zum Geburtstag Tote gibt!

Stiefengrat: Ohne weiteres scharf schießen, wäre ja noch schöner.

Wachtel: Ach Gott, Schüsse können meine Darmnerven nicht aushalten.

Stechbein: Die ganze schöne Feier wird uns verdorben.

Barde: What's this all about? Are we not going to get some beer here?

Paula: *(Flings her tray into the group of* delegates.*)* Get your own beer! *(Rushes out to the* crowd.*)*

Trankhafen: That is unbelievable.

Hornbriller: She seems to have aggressive tendencies.

Blödel: Yes, alcoholism, miserable alcoholism.

Lieutenant: Get back! *(*Officers *are pressed by the* crowd, *begin to yield.)* Get pistols out!

Niedermaier: Man, don't do something stupid!

Otti: The whole square is full of innocent bystanders.

Lieutenant: I'm telling you to get out of the way!

Niedermaier: Lieutenant! I am Weather Councillor Niedermaier.

Lieutenant: *(Stops.)* All right. I'll ask the state secretary whether I should let these people through. *(Speaks quietly with an* officer, *who then runs to the terrace.)*

Schönbrod: Well, then we'll just wait here for a moment. *(The* crowd *stands still, threateningly.)*

Policeman: *(in front of the terrace)* The lieutenant requests permission to use firearms.

Barde: Well, of course.

Krampf: You want to start shooting? We need to carefully consider any objections to that first.

Hustenreiz: I would warn you against taking rash measures.

Krachhahn: Don't show that mob any weakness!

Möhre: Let's please not have dead bodies on this birthday!

Stiefengrat: I think it would be better to go ahead and shoot without delay.

Wachtel: Oh God, my stomach can't stand it if there's shooting.

Stechbein: This whole celebration is going to be spoiled.

Blödel: Wenn ich nicht irre, ist da an der Spitze der weißbärtige Unruhestifter von der Jubiläumsfeier wieder.

Trankhafen: Sie sind alle dabei, natürlich auch das rothaarige Frauenzimmer, ich habe sie eben deutlich erkannt.

Schutzmann: Soll denn nun geschossen werden?

Speicherer: Soll doch der Herr Staatspräsident selbst entscheiden. Ach so, er schläft.

Trankhafen: Um Gottes Willen, da läuft ja eine Fee mitten über den Platz.

Hornbriller: Das Terrain müßte vor der Offensiven sondiert werden, damit keine Passanten blessiert werden.

Selters: Der Herr Regierungsassessor sollte mit den Leuten verhandeln.

Biederhold: Vor allem, damit uns der Weg zur Kirche nicht versperrt wird.

Hornbriller: Disponieren Sie also, ob sie mich als Parlamentär zu den Demonstranten delegieren wollen.

Krampf: Widerspruch erhebt sich nicht.

Trankhafen: Ich will lieber mitgehn.

Krachhahn: Ein Dolmetscher wird nötig sein. *(Schutzmann mit* Hornbriller *und* Trankhafen *zur Polizeikette)*

Hornbriller: Ich kann es nur als Infamie charakterisieren, inmitten der Gratulationscour Tumulte zu inszenieren.

Schönbrod: Was wollen Sie hier? Wir wollen mit dem Minister sprechen.

Hornbriller: Ich bin als Mandatar der Regierung designiert. Dekuvrieren Sie Ihre Querelen.

Niedermaier: Unter vorgehaltenen Pistolen verhandeln wir nicht.

Trankhafen: Herr Polizeileutnant, lassen Sie die Waffen wegstecken. Der herr Staatspräsident wünscht an seinem Geburtstage keine Leichen.

Leutnant: Dann lehne ich jede Verantwortung ab.

Blödel: If I'm not mistaken, the ringleader is that white-haired rabblerouser from the cornerstone celebration once again.

Trankhafen: They're all there, including that red-haired woman, I saw her clearly.

Policeman: So should we shoot?

Speicherer: That's something for the state president to decide himself. Ah, wait, he's sleeping.

Trankhafen: Oh my God, there's a fairy running across the square.

Hornbriller: That area needs to be cordoned off from the area of the offensive, so that no passers-by are wounded.

Selters: The government assessor should negotiate with these people.

Biederhold: Just make sure that the path to the church is not blocked off.

Hornbriller: Decide among yourselves whether you wish to send me as a parliamentarian to speak with the demonstrators.

Krampf: I hear no objection.

Trankhafen: I'd like to come along.

Krachhahn: Yes, he'll need an interpreter. *(The* officer *goes with* Hornbriller *and* Trankhafen *to the police line.)*

Hornbriller: I can only characterize this as an infamy, the way you have staged this tumult in the middle of the congratulatory ceremony.

Schönbrod: What are you doing here? We want to speak with the minister.

Hornbriller: I have been delegated with a mandate from the government. What are your grievances?

Niedermaier: We will not negotiate with pistols pointed at us.

Trankhafen: Herr Lieutenant, have your men put their guns away. The president does not want any corpses on his birthday.

Lieutenant: Then I don't take any responsibility for what happens.

Hornbriller: Wer ist der spiritus rector der manifestation?

Schönbrod: Mit Ihnen haben wir nichts zu schaffen. Hundertmal haben wir nach einem von den Herren gefragt. Ja, Husten. Wenn die Geheimräte und Generäle vorfahren, dann springen sie alle. Heute sollen sie mal hören, was der Bauer denkt.

Niedermaier: Die Abordnung muß unbedingt vorgelassen werden. Werktätige, Erwerbslose, brotlos gemachte Landarbeiter fordern täglich Gehör bei denen, die sie zugrunde richten. Entschließungen gegen das Wetter werden massenhaft an das Wetteramt, an den Landtag, an die Regierung gesandt—

Otti: —und garnicht gelesen.

Niedermaier: Zu uns kommen sie dann und klagen. Aber wir müssen ja die Befehle des Amtes ausführen, so blödsinnig und verbrecherisch sie sind.

Hornbriller: Herr Diplomingenieur, Sie wählen despektierliche Vokabeln. Ich bin konsterniert, Sie als Advokaten für diese Revolteure plädieren zu hören.

Trankhafen: Ihr Auftreten hat natürlich die fristlose Entlassung zur Folge.

Fischer: Dann schmeißen Sie uns nur alle raus. Das ganze Werk steht hinter Herrn Niedermaier.

Trankhafen: Wer an diesem Aufruhr teilnimmt, kann sich als entlassen betrachten. *(Gelächter)*

Otti: Morgen stellen Sie sich wohl an die Maschine.

Trankhafen: Kein Mensch ist unersetzlich.

Paula: Sie bei Ihrem Stechbein gewiß nicht.

Annie: Der will mit jeder schmieren.

Trankhafen: Elende!

Hornbriller: Auf der Basis ordinärer Insinuationen können wir nicht diskutieren.

Hornbriller: Who is the *spiritus rector* of this demonstration?

Schönbrod: We don't have any business to conduct with you. We have asked to speak with one of these gentlemen a hundred times or more. Yes, go ahead and cough. When the privy councillors and generals drive past they all jump. Today they're going to hear what farmers think.

Niedermaier: This delegation absolutely must be allowed to proceed through. Day in and day out these workers, these unemployed people, these starving farmers have been demanding a hearing before those that are causing them ruin. Resolutions and petitions against the weather have been sent in bundles to the Weather Bureau, to the provincial parliament, to the government—

Otti: —and they're never even read.

Niedermaier: Then the people come to us and complain. But we are required to carry out the orders of the Bureau, even if these orders are stupid and criminal.

Hornbriller: Herr Engineer, your choice of words is quite disrespectful. It consternates me to hear you plead as an advocate of these rebels.

Trankhafen: The consequence of your appearance here will be, of course, your immediate dismissal.

Fischer: Then you'll have to throw us all out. The whole weather works stands with Herr Niedermaier.

Trankhafen: Whoever takes part in this uprising can consider himself fired. *(laughter)*

Otti: And I suppose you'll be standing in front of the machines tomorrow?

Trankhafen: No one is indispensable.

Paula: You certainly aren't as far as Stechbein's concerned.

Annie: He's trying to seduce every woman in the place.

Trankhafen: You miserable rabble!

Hornbriller: We cannot continue this discussion on the basis of these common insinuations.

Schönbrod: Wir haben ihr Geschnack auch längst satt. Sollen wir nu zu den Herren hin oder nicht?

Trankhafen: Das kann gar nicht in Betracht kommen.

Hornbriller: Ein kompletter Nonsense.

Schönbrod: Also los, Kinnings! *(Lärm. Die* Schutzleute *werden abgedrängt. Die* Masse *dringt vor.)*

Hornbriller: Herr Polizeileutnant, kommandieren Sie doch zur Attacke.

Leutnant: Wenn ich nicht schießen lassen kann, geht mich die ganze Geschichte nichts weiter an. Antreten. Links um—marsch! *(Die Polizei marschiert ab. Die Menge geht mit dem Ausdruck verhaltener Entschlossenheit bis etwa zur Leiter. Die Beamten neben der Terrasse drücken sich nach rückwärts, viele verschwinden. Vereinzelte Masken schwirren ängstlich umher.)*

Stechbein: Was soll das bedeuten?

Steinbott: O, wir wolln bloß auch'n bißchen was abhaben von der Geburtstagsfeier.

Wimmerzahn: Wollen gewiß gratulieren kommen, die guten Leute, natürlich ja. Danke, danke schön.

Blödel: Aber es ist offener Aufstand, Herr Präsident!

Wimmerzahn: Aufstand? Nicht möglich, Herr Minister Blödel. Sehr gut, Aufstand! Nein doch, sehr gut.

Stiefengrat: Warum geschieht denn nichts zur Abwehr? Werde mal selber—*(geht hinunter)* Wer wagt hier, sich gegen die Obrigkeit aufzulehnen? Unerhörte Frechheit! Ich befehle—

Wolff: Hanswurst! *(gibt ihm eine Ohrfeige)*

Stiefengrat: *(taumelt zurück)* Das mir! Herr Staatspräsidcent, verhängen Sie augenblicklich das Standrecht!

Wachtel: Entsetzlich! Fräulein—ach Gott, wo ist denn das Fräulein? Den Schlüssel bitte! *(irrt suchend ins Lokal)*

Schönbrod: *(ist auf die Leiter gestiegen)* Ruhe mal!

Paula: Ruhe für Vater Schönbrod!

Schönbrod: We're tired of your good manners. Are we going to speak to the gentlemen or not?

Trankhafen: That is out of the question.

Hornbriller: Absolute nonsense.

Schönbrod: All right, let's go, kids! *(Noise. The* police *are pushed back. The* mob *presses forward.)*

Hornbriller: Lieutenant, prepare to attack!

Lieutenant: If I can't let them shoot, then I'll have nothing more to do with this thing. Attention! Left face! Forward march! *(The* police *march offstage. The* crowd *moves resolutely up to approximately where the ladder stands. The* bureaucrats *next to the terrace withdraw, many of them disappear. A few* participants *in the parade mill about nervously.)*

Stechbein: What does this mean?

Steinbott: Oh, we just wanted to join in the birthday celebration a little bit.

Wimmerzahn: I'm sure they want to come and congratulate me, the good people. Of course, yes. Thank you, thank you very much.

Blödel: But this is an open rebellion, Herr President!

Wimmerzahn: Rebellion? Impossible, Minister Blödel! That's funny, rebellion! Really, that's very funny.

Stiefengrat: Why are no defensive measures being taken? I'll go myself— *(Goes down.)* Who here dares to defy the authorities? This is unheard of! I order you—

Wolff: You clown! *(Slaps him.)*

Stiefengrat: *(Stumbles backwards.)* What are you doing to me? Herr President, declare martial law immediately!

Wachtel: This is terrible! Waitress! — Oh God, where is the waitress? The key, please! *(Stumbles around in the restaurant, searching.)*

Schönbrod: *(He has climbed up onto the ladder.)* Quiet!

Paula: Quiet for Grandpa Schönbrod!

Stechbein: *(vor der Terrasse)* Der Herr Ortsschulze wünscht, sein Anliegen vorzutragen.

Biederhold: Läßt sich das nicht hinausschieben? Wir wollten doch grade zum Gottesdienst aufbrechen.

Otti: Ihr Herrgott wird wohl in einer halben Stunde auch noch zu sprechen sein.

Schönbrod: Hätten Sie uns gleich vorgelassen, und nicht die Polizei gegen uns gejagt, dann hätten wir auch mit uns sprechen lassen. Jetzt reden wir, wann und wie wir das bestimmen. Das Maß ist voll.

Hantke: Ja, das Maß ist voll.

Schönbrod: Ihr Präsident soll das selber hören.

Peters: Der schläft ja.

Schönbrod: Auch recht. Ich wollt' bloß sagen, als der auf die Welt kam vor vierundsiebzig Jahren, da hab' ich hier in meinem Heimatdorf all Vieh gehütet. Hier bin ich Knecht gewesen und Großknecht und Bauer geworden und das ist über dreißig Jahr, daß sie mich zum Schulzen gewählt haben. Ich weiß hier Bescheid. Denn ein Dorfschulze ist kein Bonze, wie man das wohl nennt. Der karrt seinen Mist auf den Acker wie alle. Das ist kein leichtes Brot und dazumal konnten sie das Wetter noch nicht selber machen. Denn gab es mal zuviel Naß für die Kartoffeln und denn verhagelte mal der Hafer, oder daß die Hitze zu doll war und immer bloß Sonne so wie jetzt, und eh daß wir heuen und ernten konnten, war alles verbrannt. Das kam ja vor, aber im allgemeinen war Verlaß auf die Natur und wir wußten doch, wann Frühling und Herbst war und Sommer und Winter. Aber nach dem großen Krieg ist der Himmel ja wohl selber verrückt geworden. Hatten sie nu mit all dem Knallen die Stratosphäre oder wie das Ding heißt, durcheinander gefuhrwerkt oder kommt das von dem Radio, wo sie um die ganze Erde mit rumfunken. Ich weiß das nicht. Na, zu Niedermaier seiner Erfindung war es nachgrade hohe Zeit, und da hatten wir ja das Glück, daß wir den Turm hierher kriegten. Die paar Jahre, wo der hier das Wetter bestellt hat mit der roten Otti und Peilmeister Peters und allen andern, und wir all zusammen das in der Genossenschaft besprachen, und daß auch anderswo immer die rechte Zeit war, das waren die schönsten Jahre in meinem langen Leben. Nicht eine

Stechbein: *(in front of the terrace)* The village mayor wishes to present his concerns.

Biederhold: Can't that be postponed? We need to get over to the church service.

Otti: You'll still be able to speak to your Lord God in a half an hour.

Schönbrod: If you had let us through right away and not sent the police against us, then we would have discussed it with you. Now we are going to speak whenever and wherever we want. We've had enough.

Hantke: Yes, we've had enough.

Schönbrod: Your president might want to hear this himself.

Peters: He's asleep.

Schönbrod: Well, never mind. I just wanted to say that when he came into the world seventy-four years ago, I was tending cows here in my village. I was a farm-hand, then a farm foreman and then a farmer, and thirty years ago they elected me village mayor. I know what's going on here. See, a village mayor isn't a politico, as we say. He spreads his manure on his own fields like everybody else. That's not an easy way to make a living, and on top of that we couldn't do anything about the weather back then. Sometimes it was too wet for potatoes, or sometimes hailstorms knocked down our oats, or sometimes there was nothing but heat and sunshine all the time, just like now. And before we could make hay and get in the harvest everything was burned up in the field. That happened sometimes. But mostly we went along with nature, and we knew when spring was, and fall and summer and winter. But after the great war the skies seemed to go crazy. Maybe all that banging and shooting messed up something in the stratosphere, or whatever it's called, or maybe it comes from radio, the way they send their signals all around the earth. I don't know anything about that. Well, when Niedermaier came up with his invention it was high time for it, and we were lucky enough to get the weather tower right here. Those couple of years when he was controlling the weather with Red Otti and Peters the soundings man and everybody else, and when we all got together in the collective and talked it over, and when it worked out for people everywhere else—those were the best years of my whole

Mißernte, nein, der Boden gab dreimal mehr her und im ganzen Land
haben sie fremde Früchte angebaut, die sonst wohl bloß da wachsen,
wo der Doktor da seine Sprache gelernt hat. *(Heiterkeit)* Na, und
danach haben Sie uns ja die Kirche hergesetzt und die Terrasse da und
den Steinbaukasten und den ganzen Kram, und das Werk haben Sie
von der Gemeinde weggerissen, wenn Ihnen das auch man schwach
geglückt ist, denn zusammenstehn tun wir doch, das sehn Sie ja. Aber
unserm Niedermaier haben Sie sein eigen Werk aus den Fingern
gespielt und er muß das mit ansehn, wie hier die Regierungsräte und
Parteisekretäre umspringen und das ganze Pack, das da mit
Zylinderhüten rumsteht und sich weiß Gott was einbildet auf
Dummheit und Niedertracht.

Krampf: So dürfen Sie aber nicht von ehrenwerten Beamten sprechen.

Schönbrod: Ich sprech' wie mir der Schnabel gewachsen ist. Und die
ehrenwerten Beamten! Wie sieht es auf unsern Feldern aus? Zur
Aussaat eine Sandwüste und zur Erntezeit ein Schwimmbad. Und so
im ganzen Land. Was waren hier frohe Menschen. Und jetzt? Die
Genossenschaft kann keinen Auftrag mehr weggeben. Die Männer
arbeitslos, die Frauen schleichen rum und wissen nicht, wie sie 'ne
Suppe auf den Tisch bringen. Und die Kinder haben Hunger und die
englische Krankheit. Das hat nu aber lange genug gedauert. Wem
keiner helfen will, muß sich selber helfen. Sonst ist ihm nicht zu
helfen.

Jenny: Selbsthilfe, ja!

Wolff: Aber nicht wieder bis wer weiß wann warten.

Stechbein: Drohungen haben doch keinen Wert. Nennen Sie Ihre
Forderungen. Das Wetteramt wird sich nicht unzugänglich zeigen.

Schönbrod: Bis jetzt hat das Wetteramt seine gepolsterten Kanzleitüren
noch nie für uns aufgemacht. Und nun wollen Sie wissen, was wir
verlangen. Das will ich Ihnen sagen. Die Leute, die das Werk
geschaffen haben, sollen auch im Werk zu sagen haben. Der Turm
kommt an das Volk zurück, und wie das Wetter wird, bestimmen wir
selber. Der Staatssekretär mit allen Schüsselfressern, mit allen
Nichtstuern und Antreibern und Klugscheißern, die nichts gelernt
haben als Papier vollschmieren, Feste feiern und den Armen die Haut
von den Knochen ziehn,—die gehen allesamt dahin zurück, wo sie

life. Never a bad harvest, the earth gave us three times as much as before, and all over the country they planted foreign fruits, things that otherwise only grow where that doctor there learned to speak. *(Laughter.)* Well, and then they came and built that church there and the terrace and those concrete boxes and this whole mess, and they tore the weather works away from the village. Of course, that didn't do you much good, because you can see that we still stand together. But you took our friend Niedermaier's very own weather works out of his hands. Now he has to stand here and watch all these government councillors and party secretaries hop around here, and this whole bunch of big shots with their top hats standing around thinking up God knows what kind of idiocy.

Krampf: You may not speak this way about worthy civil servants.

Schönbrod: I'll speak whatever way it comes out of my mouth. And the honorable bureaucrats! What does it look like now in our fields? When we're sowing it's a desert, and when we're harvesting it's a swimming pool. And it's like this all over the country. We were once happy people here. And now? We can't even give away contracts on our crops. The men are all out of work, the women mope around and don't know how they're going to put soup on the table. And the children are all starving and have rickets. That's gone on now for too long. If no one will help us, we have to help ourselves. Otherwise we'll get no help.

Jenny: Yeah, self-help!

Wolff: But we're not going to keep waiting till who knows when.

Stechbein: Threats will get you nowhere. State your demands. The Weather Bureau will prove capable of responding.

Schönbrod: Up to now the Weather Bureau hasn't even opened its upholstered chancery doors for us. And now you want to know what we demand. I'll tell you what. The people who made these weather works should also have a say in how they're run. The tower needs to be returned to the people, and we'll decide ourselves what the weather will be. As far as the state secretary is concerned, with all his idlers and whip-crackers and know-it-alls who never learned anything but how to fill out forms, go to parties, and cheat the poor—these guys all need to go back where they came from. The collective gets all its rights back

hergekommen sind. Die Genossenschaft wird in alle Rechte wieder eingesetzt und morgen früh ist Herr Niedermaier Leiter der ganzen Anlagen   und läßt endlich den Regen fallen, den unser Acker und unser Vieh braucht. *(Steigt von der Leiter herunter. Viele schütteln ihm die Hand.)*

Hantke: Jetzt müssen wir aber dahinter stehen. Genossen, ich bin Landarbeiter, und das sollen die Herrschaften da sich merken: unter uns hier ist nicht einer, Bauer oder Arbeiter, Mann oder Frau, der nicht wüßte, was er zu tun hat, wenn es hier nicht sofort anders wird.

Speicherer: Das ist ja allerlei.

Stechbein: Sie wollen uns doch nicht im Ernst zumuten, daß wir die uns auf Grund der Verfassung anvertrauten Ämter einfach im Stich lassen!

Otti: Grade das muten wir Ihnen zu. Und zwar fristlos.

Hornbriller: Ein rabiates, auf dem Vulgäreffekt spekulierendes Ultimatum.

Möhre: Wie Menschen nur so undankbar sein können!

Hustenreiz: Die Bewegung zeigt, daß das Wetteramt unter andre Leitung gehört.

Niedermaier: *(ist auf die Leiter gestiegen)* Freunde! Genossen!

Rufe: Hoch Niedermaier! Nieder mit dem Wetteramt! Nieder mit der Regierung!

Niedermaier: Der Staatssekretär hat sich auf die demokratische Verfassung bezogen. Die Demokratie gilt für die herrschende Macht grade so lange, wie sie ihr nützt. Die Partei, die eben die demokratische Mehrheit hat, ist, weil die Arbeiter sie gewählt haben, einfach von jeder Mitbestimmung ausgeschlossen worden. An diesen Methoden ändern wir nichts, wenn wir den demokratischen Einrichtungen andre Leiter geben. Die Staatsämter sind nur dazu da, Bonzen zu ernähren, und das Wetteramt hat gewiß keine edleren Aufgaben. Wir brauchen keinen Ersatz für den Staatssekretär Stechbein und die Ministerialrätin Dr. Trankhafen. Ein Chauffeur auf dem Bock macht aus einer Eselsfuhre kein Automobil. Weg mit der ganzen Bescherung! Weg mit der Kuponschere von unserer Arbeit!

again, and tomorrow morning Herr Niedermaier will be the director of the whole operation, so he can finally bring the rain we need for our fields and livestock. *(Climbs down from the ladder. Several people shake his hand.)*

Hantke: But now we need to stand behind that statement. Comrades, I'm a farm worker, and I say the gentlemen need to mark this: there's not a single person here among us, farmer or worker, man or woman, who doesn't know what will have to be done if things don't change around here right now.

Speicherer: That's really a bit much.

Stechbein: You certainly don't seriously expect us to simply give up these offices which were assigned to us according to the constitution!

Otti: That's exactly what we expect. Immediately.

Hornbriller: What a rabid, vulgar ultimatum! She's just playing to the crowd!

Möhre: How ungrateful people can be!

Hustenreiz: This movement shows that the Weather Bureau should be under different leadership.

Niedermaier: *(He has climbed onto the ladder.)* Friends! Comrades!

Shouts: Hurrah for Niedermaier! Down with the Weather Bureau! Down with the government!

Niedermaier: The state secretary just referred to the democratic constitution. The ruling class is all for democracy, but only as long as it's to their advantage. The party that has a democratic majority right now has been excluded from any decision making, only because workers elected it. We won't change anything about these methods as long as we just put new leaders into these "democratic institutions." State offices just exist so that big shots can make a living, and the Weather Bureau doesn't have any more noble purpose than that. We don't need a replacement for State Secretary Stechbein and Ministerial Advisor Trankhafen. A chauffeur in the driver's seat can't turn a donkey cart into an automobile. Let's do away with the whole mess! Let's do away with all this speculation on our labor!

Rufe: Nieder! Weg damit!

Niedermaier: Wo ein Amt waltet, hat das leben keinen Atem. Bürolampen schaffen keinen Sonnenschein, aus Tintenfässern fließt kein fruchtbarer Regen, von Aktenstaub steigt kein frischer Wind auf. Unsere Hand hat die Wettermaschinen entworfen, unsere Hand stellt ihre Hebel. Aber Bürokratie und politischer Schacher hat Fesseln um unsere Hand gelegt, und so ist aus dem Segen der Menschheit ein Fluch der Menschheit geworden. Wir wollten die Fruchtbarkeit des Bodens vervielfachen um der Freiheit des Volkes willen; sie aber schänden das Werk und lassen künstlich die Erde verdorren, um des Wuchers willen, um dem Volk das Brot, den Kindern die Milch zu verteuern. Wir haben gewarnt und man wollte nicht hören. Wir haben gefordert und man hat uns die Tür gewiesen. Zum ersten Male stehen wir den Spitzen des Staates und der Wetterbehörde Auge in Auge gegenüber. Wir mußten uns den Zugang zu ihnen gewaltsam erzwingen. Jetzt aber frage ich die Regierung: Wollen Sie, die Sie nicht zur Arbeit hier versammelt sind, sondern zur Geburtstagsfeier—wollen Sie gutwillig dem Volke zurückgeben, was dem Volke gehört? Wollen Sie widerstandslos das Werk, das Sie nicht geschaffen haben und das Sie nicht braucht, verlassen, damit es die Zwecke erfüllen kann, für die es bestimmt ist und die fern von Ihren Zwecken und Gedanken sind? Wollen Sie ohne zu feilschen und bedingungslos den Platz räumen, der Ihnen nicht gebührt und den Sie ohne die Hilfe vom Geld- und Waffenmacht niemals hätten besetzen können? Die Bauern und Arbeiter hier sind die wahren Besizter dieser Anlagen, sie sind die Träger der Genossenschaft, der sie die Früchte ernster und freudiger Arbeit geraubt haben. Diese Arbeiter und Bauern sind entschlossen, heute das ihrige zurückzunehmen. Ihre Geduld ist am Ende, ihr Ingrimm groß. Sie kennen jetzt unsere Forderungen, entscheiden Sie sich!

Hornbriller: Ein Nonplusultra der Arroganz!

Hustenreiz: Wir müssen uns doch wenigstens beraten können.

Niedermaier: Wenn es sehr schnell geht, bitte. Aber wir spaßen nicht.

Krampf: Wir unterbrechen demzufolge die Geburtstagsordnung und treten in die Aussprache ein. *(Die* Demonstranten *verteilen sich in losen Gruppen über den Platz.)*

Shouts: Down with it! Throw it out!

Niedermaier: Wherever an office runs the show, then life can't flourish. Desk lamps don't make sunshine, rain doesn't fall from inkwells, wind doesn't blow through dusty file folders. Our hands designed the weather machines, our hands turned the switches. But the bureaucrats and political players have locked our hands in chains, and so this blessing to humanity has become a curse on humanity. We wanted to multiply the fruits of the earth for the sake of the people; but they have desecrated these weather works and artificially caused a drought for the sake of money, in order to make bread more expensive for the common people, to make milk too expensive for children. We warned them and they didn't listen to us. We made demands and they showed us the door. For the first time we are standing face to face with the leaders of the state and the weather authorities. We had to force them to give us access to them. But now I ask the government: will you politicians, who are gathered here not to work but to celebrate a birthday—will you willingly give back to the people that which belongs to the people? Will you leave this installation without resisting us, this operation that you didn't build and that you don't need, will you leave here so that it can fulfill its purpose for the ones for whom it was created, those whose goals and thoughts are so far from your own? Will you leave this place unconditionally, without haggling, this place that is not meant for you, this place you would never have been able to occupy without the power of your money and weapons? The farmers and workers are the true owners of this installation, they are the members of the collective from which you robbed the fruits of honest and cheerful labor. These farmers and workers are determined to retake that which belongs to them today. Their patience is at an end, their anger is great. Now you know our demands, make a decision!

Hornbriller: This is the *ne plus ultra* of arrogance!

Hustenreiz: We at least need to talk it over.

Niedermaier: If you can do it quickly, go ahead. But we aren't joking.

Krampf: We'll interrupt the birthday celebration and convene a discussion. *(The* demonstrators *disperse into small groups on the square.)*

Selters: Angesichts der bedrohlichen Lage werden wir gezwungen-ermaßen einlenken müssen.

Speicherer: Es kommt in diesem Augenblick nur auf eins an: Zeit gewinnen!

Möhre: Vielleicht können wir sie bis nach dem Kirchgang hinhalten.

Stechbein: Den Schein unserer Autorität müssen wir um jeden Preis wahren.

Hornbriller: Ein prekäres Problem. Durch blamable Konzessionen könnte sich die Regierung irreparabel diskreditieren.

Stiefengrat: Man muß die Unbotmäßigen zu Paaren treiben.

Hornbriller: Die Statuierung eines Exempels wäre allerdings ein Risiko; ein Desaster wäre eine Katastrophe von garnicht taxierbaren Dimensionen.

Stiefengrat: Mit der Krapüle verhandelt man nicht.

Hustenreiz: Exzellenz, ich bin immerhin Sozialist.

Barde: *(hüstelnd)* Auch ich möchte darauf hinweisen, daß mich das Programm meiner Partei zu einer gewissen Arbeiterfreundlichkeit verpflichtet.

Krachhahn: Wenn die Geschichte allerdings schon so steht, dann werden wir ja wohl erst mit dem Zuckerbrot kommen müssen. Wie wär's denn, wenn der Herr Staatssekretär oder meinetwegen der Minister selbst erklären würde, daß morgen ein Ministerrat die Angelegenheit in besonderer Sitzung beschnarchen wird?

Trankhafen: Der Herr Abgeordnete von Krachhahn täuscht sich über den Ernst der Lage. Die Leute sind viel zu gereizt, als daß sie ohne Zusage auseinander gehen. würden.

Stechbein: Ich kann doch aber nicht hier auf dem Festplatz ohne weiteres das Wetteramt auflösen und die Beamten, die sich grade zum Kirchgang rüsten, ihre Entlassung mitteilen.

Hornbriller: Eine groteske Idee, die Administration solle stante pede in corpore san façon demissionieren. Direkt ridikül.

Selters: In view of our precarious situation we are forced to yield somewhat.

Speicherer: There is only one thing to do right now: play for time!

Möhre: Maybe we can hold them off until the next church service.

Stechbein: We must preserve the appearance of our authority in any event.

Hornbriller: This is a tricky problem. The government could discredit itself irreparably by making embarrassing concessions.

Stiefengrat: We need to back these insubordinates up against a wall.

Hornbriller: To be sure, staging an example would be a great risk. If it turned bad we would have a catastrophe of unimaginable dimensions.

Stiefengrat: You don't have to negotiate with corpses.

Hustenreiz: Your Excellency, I am a Socialist after all.

Barde: *(clearing his throat)* I would like to point out, too, that my party's platform calls for a certain friendliness to workers.

Krachhahn: If the situation is already this bad, then we probably need to come back to them with some tidbit. How about if the state secretary, or even the minister himself, declares that a ministerial council would take up the matter tomorrow morning in a special session?

Trankhafen: Delegate von Krachhahn is deceiving himself as to the seriousness of the situation. These people are already much too excited to leave without receiving acceptance of their demands.

Stechbein: But I can't just go ahead on my own and dissolve the Weather Bureau here on the square and dismiss all the bureaucrats. They're getting ready for the church service even as we speak.

Hornbriller: A grotesque idea, that the administration should be decommissioned *stante pede in corpore sans façon.* Absolutely ridiculous.

Biederhold: Wenn der Herr Minister für Ruhe, Ordnung und Sicherheit dazu bereit wäre, so glaube ich, wird es am zweckdienlichsten sein, er gäbe namens des Staatspräsidenten—wir brauchen ihn dazu nicht im Schlummer zu stören—die Erklärung ab, die Staatsregierung werde morgen zusammentreten und die Forderungen in wohlwollende Erwägung ziehen. Er kann dabei nötigenfalls gleich zusichern, daß von Maßregelungen Abstand genommen werden soll.

Selters: Ausgezeichnet. Das ist ein in jeder Hinsicht befriedigender Vorschlag.

Speicherer: Ja, so geben wir nichts aus der Hand und gewinnen Zeit.

Hustenreiz: Würdige Festigkeit gepaart mit weiser Mäßigung.

Hornbriller: Und im Effekt mit eminenter Psychologie auf die Massenmentalität ausbalanziert.

Blödel: Der Herr Staatssekretär wird mir wohl bei dem schweren Gang zur Seite stehen.

Krampf: Wenn sich kein Widerspruch erhebt—

Stiefengrat: Elende Krebserei! Ich telephoniere nach Truppen. *(Ab.* Blödel *und* Stechbein *treten vor die Terrasse.)*

Wolff: Genossen! Aufpassen! *(Die* Menge *sammelt sich.)*

Brunner: Letztes Auftreten der Wetterborner Komiker!

Stechbein: Der Herr Minister für Ruhe, Ordnung und Sicherheit, Herr Doktor Blödel, wünscht im Namen des Herrn Staatspräsidenten—

Paula: Der schläft ja.

Stechbein: —sowie der Regierung eine Erklärung abzugeben.

Steinbott: Man zu!

Blödel: Die Staatsregierung als die Sachverwalterin und Vertraute des ganzen Volkes—

Jenny: So seht ihr aus.

Blödel: —ist von jeher von dem Bestreben erfüllt, berechtigten Wünschen desselben weittunlichst Rechnung zu tragen. Sie verschließt

Biederhold: If the minister for law, order and security were willing, I believe it would be most expedient if he made a declaration on behalf of the president—we don't need to rouse him from his slumber—stating that the state government will convene tomorrow and favorably consider the demands. If necessary he can assure at the same time that we will desist from applying any disciplinary measures.

Selters: Excellent. That is a satisfactory solution in every respect.

Speicherer: Yes, this way we don't give up anything right away, and we gain time.

Hustenreiz: Dignified resolution coupled with wise moderation.

Hornbriller: And balanced with the psychological principles of mass thinking.

Blödel: I trust that the state secretary will stand at my side as I make this very difficult walk.

Krampf: If there is no objection—

Stiefengrat: Miserable cowards! I'll telephone for troops. *(Off.* Blödel *and* Stechbein *step onto the terrace.)*

Wolff: Comrades! Listen! *(A* crowd *assembles.)*

Brunner: The last appearance of the comedians of Weatherspring!

Stechbein: The minsiter for law, order and security, Dr. Blödel, on behalf of the state president—

Paula: He's asleep.

Stechbein: —as well as the government, would now like to make a declaration.

Steinbott: Let's hear it!

Blödel: The state government, as the protector and voice of the people—

Jenny: That's just what you look like.

Blödel: —will endeavour from this moment on to give full consideration to the legitimate wishes of the people. Therefore the

sich daher keineswegs der Erwägung, daß das bei der gegenwärtigen freudigen Veranlassung zutage getretene Mißvergnügen einiger ortsansäßiger Personen—

Hantke: Aller!

Blödel: —sowie eines Teiles der technischen Belegschaft des Wetterturms—

Fischer: Der ganzen!

Blödel: —in gewisser Hinsicht vielleicht nicht vollständig jeder Begründung entbehren mag.

Otti: Zu gütig.

Blödel: Es ist daher in gemeinsamer Beratung mit der Leitung des Wetteramtes und den Vertretern sämtlicher staatsbejahender Landtagsparteien von dem Herrn Staatspräsidenten das folgende angeordnet worden: Bereits am morgigen Tag tritt der Ministerrat unter Vorsitz des Herrn Staatspräsidenten und unter Hinzuziehung aller in Betracht kommenden Behörden und Wirtschaftsvertretungen zu einer außerordentlichen Sitzung zusammen *(Gelächter)*, um eingehend zu den hier vorgebrachten Anregungen Stellung zu nehmen *(verstärktes Lachen, Pfiffe)*. Ich will gleich bemerken, daß die Regierung gewillt ist, nicht nur Ihre Wünsche in wohlwollende Erwägung zu ziehen *(stürmisches Gelächter)*, sondern auch von Maßregelungen wegen der Zusammenrottung hier in hochherziger Weise Abstand zu nehmen. *(brausendes Gelächter, großer Lärm)*

Niedermaier: Das ist alles?

Stechbein: Das ist wohl ein Höchstmaß des Entgegenkommens. *(wendet sich mit* Blödel *zur Terrasse zurück)*

Niedermaier: Otti, du weißt Bescheid. Peters, Fischer—marsch! *(*Niedermaier, Peters *und* Fischer *im Laufschritt in den Turm)*

Stechbein: Diese Menschen sind anscheinend noch immer nicht zufrieden.

Blödel: Unbegreiflich.

Wolff: Jetzt rauf zur Terrasse!

government can by no means overlook the fact that certain unpleasant incidents caused by some residents of this village—

Hantke: By all of them!

Blödel: —as well as by a part of the technical staff of the weather tower—

Fischer: The whole staff!

Blödel: —may well not have been entirely without valid reasons.

Otti: You're too kind.

Blödel: Therefore, in joint consultation with the management of the Weather Bureau and the representatives of all parties of the provincial parliament that are loyal to the state, the following has been resolved by the state president, to wit: no later than tomorrow the ministerial council, under the chairmanship of the state president and including all pertinent authorities and representatives of economic interests, will convene in extraordinary session *(laughter)*, for the purpose of establishing the government's position on the requests that have been made here. *(louder laughter, whistles, boos)* I would like to note that the government is not only willing to give favorable consideration to these wishes *(roaring laughter)*, but also generously to defer any disciplinary action related to today's mass demonstration. *(thunderous laughter, loud noise)*

Niedermaier: That's all?!?

Stechbein: We are being extraordinarily obliging. *(Returns with* Blödel *to the terrace.)*

Niedermaier: Otti, you know what to do. Peters, Fischer—forward march! (Niedermaier, Peters, *and* Fischer *run to the tower.)*

Stechbein: Apparently these people still aren't satisfied.

Blödel: Unbelievable.

Wolff: Let's go up to the terrace!

Steinbott: Holt die Sensen!

Berta: Zündet die Bude an!

Hantke: Ruhig Blut. Nicht jeder einzeln vorgehn. Was geschieht, müssen wir gemeinsam machen. *(Lebhafte Auseinandersetzungen)*

Otti: Vater Schönbrod, ein Wort bitte. *(spricht leise mit ihm)*

Trankhafen: Es scheint leider noch keine Beruhigung eingetreten zu sein.

Wachtel: *(aus dem Innern des Lokals tretend)* Und keine Bedienung. Ich habe schon die Herrentoilette benutzen müssen.

Hustenreiz: Was wollen wir tun? Ich fürchte das Schlimmste.

Krachhahn: Quatsch! Bloß nicht nie Nerven verlieren!

Hornbriller: Contenance!

Möhre: Wir wollen lieber beten.

Biederhold: Gottvertrauen—das ist das Gebot der Stunde.

Otti: Kommt mal näher, Genossen. Hört zu. Dichter heran, die brauchen nicht zu hören.

Annie: Kommt doch, hört, was Otti sagt. *(Getuschel)*

Speicherer: Die sind ja so still geworden.

Stechbein: Sie beraten. Dann ist noch nichts verloren.

Hornbriller: Ein Symptom, daß sie deroutiert sind.

Blödel: So hat die Erklärung doch ihren Eindruck nicht verfehlt.

Stiefengrat: *(kommt wütend aus dem Lokal)* Sauwirtschaft! Die Leitung ist entzwei. Ich kriege keine Verbindung mit den militärischen Stellen.

Otti: Genossen, nehmt euch zusammen. Jetzt keine Gewalt. Es wird alles recht werden.

Jenny: Wir dürfen ihnen doch keine Zeit lassen, bis sie nach Soldaten telefoniert haben.

Paula: Das können sie nicht, ich habe die Leitung durchgeschnitten.

Schönbrod: Das war nicht dumm von dir, lütte Paula.

Steinbott: Get the scythes!

Berta: Burn the place down!

Hantke: Wait, settle down. Don't everyone go off on your own. Whatever we do, we must do together. *(animated arguments)*

Otti: Grandpa Schönbrod, could I have a word with you? *(She speaks with him quietly.)*

Trankhafen: Unfortunately it seems that they haven't yet gotten quiet.

Wachtel: *(coming out from inside the restaurant)* And no service. I had to use the men's toilet.

Hustenreiz: What should we do? I fear the worst.

Krachhahn: Nonsense! Just don't lose your nerve!

Hornbriller: Contenance! We must maintain our composure.

Möhre: We'd be better off praying.

Biederhold: Trust in God—that's our motto now.

Otti: Come here, comrades, gather around. Come closer, we don't need them to hear this.

Annie: Come on, listen to what Otti's saying. *(whispering)*

Speicherer: They've gotten so quiet all of a sudden.

Stechbein: They're discussing the matter. We haven't lost anything yet.

Hornbriller: A sign that they are distracted.

Blödel: So our declaration did have an effect, after all.

Stiefengrat: *(Comes out of the restaurant furiously.)* This hole of a restaurant! The connection is broken! I can't get through to the military positions!

Otti: Comrades, stick together. We don't need violence now. Everything will be all right.

Jenny: We mustn't give them enough time for them to call for troops.

Paula: They can't do that, I cut the lines.

Schönbrod: That was pretty smart, little Paula.

Otti: Laßt mich mal mit ihnen tun, was ich will.

Steinbott: Wir haben doch jetzt nichts mehr mit denen zu bereden.

Schönbrod: Wenn ihr meint, ihr müßt nu zuerst hinlaufen und Feuer anlegen, eh ihr auch bloß gefragt habt, wo Niedermaier hin ist, kann ich euch nicht von abhalten. Aber wenn ihr auf mich hören wollt, denn sag' ich euch, laßt die rote Otti man machen. Ich steh' dafür gut, daß das nicht zu euerm Schaden sein soll.

Hantke: Wir wollen es mal Otti überlassen. Nachher können wir immer noch tun, was wir mögen.

Otti: (*zur Terrasse gewendet*) Wenn die Herrschaften noch zur Kirche wollen, werden Sie in keiner Weise gestört werden.

Jenny: Otti! Was fällt dir ein?

Wolff: Die ist wohl verrückt geworden.

Stechbein: Allerdings eine überraschende Wendung.

Trankhafen: Sie hat Angst bekommen um ihre Stellung.

Berta: Kuckt, sie will noch mehr sagen. Ich kann das nicht begreifen.

Hantke: Sie wird wohl wissen, was sie vorhat.

Wolff: Sie hat uns so wenig zu sagen, wie sonst jemand.

Schönbrod: Ich sag' euch nochmal, ich sag' gut für Otti. Aber ihr dürft keinen Mucks tun, was sie auch sagt. Wundern könnt ihr euch im Stillen.

Steinbott: Da kann ich nicht aus klug werden.

Jenny: Ich auch nicht.

Paula: Weil ihr Schafsköpfe seid. Oder meint ihr, die Hampelmänner da wären klüger als wir?

Annie: Jetzt versteh' ich. Weil sie uns für so dumm genommen haben, sind sie es selber.

Brunner: Jetzt soll Otti aber endlich die Hampelmänner strampeln lassen.

Otti: Let me do what I want to with them.

Steinbott: But we don't have anything to discuss with them.

Schönbrod: If you all think you need to run and start a fire before you even know where Niedermaier went, then I can't stop you. But if you'll listen to me, then I'll tell you: you all let Otti do as she sees fit. I'll guarantee that you won't get hurt.

Hantke: Let's leave it up to Otti. Afterwards we can still do whatever we want.

Otti: *(turned toward the terrace)* If the ladies and gentlemen wish to go to church, they won't find anything stopping them.

Jenny: Otti! What can you be thinking!

Wolff: She's gone crazy.

Stechbein: This certainly is a surprising turn of events.

Trankhafen: She's afraid.

Berta: Look, she's going to say more. I really can't understand this.

Hantke: She must know what she's doing.

Wolff: She didn't tell us any more than anyone else did.

Schönbrod: I'll tell you one more time, I'll vouch for Otti. You all mustn't do anything, no matter what you hear her say. You can just wonder about it to yourselves.

Steinbott: I just don't get it.

Jenny: Me neither.

Paula: Because you're acting like numbskulls. Or do you think those puppets over there are smarter than we are?

Annie: I think I understand now. They are the dumb ones, because they took us all for dumb.

Brunner: Now Otti's going to finally make those puppets dance.

Otti: Meine Freunde haben mich beauftragt, sie wegen ihres unpassenden Betragens um Entschuldigung zu bitten.

Speicherer: Hört! Hört!

Otti: Niemand konnte natürlich erwarten, daß die Regierung sofort zu den in der ersten Aufregung gestellten überspannten Forderungen Ja und Amen sagen würde. Umsomehr sind wir beschämt und gerührt, daß der Herr Minister so ein großes Verständnis für die Bitten der Belegschaft und der Bevölkerung gezeigt hat. Daß unsere Wünsche von der Regierung in wohlwollende Erwägung gezogen werden sollen, ja, daß sogar dabei von Maßregelungen abgesehen werden soll, ist mehr als wir erwarten konnten, vielleicht mehr als wir verdient haben. Man darf nichts Unmögliches fordern, und wir erkennen die höhere Einsicht der vom Vertrauen des ganzen Volkes getragenen Führer unsere Vaterlandes dankbar und ehrfurchtsvoll an und werden uns freudig und gehorsam in alle ihre Entscheidungen fügen.

Krachhahn: Sieh mal an!

Biederhold: Welche Wendung durch Gottes Fügung.

Hantke: Ob sie das nicht merken werden?

Brunner: Keine Angst. Butter und Schmeichelei müssen dick aufgetragen werden.

Otti: Wir hätten noch eine Bitte. Auch wir möchten nicht länger zurückstehn und unsre Verehrung für den weisen Staatslenker, Herrn Präsidenten Wimmerzahn an seinem Geburstage—

Wimmerzahn: *(wacht auf)* Wie bitte? Ach ja, das Fräulein sagt ein Gedicht auf, ja, sehr schön, wirklich poetisch. Danke, liebes Fräulein, danke recht schön.

Otti: —durch den Vortrag eines Liedchens zum Ausdruck bringen. Dürfen wir das?

Blödel: Aber gewiß, gutes Kind. Wir freuen uns sehr darauf.

Otti: Jugendchor, antreten!

Trankhafen: Lassen Sie sich umarmen, Fräulein Jungleib. Es soll alles vergeben und vergessen sein. (Otti *beginnt, den* Chor *zu ordnen.)*

Otti: My friends asked me to beg your pardon for their inappropriate behavior.

Speicherer: Hear, hear!

Otti: Of course, no one should have expected that the government would immediately say "yes" and "amen" to our demands that were drawn up in the heat of the moment. We are all the more embarrassed and touched by the fact that the minister showed such understanding for the requests made by our staff and population. The fact that the government is going to give favorable consideration to our requests and defer disciplinary action is really more than we could have hoped for, perhaps more than we deserved. One should not ask for impossible things, and we gratefully and respectfully acknowledge the great insight offered by the leader of our fatherland, in whom the people place their trust. We will gladly and obediently abide by all his decisions.

Krachhahn: Would you listen to that!

Biederhold: What a wonderful development, through the grace of God.

Hantke: Don't you think they'll notice?

Brunner: Don't worry, both butter and flattery have to be laid on thick.

Otti: We have one more request. We too would like to step forth and express our admiration for our wise captain of the ship of state, President Wimmerzahn, on his birthday—

Wimmerzahn: (*Wakes up.*) What's that? Oh, yes, the young lady is reciting a poem, yes, very nice, really poetic. Thank you, dear lady, thank you very much.

Otti: —by singing a little song. May we?

Blödel: But of course, my dear child. We look forward to it.

Otti: Youth choir, assemble, please!

Trankhafen: Let me embrace you, Fräulein Jungleib. All is forgiven and forgotten. (*Otti begins to arrange the* choir.)

Paula: *(sich die Seiten haltend)* Otti, sowas Komisches hab' ich noch nie erlebt.

Otti: Ihr seid mir also nicht böse?

Steinbott: Ich kann bloß noch nicht sehn, wo das hinaus soll.

Schönbrod: Wenn das nicht zum Guten hinausgeht, könnt ihr heut abend Otti und mich alle beide mit dem Dreschflegel totschlagen.

Stechbein: So glücklich und reibungslos hätte ich mir den Ausgang selbst nicht erhofft.

Hornbriller: Eine höchst loyale Deklaration. Alles all right.

Hustenreiz: Aber die Ministerratssitzung morgen ist zugesagt und muß stattfinden. Die Regierung wird dabei unbedingt eine Lösung finden müssen, die ein Einlenken in der Richtung der vorgebrachten Forderungen mindestens andeutet.

Krachhahn: Wir sollen dem Geschmeiß wohl auf Staatskosten Speckklöße in den Rachen stopfen?

Selters: Als Aufsichtsratsmitglied muß ich auf jeden Fall Wert darauf legen, daß die etwas leichtfertig erweckten Hoffnungen der Leute nicht etwa auf Kosten der Pfandbriefinhaber erfüllt werden.

Speicherer: Im Gegenteil müssen bei einer Änderung in der Verwaltung die Belange der Wirtschaft noch stärker berücksichtigt werden als bisher.

Trankhafen: Wir dürfen die begrüßenswerte Wandlung in der Stimmung dieser unberechenbaren Menschen nicht leichtfertig wieder aufs Spiel setzen. Vielleicht empfiehlt sich sogar eine unverbindliche Fühlungnahme mit den Unversöhnlichen.

Stechbein: Hätten wir sie gleich heute mit zur Feier zugezogen, so wären uns die unliebsamen Auftritte wahrscheinlich erspart geblieben.

Krampf: Aber der Herr Abgeordnete Widerborst hätte sicherlich wieder durch gröblich die Ordnung verletzende Reden dem Geist der Verfassung zuwidergehandelt.

Hornbriller: Der Minister hat sich in seiner modifizierten Dialektik so wohl salviert, daß von einer kategorischen Obligation der Regierung

Paula: *(holding her sides)* Otti, I've never seen anything so funny.

Otti: So you all aren't mad at me?

Steinbott: I just can't see what's going to come of this.

Schönbrod: If this doesn't work out for the best, you all can take Otti and me out this evening and flail us to death.

Stechbein: I never would have hoped that things would turn out so happily.

Hornbriller: An admirable declaration of loyalty. All is well.

Hustenreiz: But the meeting of the ministerial council tomorrow is confirmed, and it has to take place. The government will have to find a solution by all means, one that at least hints at a concession in the direction of their demands.

Krachhahn: So we are supposed to feed them all the steak they're asking for at the state's expense?

Selters: As a member of the advisory council I must point out how important it is that these people's carelessly aroused hopes not be answered to the detriment of the bond market.

Speicherer: On the contrary, if we make changes in the administration, we ought to give economic considerations even higher priority than before.

Trankhafen: We must be careful not to jeopardize this welcome change in the mood of these unpredictable people. It might even be advisable to adopt a non-binding compact with the Intransigents.

Stechbein: If we had brought them along today to this celebration, we probably would have been spared this unfortunate scene.

Krampf: But Delegate Widerborst would certainly have violated the spirit of the constitution with his crude, subversive speeches.

Hornbriller: The minister, by making his modified offer, has very likely ensured that any categorical obligations on the part of the government

zur Realisierung der fundamentalen Reorganisation des Wetteramtes nur cum grano salis die Rede sein kann. Die dilatorische Behandlung des Projektes wird die Emotionen der moussierenden Volkspsyche peu-à-peu wieder zur Subordination bringen. Man muß die Courage zur Unpopularität haben.

Barde: (*erhebt sich*) Meine Damen und Herren! Die Ereignisse des heutigen Tages zwingen zu durchgreifenden Entschlüssen.

Biederhold: Wo will das hinaus?

Barde: Es waren Volksgenossen, die die Notlage des Vaterlandes hier vor uns zum Ausdruck gebracht haben. Die Arbeiterrassenpartei erblickt in dem Vorgang den Auftakt zur nationalen Revolution und sie versteht den Ruf, der damit aus den Tiefen an sie als die Retterin des Volkes ergeht. Die Erneuerung des Staates muß erfolgen an Haupt und Gliedern. Wir fordern daher unverzüglich die Abdankung der Regierung, die Auflösung des Landtags, die Entjudung des Vaterlandes und die Brechunng der Zinsknechtschaft. Vom morgigen Tage ab liegt die gesamte gesetzgebende und vollziehende Gewalt in den Händen unseres großen Führers Kajetan Teutsch. Das Wetteramt wird sofort allen landfremden Einflüssen entzogen. Um eine den völkischen Belangen gemäße judenreine Wetterbildung zu gewährleisten, übernehme ich selbst die Leitung und gelobe, daß ich die Gestaltung des Wetters von nun an voll und ganz den Anforderungen der Vaterlandsverteidigung anpassen werde. Heil!

Stiefengrat: Das ist der Weg zur Rettung!

Krachhahn: Ohne Zweifel der beste Weg.

Speicherer: Jedenfalls ein gangbarer Weg.

Selters: Die Beschreitung dieses Weges wird von einer Befragung des Aufsichtrates über die Rückwirkungen auf die Kurse der Wetterpapiere abhängig zu machen sein.

Biederhold: Die Kirchenpartei wird sich alle Wege offen halten.

Hustenreiz: Der verfassungsmäßige Weg darf keinesfalls verlassen werden.

pertaining to the reorganization of the Weather Bureau can only be considered *cum grano salis*. To defer dealing with this matter will *peu-à-peu* bring the mood of the popular psyche here to a state of subordination. We must have the courage to be unpopular.

Barde: (*Rises.*) Ladies and gentlemen! Today's events force us to take drastic measures.

Biederhold: I wonder where this is leading?

Barde: These were true Germans who expressed to us today the emergency our fatherland is facing. The Workers' Race Party sees in these events the beginning of a national revolution, and it understands that the cries for help from the depths of the popular spirit are cries for the party to come to the people's rescue. The result must be the renewal of the state in every respect. Therefore we demand the immediate abdication of the government, the dissolution of the provincial parliament, the removal of all Jews from the fatherland, and the abolition of interest slavery. Starting tomorrow the legislative and executive power will lie in the hands of our great leader, Kajetan Teutsch. All alien influences will be removed from the Weather Bureau immediately. In order to guarantee a non-Jewish administration of the weather, in accordance with the people's interests, I myself will take over its management, and I vow that from now on the determination of the weather will fulfill the needs of the defense of the fatherland! *Heil*!

Stiefengrat: This is the way to our salvation!

Krachhahn: Without a doubt, this is the best way.

Speicherer: At any rate it's a way we can follow.

Selters: As we follow this course we must ask the supervisory council about the reaction of the equities markets.

Biederhold: The Church Party remains open to all possibilities.

Hustenreiz: We must by no means forsake the constitutional course.

Blödel: Der Regierung wird es obliegen zu prüfen, ob der Weg der Diktatur mit der in der Verfassung festgelegten Demokratie in Einklang steht.

Stechbein: Die eingearbeitete Verwaltung des Wetteramtes würde jedenfalls die Geschäfte zunächst weiterführen. Einen andern Weg, die Pensionsansprüche festzustellen, sehe ich nicht.

Trankhafen: Wenn wir uns vom Wege des Rechtes entfernen, ist eine Erschütterung der Verfassung unausbleiblich.

Wachtel: Ich bin durch alle die Erschütterungen in einer schrecklichen Verfassung, vollständig erschöpft.

Krampf: Damit wäre die Rednerliste gleichfalls erschöpft.

Möhre: Ob wir nicht den Herrn Staatspräsidenten wecken sollten?

Otti: *(marschiert mit dem* Jugendchor *auf)* Also das "Lied der Jugend", aber nicht lachen beim Singen!

Möhre: Herr Präsident! *(rüttelt ihn)*

Wimmerzahn: Ja, so. Also nächste Woche wieder warm und trocken. Einverstanden, jawohl.

Trankhafen: Herr Präsident, erwachen Sie doch!

Chor: Erwache, Jugend, es dämmert der Tag.
Steh auf und führ deinen ersten Hammerschlag.
Schlag kräftig an des Zeitenturms Tor.
Auf, auf! die Jugend drängt vor.

Und will Verwesung sperren dir den Turm,
Erzwing, o Jugend, den Zugang dir im Sturm!
Entwinde den Gespenstern ihren Schatz!
Woran! Die Jugend will den Platz.

Den Alten ziemt's mit den Jungen zu gehn.
Steht nicht im Weg; was geschehn muß, laßt geschehn.
Zurück bleibt, wer den Augenblick verpaßt.
Die Jugend hält keine Rast!

Blödel: It is incumbent on the government to verify whether pursuing a dictatorship is consistent with the constitution's definition of democracy.

Stechbein: The established administrators of the Weather Bureau would initially continue running it, at any rate. I can't see any other way to establish pension claims.

Trankhafen: If we distance ourselves from the legal course, then the constitution will inevitably suffer a shock.

Wachtel: My constitution is completely exhausted from all these shocks.

Krampf: I believe the list of speakers has also been exhausted.

Möhre: Shouldn't we wake the state president?

Otti: *(Marches on with the* youth choir.*)* All right, the "Song of Youth," but don't laugh while you're singing!

Möhre: Herr President! *(Shakes him.)*

Wimmerzahn: Yes, of course. So next week it will once again be warm and dry. Yes, I agree, indeed.

Trankhafen: Herr President, wake up!

Choir: Wake up, O youth, it's the dawn of the day.
         Rise up, take your hammer, and swing away.
         Strike strong upon the age's gate.
         Arise, o youth, there's no time to wait.

         And if decay is blocking your view,
         Then, youth, you must force your way through!
         Drive out the ghosts that linger here!
         We'll take our place! The way is clear!

         You older ones, march with us youth.
         Don't stand in our way! Come hear the truth!
         If you stay behind, then you miss the chance,
         And youth, rest not: advance, advance!

Was braucht denn jeden Tag Sonne zu sein?
Es fahr auch einmal ein Donnerwetter drein!
Das Leben wächst. Es sterbe was zerfällt.
Der Jugend Zukunft und Welt!

Betroffene Gesichter. Einsetzender Beifall verstummt sofort. Otti *führt
den* Chor *hinter die Leiter, wo er mit Händeklatschen begrüßt wird.*

Hustenreiz: Das war ein sonderbares Lied.

Krachhahn: Haarsträubendes Zeug.

Trankhafen: Sowas Jugendlichen einzuüben.

Biederhold: Wahrlich, es sind traurige Zeichen des sittlichen
   Niederganges.

Möhre: Ich hab' ja nicht alles verstanden, aber ich fand es empörend.

Selters: Verglichen mit ihrem allerliebsten Märchenspiel—

Hornbriller: Inkommensurable Qualitäten. In ihrem Opus humorvolle
   Symbolik, hier ein typisches Tendenzelaborat dilettierdner Amateure.

Stechbein: Was macht denn das Windrad da für Bewegungen?

*Alle sehen hinauf. Der Schwanzflügel des Windrades, der bis jetzt
unbewegt nach rechts stand, ist in starke Bewegung geraten, schleudert
das Rad eine Zeitlang hin und her und bleibt endlich, nach der
entgegengesetzten Richtung zeigend, stehen. Die Radscheibe gerät mit
wachsender Geschwindigkeit in Drehung.*

Otti: Das Windrad, seht doch!

Hantke: Und die Windrose! (*Der Zeiger der Windrose schwankt heftig,
   dreht sich mehrmals um das ganze Blatt, wendet sich schließlich nach
   unten.*)

Steinbott: Es gibt Regen, Kinder!

Berta: Und Wind! Da zieht es sich schon zusammen.

Schönbrod: Da wird am Ende noch mehr aus als Regen und Wind.

Jenny: Wo ist eigentlich Niedermaier?

Why constant sun in these temperate climes?
We also need thunderstorms at times!
Living things grow; death takes them away.
To the youth grant the world and the coming day!

Embarrassed faces. The beginnings of applause quickly fall silent. Otti leads the choir *around behind the ladder, where they are welcomed with handclapping.*

Hustenreiz: That was a strange song.

Krachhahn: Really hair-raising stuff.

Trankhafen: Imagine teaching that kind of thing to young people.

Biederhold: Truly, this a sad sign of moral decay.

Möhre: I didn't understand it all, but I found it shocking.

Selters: When one compares this with that lovely fairy play—

Hornbriller: One cannot even compare the two. In their earlier opus there was much humorous symbolism, here we see the tendentious ramblings of amateurs.

Stechbein: Why is the wind wheel moving like that?

Everyone looks up. The rudder of the wind wheel, which up to now has pointed to the right without moving, has started moving vigorously, swings the wheel back and forth for awhile, and finally stops, pointing in the opposite direction. The wheel begins turning with increasing speed.

Otti: Look, the wind wheel!

Hantke: And the weather vane! (*The pointer of the weather vane swings vigorously, turns around completely several times, and finally turns downward.*)

Steinbott: It's going to rain, kids!

Berta: And wind! It's coming together already.

Schönbrod: This is going to give us more than just rain and wind.

Jenny: Where is Niedermaier?

Annie: Mit Peters und Fischer im Turm. Sie machen Wetter!

Otti: Habt ihr endlich begriffen?

Wachtel: Ich weiß nicht, es zieht auf einmal so. *(Der Himmel überzieht sich mit dunkeln Wolken.)*

Biederhold: Es wird Zeit, zur Kirche aufzubrechen.

Barde: Das dritte Reich einzusegnen. *(Wetterleuchten)*

Möhre: Allmächtiger, es gibt ein Gewitter.

Stechbein: Das ist undenkbar. Die Apparate sind doch für zehn Tage auf Fortbestand der wolkenlosen Witterung eingestellt.

Hornbriller: Funktionieren denn diese sensitiven Apparate auch mit garantiert exakter Präzision?

Stechbein: Unbedingt. Wo ist der Peilmeister? *(Pfeifender Wind. Die Szene verdunkelt sich etwas. Die noch herumstehenden* Beamten *und* Zuschauer *ziehen sich mit Zeichen der Unruhe zurück.)*

Trankhafen: Da kommt ja der Wetterrat mit dem Peilmeister und dem Monteur aus dem Turm.

Hustenreiz: Dann erklärt sich alles.

Hornbriller: Sabotage! Obstruktion!

Biederhold: Was treibt denn die Menge da? *(Die* Masse *bewegt sich drohend auf die Terrasse zu. Das Licht wird schwächer.)*

Möhre: Sie kommen auf uns zu! Polizei!

Hornbriller: Man muß Militär requirieren. Terror!

Stiefengrat: Sie haben das Telefon abgeschnitten. Wir sind machtlos.

Biederhold: Ich gehe, ein stilles Gebet zu verrichten. *(Ab. Fortgesetztes Blitzen, ferner Donner, verstärkter Sturm. Die* Masse *rückt näher.)*

Niedermaier: *(tritt vor die Terrasse)* Beeilen Sie sich, wenn Sie noch gesund weiter kommen wollen. *(Donnerschlag)*

Wachtel: Mein Magen kann kein Gewitter vertragen. Stellen Sie doch das Wetter um!

Annie: With Peters and Fischer in the tower. They're making weather!

Otti: Do you understand now?

Wachtel: I don't know, suddenly there's such a draft. *(The sky becomes filled with dark clouds.)*

Biederhold: It's time to go to church.

Barde: So that we can bless the Third Reich. *(lightning flash)*

Möhre: My God, it's a thunderstorm.

Stechbein: That's impossible. We already had the apparatus set for ten days of cloudless weather.

Hornbriller: Does this sensitive equipment function with guaranteed accuracy?

Stechbein: Absolutely. Where is the soundings chief? *(Wind begins to whistle. The stage gets somewhat darker. The* bureaucrats *and* audience members *who are still onstage begin to withdraw at signs of the storm.)*

Trankhafen: There come the weather councillor with the soundings chief and the mechanic out of the tower.

Hustenreiz: That explains everything.

Hornbriller: Sabotage! Obstruction!

Biederhold: What's that crowd doing over there? *(The* mass of people *moves threateningly toward the terrace. It gets darker.)*

Möhre: They're coming toward us! Police!

Hornbriller: We require the military. Terrorists!

Stiefengrat: They've cut the telephone lines. We are powerless.

Biederhold: I will go pray silently. *(Off. Continued flashes of lightning, distant thunder, the storm gets stronger. The* crowd *comes nearer.)*

Niedermaier: *(Steps in front of the terrace.)* You'd better hurry if you want to get out of here safely. *(clap of thunder)*

Wachtel: My stomach can't take a thunderstorm. Please change the weather!

Wimmerzahn: *(aufwachend)* Sehr unruhig heute Nacht, wirklich recht unruhig.

Krampf: Herr Präsident, kommen Sie rasch zum Auto. Die Sitzung ist aufgehoben. Herr Minister, bitte. *(*Krampf *und* Blödel *nehmen* Wimmerzahn *unter die Arme und führen ihn ins Lokal. Die Terrasse entleert sich schnell.)*

Möhre: Wo ist Regierungsassessor Hornbriller?

Trankhafen: Wo ist Staatssekretär Stechbein? *(Die Dunkelheit nimmt zu.)*

Stiefengrat: Hätte ich nur Soldaten—ich wollte euch helfen!

Schönbrod: Und wenn Sie alle Kanonen der Welt hätten—*(zeigt zum Himmel)*—vor unserm Geschütz ist das man ein Spielzeug. *(Greller Blitz und krachender Donner.* Stiefengrat *geht schlotternd ab.* Stechbein *und* Trankhafen *erscheinen an der Brüstung.)*

Trankhafen: Freunde! Hört! Wir haben eine wichtige Botschaft. Die Regierung bewilligt alle Ihre Forderungen. Sie stellt sich voll und ganz auf den Boden der gegebenen Tatsachen. *(Schallendes Gelächter, das sich in einem heranbrüllenden Windstoß mischt und die beiden wegzuwehen scheint.)*

Barde: *(tritt mit Faschistengruß an die Brüstung der Terrasse)* Volksgenossen! Die Arbeiterrassenpartei erhebt mit euch das Banner der Revolution. Auch wir sind Arbeiter—

Paula: Mit Bügelfalten!

Barde: Wir übernehmen die Führung im Lande. Hiermit rufe ich Kajetan Teutsch zum Diktator an!

Brunner: Er soll herkommen, wenn er gern am Windrad bammeln mag. *(Ein Windstoß dreht* Barde *um und schmeißt ihn durch die Tür ins Lokal.)*

Schönbrod: Präsidenten und Regierungen und Parlamente und wie das Teufelszeug all heißt, alle wollen man bloß dem Volke helfen, und nu sollen wir das auch noch dem Kerl glauben, der uns allein vom hohen Pferd runter kommandieren will.

Wimmerzahn: *(waking up)* A restless night, really quite restless.

Krampf: Herr President, come along quickly to the car. The session has been suspended. Herr Minister, please. *(*Krampf *and* Blödel *take* Wimmerzahn *under the arms and lead him into the restaurant. The terrace empties quickly.)*

Möhre: Where is Government Assessor Hornbriller?

Trankhafen: Where is State Secretary Stechbein? *(It gets darker and darker.)*

Stiefengrat: If only I had soldiers! I would try to help you!

Schönbrod: Even if you had all the cannons in the world— *(Points to the sky.)* —they would be just toys in the face of our artillery. *(Blinding flash of lightning, sharp crack of thunder.* Stiefengrat *exits trembling.* Stechbein *and* Trankhafen *appear on the balustrade.)*

Trankhafen: Friends! Listen! We have an important message! The government has approved all your demands. It accedes to the facts as they are right now. *(Peals of laughter, mixed with a gust of wind that blows through, and the two noises seem to sweep* Stechbein *and* Trankhafen *away.)*

Barde: *(Appears with the fascist salute at the balustrade of the terrace.)* Comrades! The Workers' Race Party joins you in raising the banner of the revolution! We too are workers—

Paula: With brown uniforms!

Barde: We are taking over leadership of the country. I hereby declare Kajetan Teutsch dictator!

Brunner: If he comes here he'll dangle from the wind wheel. *(A gust of wind turns* Barde *around and throws him through the door into the restaurant.)*

Schönbrod: Presidents and governments and parliaments and whatever all that stuff is called, they all want to help the people, and now we're supposed to believe this guy who is going to give us all commands from up on his high horse.

Niedermaier: Das Wetter muß gleich hier sein. Es wird auch für uns Zeit. *(Schönwetterchen tritt weinend auf.)*

Schönwetter.: Ich kann Sonnenscheinchen nicht finden.

Berta: Was fehlt dir denn, Lütting?

Schönwetter.:   Ich bin doch Schönwetterchen; ich bin bei Sonnenscheinchen zu Besuch.

Peters: O weh, Sonnenscheinchen ist weg und Schönwetterchen hat sich verlaufen. Was machen wir da?

Paula: Komm' mit mir. Wenn Sausewindchen und Gewitterchen weg sind, gehn wir zusammen, Sonnenscheinchen suchen. *(Die Bühne ist nur noch schwach beleuchtet. Wind und Regen peitschen heftiger. Alle verlassen die Szene.)*

Fischer: *(im Abgehen)* Wer wird wohl morgen der erste sein, der sich den Arbeitern und Bauern anschmieren will?

Otti: *(im Abgehen)* Alle Macht den Räten! *(In der Ferne jubelnde Stimmen, die sich in Donner und Sturm verlieren. Es wird noch dunkler, das Wetter lärmender.* Stechbein *und* Trankhafen *tasten von der Terrasse her über die Bühne.)*

Stechbein: Nur schnell unter Dach! Der Sturm entwurzelt uns.

Trankhafen: Wohin, mein Theodor? Es ist schwarz rundum, und das Amt wird vom Feinde besetzt sein. Der Boden wankt unter mir. O, Geliebter!

Stechbein: Hinweg, Henriette! Auf festerem Grunde will ich Fuß fassen. Die Revolution ist sieghaft. Deine Partei hat das Volk verraten. Noch morgen vollziehe ich meinen Eintritt in die Partei der Unversöhnlichen. Leb' Wohl, Henriette!

Trankhafen: Wehe! Wehe! *(aus der Ferne)* Theodor! *(Beide verschwinden.)*

Wachtel: *(läuft über die Bühne)* Der Leib der Erde kracht. Kein Fleckchen mehr, wohin ich mich verkriechen kann! O, meine Not. Ich unselige! *(Verschwindet.* Möhre *und* Hornbriller *irren miteinander über die Bühne.)*

Niedermaier: The weather ought to be here soon. Now it's our time. *(*Little Blue-Skies *enters crying.)*

Blue-Skies: I can't find Little Sunshine.

Berta: What's your problem, little man?

Blue-Skies: I am Little Blue-Skies. I'm staying with Little Sunshine.

Peters: Oh, too bad, Little Sunshine is gone and Little Blue-Skies has lost his way. What will we do about that?

Paula: Come with me. When Little Gusty-Wind and Little Thunderstorm are gone, we'll go together and find Little Sunshine. *(Now the stage is only very dimly lit. Wind and rain whip the whole area. Everyone leaves the scene.)*

Fischer: *(going off)* I wonder who'll be the first to try to cheat the workers and farmers tomorrow?

Otti: *(going off)* All power to the workers' councils! *(It gets even darker, the weather gets even noisier.* Stechbein *and* Trankhafen *grope their way from the terrace across the stage.)*

Stechbein: Get under a roof quickly! The storm is uprooting us!

Trankhafen: But where, Theodore? It's black all around us, and the office has been occupied by the enemy. I feel the earth giving way under my feet. Oh, my darling!

Stechbein: Go on, Henriette! I want to get my feet on firmer ground. The revolution is victorious. Your party betrayed the people. Tomorrow I intend to join the Party of the Intransigents. Farewell, Henriette!

Trankhafen: No! No! *(from far away)* Theodore! *(The two disappear.)*

Wachtel: *(Runs across the stage.)* The belly of the earth is breaking open! There's no place where I can crawl! Oh what misery! Poor me! *(Disappears.* Möhre *and* Hornbriller *stagger together across the stage.)*

Möhre: Schnell, schnell, mein Geliebter, das Wetter verschlingt uns.

Hornbriller: Inferno! Die Vehemenz des Orkans demoliert die Etablissements! Lasciate ogni speranza!

Möhre: Gräßlich! Entsetzlich! O, mein Norbert, wirst du ewig bei mir bleiben?

Hornbriller: Abstruse Illusion! Sauve qui peut! Adieu, Malvine!

Möhre: Wehe! Wehe! *(aus der Ferne)* Norbert! *(Beide verschwinden.)*

Völlige Finsternis. Tosender Lärm von Sturm, Hagel und Gewitter. Scheiben klirren. Gebälk kracht. Der Vorhang bleibt offen. Der Lärm wird schwächer, hört auf. Es dämmert. Schnelles Hellwerden entschleiert das vierte Bild.

Möhre: Hurry, my darling, the weather will devour us.

Hornbriller: Inferno! The vehemence of this hurricane is destroying the established order! *Lasciate ogni speranza!*

Möhre: Horrible! Terrible! Oh, my Norbert, will you stay with me forever?

Hornbriller: That's an illusion! Every man for himself! *Sauve qui peut!* Adieu, Malvine!

Möhre: Oh no! Oh no! *(from a distance)* Norbert! *(The two disappear.)*

Complete darkness. The raging sounds of a storm, with hail and thunder. Windowpanes shatter. House timbers break in two. The curtain remains open. The noise subsides, stops. Light dawns on the scene. With a sudden brightening, the veil of darkness is lifted from the stage.

Viertes Bild (Epilog)

Der Himmel ist dicht bewölkt. Das Grau der Wolken wird rasch heller. Ein Regenbogen steht über dem Windrad und dem Turm, der zusehends verblaßt und verschwindet, bevor Personen die Szene betreten. Das Windrad ist in Bewegung, der Schwanzflügel steht wie im ersten Bild, desgleichen der Zeiger der Windrose. Das Unwetter ist durch viele Spuren der Zerstörung erkennbar. Alle Girlanden sind heruntergerissen, ebenso die Flaggen; doch sind die Fahnenstangen auf dem Turm stehen geblieben. Die Terrasse und das Schweizer Häuschen sind schwer mitgenommen. An den übrigen Häusern und an der Kirche sind die Fenster entzwei. Der Kirchturm ist stark beschädigt. Auf dem Boden liegen Trümmer aller Art, Grünzeug, zerfetzte Fahnentücher, Glasscherben.

Ein zerbeulter Zylinder liegt mitten auf der Bühne.

Die Bühne ist leer. Aus dem Hintergrunde nähert sich, erst undeutlich zu verstehen, der Gesang des "Alle-Wetter-Liedes", unter Musikbegleitung:

> Haß lodert nur, wo Liebe brennt.
> So mischt die Ebbe sich der Flut,
> Hüllt Goldstaub sich in Asche grau.
> Im gleichen Wolkenbette ruht
> Der Schnee beim Hagel und beim Tau.

Der Jugendchor *wird sichtbar, geführt von* Otti. *Er betritt zwischen Wetterturm und Windrad die Szene. Zugleich treten von rechts die* Bauern und Bäuerinnen *auf, in der ersten Reihe* Schönbrod. *Sie tragen Sicheln, Sensen, Spaten und anderes Arbeitsgerät, zumeist geschultert. Von links gleichzeitig* Arbeiter und Arbeiterinnen, *in der ersten Reihe* Niedermaier. *Sie tragen Äxte, Sägen und anderes Handwerkseug in den*

Act IV (Epilog)

The sky is filled with heavy clouds. The gray of the clouds becomes suddenly brighter. There is a rainbow over the wind wheel and the tower; the rainbow becomes visibly paler and disappears before characters enter the scene. The wind wheel is moving, the rudder is as in the first act; so is the pointer of the weathervane. Signs of destruction show that a storm has been through. All the garlands and flags have been ripped down, although the flagpoles still stand on the tower. The terrace and the Swiss cottage are heavily damaged. The windows are broken in the other houses and the church. The church tower is badly damaged. There is rubble of all kinds on the ground, brush, torn bits of cloth from the flags, shards of glass.

A dented, beat-up top hat lies in the middle of the stage.

The stage is empty. The "Thunderation Song" approaches from the distance, unintelligible at first, with instrumental accompaniment:

> Hate blazes in a loving heart.
> Flood waters mix with the ebbtide.
> Gray ashes hide gold dust from view.
> In the same bed of clouds abide
> The snow, the hail, and morning's dew.

The youth choir *becomes visible, led by* Otti. *It enters the scene between the weather tower and the weather wheel. At the same time* farmers *enter from the right, with* Schönbrod *in the first row. They are carrying sickles, scythes, shovels, and other tools, most of them carried on their shoulders. From the left, at the same time, come* workers, *with* Niedermaier *in the first row. They are carrying axes, saws, and other*

283

Händen oder über den Schultern. Beide Gruppen nehmen rechts und links Aufstellung. Zwischen ihnen marschiert der Jugendchor *ein und singt:*

> Aus der Sonne dunstet Unheil.
> Aus den Blitzen zuckt Erbarmen.
> Alle Wetter, alle Wetter
> Hält der Himmel in den Armen.
>
> Nur wen des Lebens Buntheit schreckt,
> Der fürchtet sich vorm Untergehn.
> Vernichtung ist's, die Leben weckt
> Und alles Sterben ist Entstehn.
> Im müden Stamme frist der Wurm.
> Zur Sonne strebt der junge Trieb.
> Feg' ihm die Bahn, Zerstörer Sturm!
> So hat der Tod das Leben lieb.
> Wolkenbruch und Strahlengluten,
> Reif und Frost und Erdenbeben,
> Alle Wetter, alle Wetter
> Töten und erzeugen leben.

Aus jeder der drei Gruppen treten ein paar männliche und weibliche Personen *vor und räumen schnell die herumliegenden Trümmer beiseite. Der Hut rollt* Otti *vor die Füsse, die ihn aufhebt und fortwirft. Er bleibt an der Kirturmspitze hängen.*

Darauf stellt sich der Jugendchor *halbkreisförmig auf und umrahmt so das Bewegunsspiel der* Arbeiter *und* Bauern*:*

Aus jeder der beiden Gruppen lösen sich sechs Männer *und sechs* Frauen *und gehen hintereinander an den zwölf Vertretern der andern Gruppe vorbei. Die* Männer *tragen bei den Arbeitern Hämmer, bei den Bauern Sicheln über der Schulter. Die* Bauern *nehmen im Vorbeigehen je eine* Arbeiterfrau *an ihre Seite, die* Arbeiter *je eine* Bauersfrau*. Die zwölf* P a a r e *führen dan einen Bewegungstanz auf, der die Zusammengehörigkeit von Bauern und Arbeitern, von Sichel und*

hand tools, in their hands or over their shoulders. The two groups take places on the left and right. The youth choir *marches between them and sings:*

> Disaster streams forth from the sun,
> Compassion from the lightning's blaze.
> Thunderation, all the weather
> Dwells in Heaven's realm always.
>
> The ones who fear life's colors bright
> Dread also every life's demise.
> Destruction brings new life to light
> And something's born when something dies.
> The dead branch nourishes the worm
> The young sprout strives toward the sun.
> Sweep clean his way, destroyer storm!
> When death comes, then is life begun.
> Cloudbursts and the glowing sun,
> Rime and frost and earthquakes too,
> Thunderation, all the weather
> Kills and creates life anew.

From each of the three groups a few men *and* women *come forward and quickly clear out the debris. The top hat rolls over to* Otti's *feet, and she picks it up and tosses it away. It gets caught on the point of the church steeple, where it hangs.*

Then the youth choir *makes a semi-circle and surrounds the dance of the* workers *and* farmers:

From each group six men *and six* women *come forth and go behind and past the twelve from the other group. From the workers' group the* men *carry hammers, from the farmers the* men *carry sickles over their shoulders. Each* man *from the farmers pairs off with a* woman *from the workers, and vice versa. The twelve* couples *then perform a dance showing the solidarity of the workers and farmers, of the hammer and*

Hammer verdeutlicht. Hieran schließt sich ein Umzug aller drei Gruppen, der im Abmarsch zur Arbeit endet.

Der Jugendchor *singt, während ein Teil aufs Feld, ein Teil zur Werkstatt und* Niedermaier *mit den* Wetterturm-Arbeitern *und* Arbeiterinnen *in den Turm abmarschiert, während sich* Schönbrod *zur Jugend stellt.*

> Wem der Sinn der Natur ergeben ist,
> Dem gibt die Natur sich zur Braut.
> Wem das Wunder der Erde sein Leben ist,
> Der hat ihr Geheimnis erschaut.
> O Mensch, verlaß nicht der Schöpfung Spur.
> Die Erde bleibt Erde, Natur bleibt Natur.
> Nur im Bund mit der Sonne, im Bund mit dem Meer
> Lenkst die Winde du, ziehst die Wolken her.
>
> Ob die Sonne scheinen soll,
> Ob der Regen weinen soll,
> Frage Saat und Herde.
> Deiner Hände Meisterschaft,
> Alles was dein Geist erschafft,
> Bringe dar der Erde.

Auf den Fahnenstangen des Wetterturms gehen während des Singens gleichzeitig eine rote und eine schwarze Fahne hoch.

> Nur der Mensch, der nicht Herr noch Knecht sein will,
> Soll das Feld, soll den Acker bestellen.
> Nur wer Gleicher im gleichen Recht sein will,
> Dem fügen sich Winde und Wellen.
> Der Erste, der Boden sein Erbgut hieß,
> Der machte die Erde zum Knechtsverließ.
> Weh der Macht, die den Himmel zu eigen begehrt.
> Sie trifft unser Fluch, sie fällt unser Schwert.

sickle. Then a parade of all three groups forms, before marching off to work.

The youth choir *sings, during which part of them go to the fields, part to the workshops, and* Niedermaier *marches with the* workers *to the tower.* Schönbrod *stands by the* young people.

> Whoever understands Nature's story,
> Nature gives herself as his bride.
> Whoever gives himself to Nature's glory,
> From him has Nature nothing more to hide.
> O children, don't forget the lesson of creation's birth:
> Nature is Nature and the Earth is the Earth.
> If, and only if, you listen to the sun and sea
> Can you guide the winds and know just where the clouds will
> be.
>
> If the sun beams down, or the rains fall on the ground,
> It's for the wheat and barley.
> All of your hands' mastery,
> Everything your mind can see,
> Give the Earth entirely.

While this song is sung, a red and a black flag are raised on the flagpoles of the weather tower.

> Whoever wants not to be lord or vassal
> May have a say in how to plant the field.
> Whoever wants no more than to be equal
> The wind and waves to his desires must yield.
> Whoever first did say the Earth was his domain,
> He put the Earth in prison, and bound it up with chains.
> But he who arrogantly claims dominion o'er the sky
> Will hear the people's curse and feel our fury by and by.

Was der Menschengeist erschafft,
Was der Hände Meisterschaft
Wachsen läßt aus Erden;
Ob der Regen weinen soll,
Ob die Sonne scheinen soll—
Freiheit soll draus werden!

Schönbrod *legt* Otti *die Hand aufs Haar und küßt sie auf die Stirn. Ein Sonnenstrahl dringt kräftig durch die Wolken.*

VORHANG

Everything your mind can see, all of your hands' mastery
Is Nature's cultivation.
If the rain falls down, if the sun shines on the ground,
It means our liberation.

Schönbrod *lays his hand on* Otti's *hair and kisses her brow. A ray of sun shines through the clouds.*

CURTAIN